Disequilibrium macroeconomic models

Disequilibrium macroeconomic models

Theory and estimation of rationing models using business survey data

JEAN-PAUL LAMBERT

*Facultés Universitaires Saint-Louis, Brussels
and CORE, Université Catholique de Louvain*

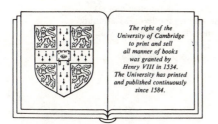

The right of the
University of Cambridge
to print and sell
all manner of books
was granted by
Henry VIII in 1534.
The University has printed
and published continuously
since 1584.

CAMBRIDGE UNIVERSITY PRESS

Cambridge
New York   New Rochelle   Melbourne   Sydney

Published by the Press Syndicate of the University of Cambridge
The Pitt Building, Trumpington Street, Cambridge CB2 1RP
32 East 57th Street, New York, NY 10022, USA
10 Stamford Road, Oakleigh, Melbourne 3166, Australia

First published 1988

Printed in Great Britain at the University Press, Cambridge

British Library cataloguing in publication data
Lambert, Jean-Paul
    Disequilibrium macroeconomic models: theory
    and estimation of rationing models using
    business survey data.
    1. Equilibrium (Economics). 2. Econometrics
    I. Title
    330′.0724   HB145

Library of Congress cataloguing in publication data
Lambert, Jean-Paul, 1952–
    Disequilibrium macroeconomic models.

    Bibliography.
    Includes index.
    1. Equilibrium (Economics) – Econometric models.
    2. Macroeconomics – Econometric models. 3. Rationing,
    Consumer – Econometric models. 4. Belgium – Manufactures –
    Econometric models. I. Title.
    HB145.L36   1987   339.5′0724   86-24966

ISBN 0 521 32209 X

HB
145
.L35
1988

MC

Contents

To Nadine, Christophe, Jean-François
and the late Elisabeth

Acknowledgements

I would like to take this opportunity to thank all those who were so helpful during the work leading to this book.

Since the book grew out of a doctoral dissertation, I want first of all to express my gratitude to Jacques H. Drèze, my thesis supervisor, for his encouragement, his expert guidance and so many stimulating discussions. Special thanks are also due to Jean-François Richard, whose help and advice proved ·invaluable at various stages of the research.

A number of people provided constructive criticisms and suggestions: Antoine d'Autume, Philippe Devillé, Peter Kooiman, John Muellbauer, Peter Stalder, Henri R. Sneessens, Gerd Weinrich and Daniel Weiserbs. To all of them I express my greatest thanks, confessing however that time, space or simply my own limitations have sometimes prevented me from doing full justice to their suggestions. Discussions with a number of people, among whom I would like to mention Michel Lubrano and Renzo Orsi, also proved valuable. Finally, I want to express my gratitude to an anonymous referee, whose comments and suggestions resulted in a considerable improvement of the original text. I, of course, remain solely responsible for the opinions expressed and for any errors made.

I would also like to thank Bart Meganck of the Belgian National Bank who provided me with some unpublished statistical data and gave expert comments on that material. Francis Bossier of the Belgian Planning Bureau and Gonzague d'Alcantara, responsible for the 'Hermes' project sponsored by the EEC, also made statistical material available to me.

This project could not have been realized without the help of various institutions: the 'Projet d'Action Concertée' conducted at CORE under the auspices of the Belgian 'Service de Programmation de la Politique Scientifique' provided the main financial support while a grant of the Belgian 'Fonds National de la Recherche Scientifique' is also gratefully acknowledged.

Most of the research was carried out at CORE (Université Catholique de Louvain) where I enjoyed (and still enjoy) a highly stimulating environment. I also benefited from a prolonged stay at the Econometric Institute at the Erasmus University of Rotterdam and I wish to thank its research staff for their hospitality. The book was finally completed at the Catholic University of Lille, where I immediately found a friendly support.

Last but not least, my thanks go to Elisabeth Pecquereau and Chantal Goossens for their skilful typing.

Introduction

Macroeconomic theory now recognizes that a number of phenomena have their origin in incomplete market-clearing. This awareness is reflected for instance in recent reports of international organizations committed to research in the field of economic policy. A report of the IMF [1982] states that:

> there is widespread concern about certain rigidities and structural problems confronting the industrial countries. This concern stems from the difficulty now being encountered in dealing with either inflation or unemployment through the use of generalized monetary and fiscal policies. (...) *Rigidities in wage bargaining and price setting* have represented perhaps the most important single set of obstacles ...

Similarly one reads in an OECD report [1982] that:

> it seems however that a series of structural factors played an important role in various countries, in particular *the noticeable and perhaps growing rigidity of labour and goods markets* ...

0.1   'Disequilibrium theory' in modern macroeconomic research

The two quotations above constitute an excellent introduction to the present study because they draw attention to the phenomenon (price and/or wage rigidity) which may be seen at the heart of most of the current debates in modern macroeconomic theory. Indeed, the highly divergent conclusions of competing schools of thought (and their models) about the appropriateness and effectiveness of economic policy may be traced back primarily to their assumptions about the speed of price/wage adjustment, an infinite value founding the 'market-clearing paradigm' while finite values (implied by the term 'rigidities' in the quotations above) are at the root of the 'non-market-clearing paradigm'. The strong opposition between these two paradigms goes back to the vigorous debate between the neo-classics and Keynes, whose 'unemployment equilibrium' rested on wage rigidity. Keynesian macroeconomics, whatever its empirical relevance, has however been frequently dismissed for its lack of microtheoretic foundations, i.e. because it did not appear to be based on rational optimizing behaviour on the part of individual agents. The 'bench-mark' model, which was considered *the* standard model in terms of which competing theories had to be expressed, was seen to be that of general equilibrium theory, the only appropriate framework for examining the conditions ensuring consistency between decisions taken by rational optimizing agents. Researchers interested in studying 'disequilibrium' economic phenomena (such as involuntary unemployment) were therefore urged to provide more robust 'microeconomic foundations to macroeconomics', i.e. to reformulate macroeconomic theory in terms of mutually consistent decisions taken by individual optimizing agents, possibly confronted with some (quantity) constraints.

Considerable efforts have been devoted to this task in recent years, resulting both in an improved understanding of the original Keynesian message and in the establishment of various models which, since they conform to a common frame of reference, are more suitable for critical confrontation and possible cross-fertilization.

This introductory section will present briefly the main models with their basic characteristics in order to put the present study into proper perspective. Reference will also be made to the earlier works which led the way for the development of the type of models to which this work belongs.[1] In the absence of a complete set of future markets (contrary to what is assumed in the Arrow–Debreu model), individuals must make decisions currently, based on expectations of an uncertain future. The different models may be termed 'general *equilibrium*' models in the sense that analysis is put on states of the economy where *current* individual decisions are mutually compatible, but these equilibria are better called '*temporary* equilibria' since no guarantee exists that individual plans will be mutually consistent at all *future* dates.

Among the 'temporary general equilibrium' models, a sharp distinction has to be made between the '*quasi-Walrasian*' models positing an infinite speed of adjustment for current prices/wages (and hence generalized 'market-clearing') and the '*non-Walrasian*' models where prices/wages are assumed to adjust too sluggishly[2] (or possibly to stop before fully adjusting) to clear all markets today (hence the widely used label 'disequilibrium' models[3]).

As Fitoussi [1983] has convincingly argued, in these different models, the typical economic agent solves an optimization problem which differs according to alternative theories by the nature and the number of constraints taken into consideration rather than by the theoretical justification of the constraints.

Indeed, the absence of any quantity constraint in the optimization problem faced by the agents in the 'quasi-Walrasian' models follows from the 'market-clearing' feature which guarantees that every agent will be able to satisfy his trade offers at the prevailing prices; but the 'market-clearing' feature itself entirely rests on the introduction of an exogenous institution, the 'auctioneer'. There is thus no *decentralized* theory of price formation in these models and the postulated instantaneous adaptation of prices/wages cannot be deduced from principles of individual behaviour.

'Non-Walrasian' models start from this observation: in the absence of an 'auctioneer' (which is the case for the vast majority of markets in modern economies), there is no assurance that the Walrasian equilibrium point will be reached and hence no guarantee that agents will be able to carry out their plans (trade offers) at prevailing prices; as a consequence, their optimization problem involves not only the traditional budget constraint but also perceived quantity constraints on the various markets they may engage in. The trade offers resulting from this more elaborate optimization problem are called *effective* to contrast them with those resulting from the 'Walrasian' optimization problem, which are called *notional* (or Walrasian) trade offers.

Early works stressing the difference between effective and notional trade offers and investigating the consequences of price rigidity were first conducted within a partial equilibrium framework.

Patinkin [1956] is generally credited with the first model which distinguishes between Walrasian and effective trade offers. Specifically, the demand for labour by firms is shown to depend on their expectation of how much output they can sell and not only on the level of real wages. Clower [1965] conducted, with more general insight, a similar analysis on household behaviour.

Barro and Grossman [1971, 1976] then combined the work of Patinkin and Clower to study individual behaviour and market non-clearance in an aggregate two-market (goods and labour) model. They used the Hicksian fix-price method (see below for critical comments on this method). In this method, a short enough period of time is considered so that prices do not change within the period, and the characteristics of an economy-wide equilibrium are looked for. Since prices cannot change, equilibrium will be established via quantity adjustments. Barro and Grossman worked out the various cases, showing that the fixed level of nominal wages and prices (and other exogenous variables) determines which side of each market will effectively experience quantity constraints.

Because of its aggregate character, Barro and Grossman's model was the one which inspired the first empirical works in 'disequilibrium' econometric modelling. We will return to this point after our brief overview of theoretical works in non-Walrasian macroeconomics.

The generalization of the Barro–Grossman model to an economy consisting of H households, F firms and N commodities was performed by Drèze [1975] and Benassy [1975], in two distinct models. Without stressing the differences between these two models, let us say that in both of them a *tâtonnement* on quantities is investigated. An equilibrium in these models is defined as a fixed point of the *tâtonnement* process in the space of effective demands.

All non-Walrasian models cited up to now are fix-price models, which does not mean that prices are considered to be invariant but rather that they are determined outside the model or, more precisely, outside the temporary equilibrium period. During the period, only quantities are free to change while prices are subject to interperiod adjustment. The fix-price methodology is to be considered as a convenient device for the analysis of economies where, because of the sluggish adjustment of prices/wages, agents have to take account of (perceived) quantity constraints (in addition to the price signals) in formulating their plans.

As such, these fix-price models allow the rigorous study of the *consequences* of sluggish price adjustment, but they leave unanswered the question of *why* prices/wages do not move quickly enough to clear markets continuously. Since they necessarily overlook longer-run issues like the possibility of *stationary* non-Walrasian equilibria, these fix-price models are to be considered as short-run models, suitable only for analyzing *temporary* equilibria characterized by disequilibrium situations on various markets. Fix-price empirical models, including the one developed later in this study, are thus to be viewed as appropriate instruments for analyzing actual short-run developments in decentralized economies (as well as in planned economies where prices are 'exogenously' fixed, sometimes for long periods of time).

Remaining at the theoretical level, the reasons behind the observed sluggishness of wages and prices have been investigated in a number of promising attempts, but the studies have not led so far to commonly agreed-upon explanations. One argument points toward the various institutional arrangements entailing price rigidities (such as administered prices, automatic wage indexation, minimum wage legislation, etc...) but this argument is of course not totally satisfactory. One of the challenges facing non-Walrasian economics is to endogenize price sluggishness by providing explanations in terms of rational behaviour of economic agents. Some first attempts are based on partial equilibrium reasoning: for example, Alchian [1970] and Okun [1981] stress the role of the high information costs which would be incurred by buyers faced with quickly and continuously adjusting prices. The body of research known under the heading of 'contract theory' (see Baily [1974] or Azariadis [1975]) also falls into this category, although it is not clear as

Negishi [1979] has pointed out, whether optimal contracts are compatible with involuntary unemployment.

Besides the arguments framed in a partial equilibrium setting, some very interesting insights have been provided by authors who attempt to go beyond the fix-price models by analyzing non-Walrasian (general equilibrium) models with endogenous prices. The starting point for their reasoning is as follows: outside Walrasian equilibrium, agents must abandon the notion that they can sell (buy) as much as they want at the going market price, but then it is no longer sensible to argue that they treat price signals parametrically. Once it is assumed that agents may modify prices in an attempt to relax the quantity constraints they face, what is the likely outcome? Is the only outcome the (assumed to be unique) Walrasian equilibrium or is there a possibility of ending up in other non-Walrasian long-run equilibria, for example the 'unemployment equilibrium', the existence of which Keynes argued to have established? Prominent works in this area are those of Benassy [1976] and Hahn [1978] (see Drazen [1980] and Fitoussi [1983] for a critical comparison).

Hahn's model appears to be the more elaborate one since it treats agents' 'monopoly power' as endogenous (i.e. an agent who does not meet any quantity constraint could accept the market price). Constrained agents are assumed to form conjectures concerning the quantities they could exchange as a function of the (by them) announced prices. A conjectural equilibrium is where agents' conjectures are confirmed, in other words a state of the economy where agents do not perceive any incentive to modify their responses to the signals they receive. Hahn proves the existence of non-Walrasian conjectural equilibrium where only one side of the market in a given commodity is rationed. Hence, in some sense, as Fitoussi [1983] argues, 'price rigidity would no longer be a cause but a consequence of underemployment equilibrium'. However, Hahn's result is sensitive to the degree of 'rationality' (by which is meant 'correctness') assumed for agents' conjectures; some 'bounded rationality' seems to be a necessary condition for a non-Walrasian equilibrium to exist. This raises the important and complex question of 'rationality': what extent of the agents' information set is compatible with rational behaviour in a world of non-zero information costs? (That is, 'global rationality', i.e. full knowledge of the entire structure of the economy as postulated by the 'Rational Expectation School', may only be compatible with rational optimizing behaviour in a world of costless information.) Further theoretical work on this subject needs to be given priority so that non-Walrasian macroeconomics can be established as offering a more appealing and rigorous approach than that offered by 'neo-classical' models.

This brief overview of theoretical advances in non-Walrasian macroeconomics is given only to put the present study into perspective. In this book, we present the results of research aiming to develop more appropriate empirical macro models along the non-Walrasian lines.

As stated above, the few empirical disequilibrium models developed so far are basically econometric transpositions of the canonical Barro–Grossman fix-price model. In that model, depending on the values of the exogenous variables, each aggregate market (goods or labour) may be characterized either by excess demand or by excess supply, so that the whole economy may find itself in one of four possible regimes: Keynesian unemployment, classical unemployment, repressed inflation or underconsumption. The traditional Keynesian model is thus reduced to a particular case of a broader framework. One of the interesting properties of this two-market disequilibrium model is that it allows a type of structural change: the economy passes through distinct regimes, in which different but stable behavioural relationships operate. The labour demand function, for instance, is not the same in the classical unemployment regime (where it corresponds to the 'notional' demand concept) as in the Keynesian unemployment regime (where it corresponds to the 'effective' demand concept). As a consequence (see Malinvaud [1977] among others), the impact of traditional policy instruments may be quite different, depending on the prevailing regime: for example, autonomous government demand exerts its full multiplier effect in the Keynesian regime but no multiplier effect at all in the classical regime, while income policy (exogenous manipulation of the real wage rate) affects unemployment oppositely in these two regimes.

Concern with effective policy making fostered the transition from theory to practice; small disequilibrium macro models were elaborated and estimated with the idea of determining, for a specific economy, which 'regimes' prevailed at each moment in the past and, above all, which regime is ruling at present.

To date, mainly because of the complexity of the new economic and econometric problems involved, there have been only a few attempts to estimate a small disequilibrium model along Barro–Grossman lines: Kooiman and Kloeck [1980, 1981] for the Netherlands, Sneessens [1981] for Belgium, Vilares [1981] and Artus, Laroque and Michel [1984] for France. The discussion of these models will be deferred until the end of chapter 1 where some of their main characteristics will be contrasted with the corresponding features of the models generated by our approach.

0.2   The 'smoothing by aggregation' approach for more realistic empirical modelling

From the above discussion one understands that, while the Barro–Grossman model provides a very useful framework for the study of theoretical issues, its simple econometric transposition is inappropriate for applied macro-economics. Indeed, the picture of the economy provided by those models remains grossly unrealistic since the whole economy can switch suddenly from one regime to another, making ineffective of even perverse the economic policy which was the most appropriate for the previous period. Also, it is impossible to account for the simultaneous existence of unemployment and vacancies or idle capacities and unfilled order in this type of model since the *min* condition is assumed to prevail at the aggregate level.

The point is that because of the heterogeneity of the goods and labour markets, the real world exhibits much more continuity than these aggregate models. At each moment, some micro markets of goods (let us briefly qualify them as products) are in excess demand while others are in excess supply; the same happens for the micro markets of labour (briefly defined as a particular combination of qualification, location, sex, etc.). As time passes, the proportion of markets in different situations of excess demand changes, but it changes in a continuous way and not in an 'all or nothing' way as in the Barro–Grossman model. Consequently, the effects of different economic policies evolve gradually over the business cycle, depending on the proportion of goods and labour markets in various disequilibria. In order to facilitate the study of policy issues, macroeconomic disequilibrium models should try to exhibit the same continuity properties as the real world where the structural change referred to above still takes place but in a continuous way.

To cope with this problem, J. Muellbauer [1978] and E. Malinvaud [1980] (in a slightly different statistical setting, however) have suggested the 'smoothing by aggregation' approach. In this approach, each aggregate market (goods or labour) is seen as consisting of a continuum of micro markets in disequilibrium, some in excess demand, some in excess supply. On each of those micro markets, the *min* condition is assumed to prevail. It can be shown that aggregation (by integration) on those micro markets results in aggregate transactions which are a continuous (though highly non-linear) function of aggregate supply and demand. The same is true for the weighted proportion of micro markets in excess demand. The precise form of the non-linear functions will of course depend on the assumptions made about the joint distribution of the microsectoral demands and supplies. Since there is no guarantee that tractable functions will emerge from this aggregation procedure, doubts have sometimes been expressed as to the usefulness of the approach (see R. E. Quandt [1982]).

However, our research suggests that this approach is completely feasible since the most reasonable assumption of jointly lognormally distributed microsectoral demands and supplies leads to very simple non-linear functional forms. Thus, this 'smoothing by aggregation' approach seems able to generate models which bear a number of interesting features, both for the study of policy analysis (see above) and from the point of view of the model builder.

First of all, and perhaps most importantly, the models provide a framework for the efficient use of extraneous information on the extent of rationing on the various markets. In conventional disequilibrium models, this role is usually played by the adjunction of price equations which are thought to help determine the prevailing regime. But the simple-minded specifications usually adopted put into question the quality and appropriateness of this 'extraneous information'. Much more direct information on the extent of rationing on the various markets is provided by regular business surveys conducted in the manufacturing sector. These surveys report on the weighted proportion of firms experiencing lack of demand for their output, insufficient capacity, constraints on the labour market, lack of raw materials and other constraints. Data from the surveys provide direct information on the weighted proportions of goods and labour micro markets in excess demand for which we were able to derive simple functional forms. So, not only does our type of model permit the use of empirical evidence on 'tension indicators', but it also tells us the appropriate way of introducing these terms into the structural equations.

Another interesting aspect of the models developed in this book is that extending the number of markets introduces no serious problem *per se*, since it only amounts to additional non-linear terms in the structural equations. This is at variance with the conventional disequilibrium models where the exponential 'multiplication of regimes' is likely to lead to insurmountable computational problems and/or prohibitive computational costs (see R. E. Quandt [1982]).

Since standard econometric techniques (for example, non-linear FIML (Full Information Maximum Likelihood)) may be used, effort can be redirected towards the search for more refined dynamic specifications – a weak point of most empirical disequilibrium models.

0.3   Plan of the book

The book is divided into three chapters covering the 'theory of aggregation' of micro markets in disequilibrium, the suitable econometric formulation of macro models intended for estimation and an empirical application to the Belgian manufacturing sector. Figure 0.1 provides a comprehensive view of how the study is organized; the text below gives more details about the book's contents.

Chapter 1 provides the theoretical foundations of the aggregation procedure and handles methodological issues related to the interpretation of business survey data. Section 1.1 applies the 'aggregation by integration'

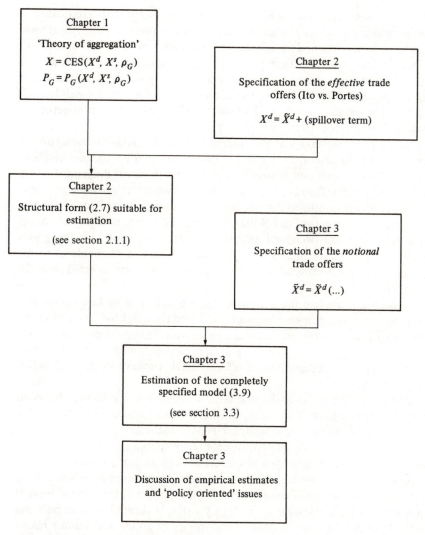

Figure 0.1. Synoptic table of contents

approach to micro markets in disequilibrium: it is shown that, with a most reasonable distributional assumption on micro demands and micro supplies, this procedure results in attractive expressions for both aggregate transactions (X) and the (weighted) proportion of micro markets in excess demand (P_G) (or conversely in excess supply). More precisely, X and P_G are seen to exhibit simple functional forms involving only one 'dispersion' parameter (ρ_G) besides their two arguments X^d (aggregate demand) and X^s (aggregate supply).

Moreover, both expressions happen to combine nicely with each other, a feature which is exploited in chapter 2 in the derivation of a structural form suitable for estimation. The 'dispersion' parameter ρ_G is shown to have an economic interpretation; it can possibly be endogenized in order to capture a type of structural change which is necessarily ignored in conventional aggregate models. The whole 'aggregation story' applies equally well to both aggregate markets – goods and labour – which are brought together in chapter 2, where the macro model is specified.

Section 1.2 shows how statistics originating from regular business surveys can be exploited in order to provide direct information on the weighted proportions of goods and labour micro markets in excess demand. First, a micro model of the firm is set up in order to examine its possible 'regimes'. Then, the survey questions directly relevant to the rationing issue are shown to be interpretable in the light of the preceding discussion, so as to yield direct information on the 'weighted proportions' statistics, both for the goods market and the labour market. Finally, the last section of chapter 1 warns against improper interpretation of the 'regime proportions' inferred from the survey data.

In order to complete the macro model, we still have to supplement our expressions for the aggregate transactions X and the weighted proportions P_G with specifications of the (effective) aggregate demands and supplies for goods and labour.[4] This is done in section 2.1 of chapter 2, where two alternative specifications of the effective trade offers (namely those of Portes and of Ito) are considered.[5]

After a brief discussion of the stochastic specification, it is shown that both models (Portes' and Ito's) are easily amenable to a structural form suitable for estimation by conventional non-linear FIML methods.

Restrictions on spillover coefficients corresponding to stability and coherency conditions are then discussed as well as the a-priori respective merits of Portes' vs. Ito's formulations. In the last subsection of section 2.1, we examine the properties of economic policy multipliers in this type of model: these multipliers are shown to be highly variable throughout the business cycle, depending on the weighted proportions of goods and labour micro markets currently in excess demand.

In section 2.2 we concern ourselves with the likely form of the aggregate short-run production function obtained by aggregation of elementary production units in a quantity rationing context. We show that explicit aggregation is feasible and results in an aggregate production function of the VES (Variable Elasticity of Substitution) type; the precise specification adopted for our aggregate model is then shown to be consistent with such a functional form.

In order to illustrate the feasibility of this approach and its potential for policy analysis, an empirical application, concerning the Belgian manufacturing sector, is presented in chapter 3.

To this end, we have to substitute precise specifications of the *notional* trade offers (like $\tilde{X}^d$, for example) which appear in the structural form derived in chapter 2.

These specifications are discussed in sections 3.1 and 3.3. Special attention is devoted to specific issues like the dynamic adjustment of aggregate technical coefficients (section 3.1), the proper specification of a 'sectoral labour supply' (section 3.3 and appendix F) and the endogenizing of the 'dispersion' parameter on the labour market (section 3.3). Section 3.2 is concerned with the relation between two concepts of aggregate capacities, one corresponding to notional output supply ($\tilde{X}^s$) and the other implicit in the business survey answers on the degree of utilization of capacities.

The complete model is then estimated by conventional non-linear FIML methods and the empirical results are commented upon in sections 3.4 to 3.6. In section 3.5 we reexamine the choice between Portes' and Ito's specifications in the light of the empirical results: Ito's specification is seen to be preferred since Portes' empirical estimates fail to satisfy the stability and coherency conditions discussed in chapter 2.

The empirical results obtained with Ito's specification are discussed at length in section 3.6. Besides the critical examination of parameter estimates, emphasis is placed on empirical results relevant for economic policy issues. Let us mention, as examples, some of these 'policy oriented' findings:

–   estimation of the actual multiplier (of an autonomous variation in demand), as a function of the 'regime proportions' and the estimated parameters.

–   assessment of the extent and persistence of the 'labour hoarding' phenomenon.

–   computation of a commonly advocated indicator of tensions on the labour market (namely the unemployment/vacancies ratio) which is usually only poorly measured by official statistics.

–   estimation of the margin of profitable capacities and the corresponding margin of 'potential employment'.

The study provides a quantified assessment of an alarming phenomenon: while the rate of capital formation in the manufacturing sector had been sufficient to absorb (or possibly reabsorb after firings) the total manufacturing labour force, it has decreased notably since the mid seventies so that a 'deficit' in available jobs is estimated to have arisen (and to be growing since then) as early as 1977–78.

1

Micro markets in disequilibrium and the use of micro data

1.1 'Smoothing by aggregation' as an alternative to the aggregate *min* condition

The *min*(imum) condition is no doubt the most characteristic feature of theoretical as well as empirical disequilibrium models following the ideas of Barro–Grossman [1971], Benassy [1975], Drèze [1975] and Malinvaud [1977]. It is the outcome of two assumptions about the rationing schemes assumed to prevail on markets in disequilibrium:

(i)   voluntary exchange (no agent may be forced to purchase more than he demands or to sell more than he supplies);

(ii)   market efficiency (all advantageous trades are carried out so that only one side of the markets is rationed).

This is illustrated in figure 1.1[1] where the *min* condition is seen to generate points on the broken line segment $X^d X^s$, so that the whole set of observations on X may be partitioned in two groups, the first being determined purely by demand and the other purely by supply.

If we ask ourselves about the empirical validity of the market efficiency assumption, we note that for it to be valid in all circumstances, all demanders must in some way meet all suppliers. This assumption is quite acceptable if the market is 'small' or centralized, but it becomes much less tenable in more extended or aggregate markets functioning in a decentralized way, as the mutual search of buyers and sellers is costly and some buyers and sellers may not meet.

More importantly from an empirical point of view, 'market inefficiency'[2]

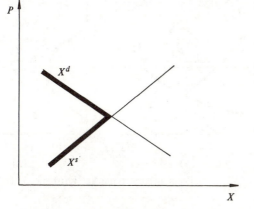

Figure 1.1. The *min* condition

may be shown to result from aggregation. At a macro level, the goods and labour markets are better viewed as heterogeneous entities obtained by aggregation over a large number of different micro markets. Let us define a *goods* micro market as the market for a specific product with all its characteristics. A *labour* micro market is similarly defined by a number of characteristics like qualifications, geographical area, experience, age, sex, etc.

Since such narrowly defined micro markets are 'small' in the sense given above, the efficiency assumption seems most acceptable at this level. Hence the *min* condition may be assumed to prevail on each micro market. But the aggregation of micro markets,[3] some of which may be in excess demand and others in excess supply, will entail the simultaneous existence of job vacancies and unemployment (or unfilled orders and idle capacities) so that the global rationing scheme will appear quite different from an aggregate *min*. This is illustrated in figure 1.2, where the following symbols are used: l^d, l^s and l respectively for labour demand, labour supply and employment; v for vacancies; u for unemployment; and w/p for the level of real wages.

Figures 1.2 (a) and (b) represent two micro labour markets which are aggregated in figure 1.2 (c) by holding relative wages fixed and varying the average real wage. Both micro markets are frictionless, so on the first micro market

$$l_1 = \min (l_1^d, l_1^s) = l_1^s$$

$$v_1 = l_1^d - l_1 = l_1^d - l_1^s$$

$$u_1 = l_1^s - l_1 = 0$$

and on the second micro market

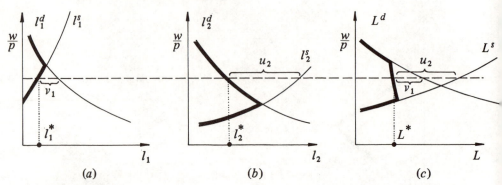

Figure 1.2. Aggregation of two micro markets: (a) micro market 1, (b) micro market 2, (c) aggregate

$$l_2 = \min (l_2^d, l_2^s) = l_2^d$$

$$v_2 = l_2^d - l_2 = 0$$

$$u_2 = l_2^s - l_2 = l_2^s - l_2^d$$

On the aggregate market

$$L^d = l_1^d + l_2^d$$

$$L^s = l_1^s + l_2^s$$

$$L = l_1 + l_2 = l_1^s + l_2^d$$

$$V = v_1 + v_2 = v_1$$

$$U = u_1 + u_2 = u_2$$

We see immediately that within some price range the aggregate transactions (L) will depart from $\min (L^d, L^s)$, so that in general $L \leq \min (L^d, L^s)$ with the possible coexistence of V (unfilled vacancies) and U (unemployment) when $L < \min (L^d, L^s)$.

Aggregating over a large number of micro markets instead of only two produces a smooth transaction curve with $L < \min (L^d, L^s)$ as shown in figure 1.3.[4]

This can be formalized as follows:

Let the joint statistical distribution of micro level labour demands l_j^d and supplies l_j^s be described by a density function $g(l^d, l^s)$ which, if the number N of micro markets is large, may be closely approximated by a smooth continuous density function.[5] We then have

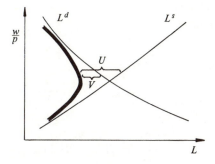

Figure 1.3. Aggregation over a large number of micro markets

$$\int_0^\infty \int_0^\infty g(l^d, l^s)\, dl^d\, dl^s = 1$$

$$\int_0^\infty \int_0^\infty l^d \cdot g(l^d, l^s)\, dl^d\, dl^s = \bar{l}^d = L^d/N$$

$$\int_0^\infty \int_0^\infty l^s \cdot g(l^d, l^s)\, dl^d\, dl^s = \bar{l}^s = L^s/N$$

where L^d and L^s are the aggregate demands and supplies and $\bar{l}^d$ and $\bar{l}^s$ are the 'average' demands and supplies over the micro markets.

If the *min* condition is assumed to prevail on each micro market, i.e. $l_j = \min(l_j^d, l_j^s)$, then the 'average' transaction $\bar{l}$ is

$$\int_0^\infty \int_{l^s}^\infty l^d \cdot g(l^d, l^s)\, dl^s\, dl^d + \int_0^\infty \int_{l^s}^\infty l^s \cdot g(l^d, l^s)\, dl^d\, dl^s = \bar{l} = L/N$$

where L is the aggregate transaction.

The proportion of micro markets in excess demand is

$$\int_0^\infty \int_{l^s}^\infty g(l^d, l^s)\, dl^d\, dl^s = \mathrm{Pr.}\,(l^d \geqslant l^s)$$

Since our observations and specifications refer to the aggregates L, L^d, L^s instead of the 'averages' $\bar{l}$, $\bar{l}^d$, $\bar{l}^s$, we want to work with the former quantities. So we may change variables from the micro (l^d, l^s) to the macro (D, S) where $D = l^d \cdot N$ and $S = l^s \cdot N$. The density function of the transformed variables is $G(D, S) = g(l^d, l^s)/N^2$ which reproduces, appropriately scaled, the distributions on the micro markets.[6]

The above expressions may now be rewritten with the macro variables:

$$L^d = \int_0^\infty \int_0^\infty D \cdot G(D, S) \, dD \, dS$$

$$L^s = \int_0^\infty \int_0^\infty S \cdot G(D, S) \, dD \, dS$$

(L^d, L^s) is thus the mean of the distribution $G(D, S)$.

The aggregate transaction is

$$L = \int_0^\infty \int_D^\infty D \cdot G(D, S) \, dS \, dD + \int_0^\infty \int_S^\infty S \cdot G(D, S) \, dD \, dS \qquad (1.1)$$

The proportion of micro markets in excess demand is

$$\text{Pr.} \, (l^d \geqslant l^s) = \text{Pr.} \, (D \geqslant S) = \int_0^\infty \int_S^\infty G(D, S) \, dD \, dS \qquad (1.2)$$

We can also calculate the 'weighted proportion' of micro markets in excess demand, where each micro market is weighted by its contribution to aggregate transaction:

$$P_w(l^d \geqslant l^s) = \frac{1}{L} \cdot \int_0^\infty \int_S^\infty S \cdot G(D, S) \, dD \, dS$$

$$= \frac{1}{1 + \dfrac{\int_0^\infty \int_D^\infty D \cdot G(D, S) \, dD \, dS}{\int_0^\infty \int_S^\infty S \cdot G(D, S) \, dD \, dS}} \qquad (1.3)$$

This statistic is much more relevant for applied work than its unweighted counterpart since the individual answers to regular surveys that we exploit have, of course, been weighted before aggregation (see section 1.2 for more details).

So L and $P_w(l^d \geqslant l^s)$ are functions of the parameters of the density $G(D, S)$. These consist of the means L^s and L^d and, in most cases, a parameter vector θ relating to higher order moments. The above equations are of the following form:

$$L = L(L^s, L^d, \theta) \quad \text{and} \quad P_w(l^d \geqslant l^s) = P_w(L^s, L^d, \theta) \qquad (1.4)$$

L and P_w are thus smooth but highly non-linear functions whose precise form will depend on the density function $G(D, S)$, i.e. on the assumptions made about the statistical distribution of the micro market demands and supplies.

The question is: can we find theoretically acceptable density functions $g(l^d, l^s)$ for the micro demands and supplies so that the aggregation (by integration) procedure just described ends up with tractable functional forms for L and P_w?

We will show that this is indeed the case if the micro demands and supplies are assumed to obey a bivariate lognormal distribution.

The choice of the lognormal distribution for the size distribution of micro demands and supplies (and hence of their ratios) seems very attractive since most results of empirical research on the size distribution of economic variables (income, wealth, firms, . . .) point towards skewed distributions like the Pareto, lognormal, Yule, Fisher's log series, etc. (See the references cited in Cramer [1969] and Ijiri and Simon [1977].) The rationale which is usually advocated for generating distributions of that type is 'Gibrat's law of proportionate effects' (see Ijiri and Simon [1977]): it invokes a great number of independently distributed factors (of finite variance) exerting a *multiplicative* (instead of an additive) action on the variable so that the central limit theorem may be applied to the *logarithm* of the variable, generating thereby a lognormal as the limiting distribution.

With the lognormality assumption, the working of micro market j may be described as

$$\begin{cases} \ln l_j^d = \lambda^d + \varepsilon_{dj} \\ \ln l_j^s = \lambda^s + \varepsilon_{sj} \\ \ln l_j = \min (\ln l_j^d, \ln l_j^s) \end{cases}$$

with

$$\begin{pmatrix} \varepsilon_d \\ \varepsilon_s \end{pmatrix} \sim N \left[\begin{pmatrix} 0 \\ 0 \end{pmatrix}, \begin{pmatrix} \sigma_{\varepsilon d}^2 & \rho_{ds} \\ \rho_{ds} & \sigma_{\varepsilon s}^2 \end{pmatrix} \right]$$

and the following expressions: for the 'average' demand

$$\bar{l}^d = \exp (\lambda^d + \tfrac{1}{2}\sigma_{\varepsilon d}^2)$$

and for the 'average' supply

$$\bar{l}^s = \exp (\lambda^s + \tfrac{1}{2}\sigma_{\varepsilon s}^2)$$

In the above expressions, λ^d and λ^s are fixed scalars while $(\varepsilon_{dj}, \varepsilon_{sj})$ represent a particular realization of the bivariate normally distributed stochastic variable $(\varepsilon_d, \varepsilon_s)$.

With these statistical assumptions, we can aggregate by integration as in equations (1.1), (1.2) and (1.3) above and get, as approximations, very simple analytical expressions for the aggregate transaction curve and for the proportions (weighted or unweighted) of micro markets in excess demand.

We present and comment here on the final results; the reader may refer to appendix A for the detailed computations.[7]

First of all, it is shown that, besides the aggregate demand and supply L^d and L^s, the only identified parameter is $\sigma_* = [\text{var} (\varepsilon_d - \varepsilon_s)]^{1/2}$. The aggregate data L

and P_w only convey information on the 'degree of mismatch' of micro demands vs. micro supplies.

The aggregate transaction curve exhibits an attractive CES-type (Constant Elasticity of Substitution) functional form:

$$L = [(L^d)^{-\rho*} + (L^s)^{-\rho*}]^{-1/\rho*} \tag{1.5}$$

The weighted proportion of micro markets in excess demand is

$$P_w(l^d \geqslant l^s) = \frac{1}{1 + (L^d/L^s)^{-\rho*}} \tag{1.6}$$

and similarly the weighted proportion of micro markets in excess supply is

$$P_w(l^d < l^s) = 1 - P_w(l^d \geqslant l^s) = \cdots = \frac{1}{1 + (L^d/L^s)^{\rho*}} \tag{1.7}$$

The single parameter ρ_* appearing in all three expressions is

$$\rho_* = -1 + \frac{2}{\sigma_*} \frac{f(-\sigma_*/2)}{F(-\sigma_*/2)}$$

$f(.)$ and $F(.)$ being the standard normal density function and the standard normal cumulative distribution function respectively.

One can show that ρ_* is inversely related to the dispersion parameter σ_* and that $\rho_* \to \infty$ when $\sigma_* \to 0$. This property permits us to present the CES transaction function as the general framework of which the aggregate *min* is only a degenerate case.

Indeed, with $\rho_* > 0$ (which is the case for all $\sigma_* > 0$ since one can show that $\lim_{\sigma_* \to \infty} \rho_* = 0$), we have

$$L = [(L^d)^{-\rho*} + (L^s)^{-\rho*}]^{-1/\rho*} < \min(L^d, L^s)$$

exhibiting a shape like that of the smooth curve of figure 1.3. The parameter ρ_* can be seen as parameterizing the position of the curve in the sense that, for given L^d and L^s, a decrease in ρ_* moves the curve away from the broken line segment (L^d, L^s). In particular, the 'inefficiency at equilibrium', i.e. the discrepancy between L and $L^d = L^s$ is computed as $L/L^d = L/L^s = 2^{-1/\rho*}$ and so depends only on ρ_*.

The conventional approach of aggregate disequilibrium models may be interpreted in the framework of our model as the limiting case of shrinking distributions for micro demands and micro supplies. Indeed, when $\sigma_* \to 0$ (or equivalently $\rho_* \to \infty$), we have

$$L = \lim_{\rho_* \to \infty} [(L^d)^{-\rho*} + (L^s)^{-\rho*}]^{-1/\rho*} = \min(L^d, L^s)$$

whereby the aggregation by integration approach appears as the most general approach encompassing the aggregate *min* as a degenerate case.

The appealing feature of this approach is that tractable functional forms with readily economically interpretable parameters emerge from explicit aggregation of micro markets in disequilibrium. This seems preferable to directly postulating (instead of deriving) attractive functional forms.

An early attempt at this is Spencer's model [1975] in which aggregate transaction is always a convex combination of aggregate demand and supply:

$$L = \lambda L^d + (1 - \lambda)L^s$$

with

$$\lambda = \frac{\exp\left[(L^s - L^d)/\sigma\right]}{1 + \exp\left[(L^s - L^d)/\sigma\right]}$$

where σ is a parameter to be estimated.

These equations lead to the generally sensible results that when excess demand (supply) is large, the value of L is close to supply (demand), and that as $\sigma \to 0$, the model reduces to the standard aggregate *min* model. But as Quandt [1982] points out, it is not clear whether Spencer's model possesses an adequate economic interpretation.

In the late 1970s, Siebrand [1979] proposed, essentially on the basis of considerations on behaviour in uncertainty and 'non-price trade conditions', that the aggregate transaction curve be situated between supply and demand (as in Spencer's model) (see figure 1.4).

He represents this by the following CES curve:

$$L = \left[\delta . (L^d)^{-\rho} + (1 - \delta) . (L^s)^{-\rho}\right]^{-1/\rho}$$

where δ and $(1 - \delta)$ represent the respective weights of demand and supply (assumed to be constant throughout the whole observation period(?)). The parameter ρ is a 'non-linearity coefficient' and does not seem to have any economic interpretation.

Both models appear to be ad-hoc constructions without direct connection to the theoretical developments of the 'quantity rationing' literature (they violate, for example, the commonly accepted assumption of voluntary exchange).

More recently, den Broeder [1983] proposed a CES-type transaction curve derived from explicit aggregation on micro markets distributed according to a Weibull-type distribution function. In this approach, micro demands and supplies are more severely restricted than in our case since they are assumed to be independently and similarly distributed. Although it is shown in appendix A that only the 'degree of mismatch' $\sigma_{(\varepsilon s - \varepsilon d)}$ is identified, the somewhat greater generality of our assumptions concerning $\sigma_{\varepsilon s}$, $\sigma_{\varepsilon d}$ and ρ_{sd} may be seen as

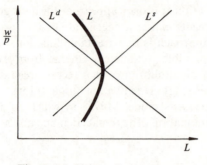

Figure 1.4. Siebrand's 'compromise' transaction curve

enriching the interpretation possibilities of our model as regards the demanders' and suppliers' behaviour. For example, it has been repeatedly argued (Muellbauer [1978]; Malinvaud [1980, 1982]) that attention should be drawn to *adjustments between micro markets experiencing different kinds of imbalance.* Workers are likely to move (geographically or by professional reorientation) from particularly depressed micro markets to others offering better prospects; employers can decide to recruit workers whose qualifications were not exactly those required; consumers may purchase one product instead of a close substitute if delivery delays appear to be substantially different, etc. (For evidence of 'quantity signals' on intersectoral flow of labour, see a.o. Pissarides [1978].)

Gouriéroux and Laroque [1983] provide an in-depth examination of the implications of such 'cross-sectoral spillovers'. In the framework of our model, these 'cross-sectoral spillovers' may be easily formalized as follows.

We start from the basic model

$$\begin{cases} \ln l_j^d = \lambda^d + \varepsilon_{dj} \\ \ln l_j^s = \lambda^s + \varepsilon_{sj} \\ \ln l_j = \min (\ln l_j^d, \ln l_j^s) \end{cases}$$

with

$$\begin{pmatrix} \varepsilon_d \\ \varepsilon_s \end{pmatrix} \sim N \left[\begin{pmatrix} 0 \\ 0 \end{pmatrix}, \begin{pmatrix} \sigma_{\varepsilon d}^2 & \rho_{ds} \\ \rho_{ds} & \sigma_{\varepsilon s}^2 \end{pmatrix} \right]$$

The 'average' imbalance between supply and demand is measured by

$$\bar{z} = \lambda^d - \lambda^s$$

and the 'local' imbalance by

$$z_j = (\lambda^d + \varepsilon_{dj}) - (\lambda^s + \varepsilon_{sj})$$

If we assume that agents tend to move from micro markets offering worse than average prospects to others offering better than average prospects and that this reaction (parameterized by γ for demanders and by δ for suppliers) takes place during the same observation period (in our empirical application, one period = one year), then the model becomes

$$
\begin{cases}
\ln l_j^d = \lambda^d + \varepsilon_{dj} - \gamma(z_j - \bar{z}) & \gamma > 0 \\
\ln l_j^s = \lambda^s + \varepsilon_{sj} + \delta(z_j - \bar{z}) & \delta > 0 \quad \text{but } (\gamma + \delta) < 1 \text{ to exclude the} \\
& \hspace{4.5cm} \text{overshooting case} \\
\ln l_j = \min (\ln l_j^d, \ln l_j^s)
\end{cases}
$$

$$
\begin{cases}
\ln l_j^d = \lambda^d + \varepsilon_{dj} - \gamma(\varepsilon_{dj} - \varepsilon_{sj}) \\
\ln l_j^s = \lambda^s + \varepsilon_{sj} + \delta(\varepsilon_{dj} - \varepsilon_{sj})
\end{cases}
$$

$$
\begin{cases}
\ln l_j^d = \lambda^d + [(1-\gamma)\varepsilon_{dj} + \gamma\varepsilon_{sj}] = \lambda^d + \varepsilon_{dj}^* \\
\ln l_j^s = \lambda^s + [\delta\varepsilon_{dj} + (1-\delta)\varepsilon_{sj}] = \lambda^s + \varepsilon_{sj}^*
\end{cases}
$$

with ε_d^* and ε_s^* representing the distributions of micro demands and supplies. One first notices that, even with $\sigma_{\varepsilon s} = \sigma_{\varepsilon d}$ and $\rho_{ds} = 0$, one gets in the general case $\sigma_{\varepsilon d}^* \neq \sigma_{\varepsilon s}^*$ and $\rho_{ds}^* \neq 0$. But the parameter of interest is

$$
\begin{aligned}
\mathrm{var}\,[\varepsilon_d^* - \varepsilon_s^*] &= \mathrm{var}\,[(1-\gamma-\delta)\varepsilon_d - (1-\gamma-\delta)\varepsilon_s] \\
&= \mathrm{var}\,[(1-\gamma-\delta)(\varepsilon_d - \varepsilon_s)] \\
&= (1-\gamma-\delta)^2 \sigma_*^2
\end{aligned}
$$

One sees immediately that a decrease in the mobility of both demanders and suppliers ($\Delta\gamma$ and/or $\Delta\delta < 0$) induces an increase of the 'degree of mismatch' $\mathrm{var}\,(\varepsilon_d^* - \varepsilon_s^*)$ and hence a decrease of the parameter ρ_*, moving the CES transaction curve away from the broken line segment $\min (L^s, L^d)$. Such a displacement of the aggregate transaction curve is reflected by an outward shift in the unfilled orders/available capacities trade-off (for the goods market) or the unemployment/vacancies trade-off (for the labour market). This last phenomenon has been effectively observed since the mid 1970s in a number of countries and the above model suggests that a possible explanation could be in terms of diminishing 'cross-sectoral' mobility. Other explanations, like the 'selectivity mechanism of unemployment', may also play a role and can be similarly modelled.[8]

The increasing (or decreasing) dispersion of demands vs. supplies at the micro level may be seen as a type of structural change which is easily modelled in the 'aggregation by integration' framework. From a practical point of view, since our approach results in particularly simple functional forms, this amounts to possibly 'endogenizing' some ρ_* parameters. However, for simplicity's sake, the ρ_* parameters will be assumed to be constant in the following discussion up to chapter 3.

Another most appealing feature of this approach, already stressed in the introduction, is its *suitability for policy analysis*. The traditional aggregate disequilibrium model is rudimentary from this point of view since, due to the aggregate *min* condition $L = \min(L^d, L^s)$, the partial multiplier $\partial L/\partial L^d$ (or $\partial L/\partial L^s$) takes the value 0 or 1 depending on the prevailing regime. One would intuitively expect that, in our approach, this partial multiplier may take any value in the range [0, 1] depending on the proportion of micro markets in one or the other regime. This is indeed the case and the simplicity of the resulting formulas makes them particularly attractive.

Taking the derivative of equation (1.5), we get

$$\frac{\partial L}{\partial L^d} = \cdots = \left(\frac{L}{L^d}\right) \cdot \left[\frac{1}{1 + (L^s/L^d)^{-\rho*}}\right]$$

which, combined with equation (1.6), gives

$$\frac{\partial \ln L}{\partial \ln L^d} = P_w(l^d < l^s) \tag{1.8}$$

The elasticity of aggregate transaction with respect to aggregate demand is thus equal to the weighted proportion of micro markets in excess supply. It should be stressed here (and is demonstrated in appendix A) that this property is not peculiar to our distributional assumptions and in fact characterizes a wider class of models.

A similar type of expression may be derived for the partial derivative. Indeed, from equations (1.5) and (1.6) we may write

$$\frac{L}{L^d} = \left[1 + \left(\frac{L^s}{L^d}\right)^{-\rho*}\right]^{-1/\rho*} = [P_w(l^d < l^s)]^{1/\rho*}$$

Combining this with equation (1.8) gives

$$\frac{\partial L}{\partial L^d} = [P_w(l^d < l^s)]^{1 + 1/\rho*} \leqslant \frac{\partial \ln L}{\partial \ln L^d} \leqslant 1 \tag{1.9}$$

which for given ρ_* is easily seen to be a continuous decreasing function of L^d/L^s in the range [0, 1].

The above expressions are those of impact multipliers. Full multiplier effects have to take into account the derived effects on – and feedback from – the labour market (for macroeconomic policy analysis) or other sectoral goods markets (for input–output analysis).

In chapter 2, after presenting the macro model, a detailed example of economic policy multiplier effects will be worked out in order to show how our approach departs from (and encompasses) both the traditional Keynesian multiplier and the 'bang-bang' multiplier of the conventional aggregate disequilibrium models.

Input–output analysis is considered in appendix C where it is shown how the traditional I–O multiplier formulas have to be modified in a quantity rationing context.

The whole discussion of this section has concentrated on one (undefined) aggregate market made up of a large number of micro markets in various disequilibrium situations. The systematic use of the letter 'L' may have suggested that we had in mind the labour market only but, as explained above, this picture applies equally well to both aggregate markets, goods and labour.

Indeed, as will be developed in detail in the next section, an aggregate macro sector may be viewed as consisting of a large number of firms facing simultaneously a goods micro market and a labour micro market. Considering micro demands and micro supplies for both types of markets, we have a four-dimensional lognormal statistical distribution.

Denoting by (η_d, η_s) and $(\varepsilon_d, \varepsilon_s)$ the stochastic terms referring to the 'size distribution' of micro demands and supplies for goods and labour, we assume the following distribution

$$
\begin{pmatrix} \eta_d \\ \eta_s \\ \varepsilon_d \\ \varepsilon_s \end{pmatrix} \sim N \left[\begin{pmatrix} 0 \\ 0 \\ 0 \\ 0 \end{pmatrix}, \begin{pmatrix} \times & \times & 0 & 0 \\ \times & \times & 0 & 0 \\ 0 & 0 & \times & \times \\ 0 & 0 & \times & \times \end{pmatrix} \right]
$$

where '$\times$' stands for a non-zero element.

The assumption of a zero correlation between the η's and the ε's is only to be seen as a convenient *theoretical hypothesis* since it allows us to perform a similar aggregation procedure separately for each aggregate market.

We do not intend to claim this assumption to be strictly compatible with factual observation; instead the main support for it stems from an 'efficiency' argument: it is a theoretical device which allows an easy derivation of an aggregate structural form which not only 'explains' actual empirical observations quite well but, much more importantly, also offers new insights into the phenomenon of rationing.

The role of such an hypothesis made *at this stage of the research* is thus merely to further the development of a (hopefully!) fruitful theoretical construct rather than to provide an accurately descriptive assumption.

Of course, when it comes to the *empirical analysis*, due account will be taken of the possibility of non-zero correlations, in order to interpret correctly the actual business survey data. This possibility will be discussed in section 1.2.3 (see note 18) and examined empirically in section 3.4.

Both aggregate markets are brought together in chapter 2 where the macro model is presented and discussed. But before that, we still have to examine how the weighted proportions of goods micro markets in excess demand $P_G \triangleq P_w(x^d > x^s)$ and labour micro markets in excess demand $P_L \triangleq P_w(l^d > l^s)$ can be derived from regular business surveys and how these statistics ought to be interpreted. This will be the subject of the next section.

1.2   The business survey data and their interpretation

In the preceding section, a micro market could be defined in rather general terms as a small segment of an aggregate macro market. The only requirement was for it to be defined at a sufficiently micro level so that the distribution of micro demands and supplies could be approximated by a continuous density function.

However, so that we can exploit statistical data yielding direct information on the weighted proportions P_G and P_L, we need to be more specific about these micro markets. This statistical information is available from the results of regular business surveys conducted within firms of the manufacturing sector.

The unit of observation is thus the individual firm. Hence, before describing the surveys and discussing the interpretation of their results, we sketch briefly the model of the typical firm in order to distinguish the various regimes in which it may find itself. The presentation adopted here mainly follows the line of Kooiman [1982, 1984].

1.2.1   The firm and its possible 'regimes'

An aggregate macro sector (in our empirical application, the Belgian manufacturing sector) is considered to consist of a large number of production units, the firms, each firm manufacturing a single product.[9]

The firm is seen to face simultaneously two micro markets: a goods micro market on which it sells its product and a labour micro market from which it draws its labour force. The time period we consider is basically the short-run: the firm's installed capital stock is hence assumed to be given and is combined with labour to produce output[10] during the period. As is characteristic of this type of model, the price of the product and the wage are assumed to be announced (possibly set by the firm itself) at the start of the period but then stay fixed, so that the burden of the adjustment falls entirely on quantities during the period.

The adoption here of the extreme fix-price assumption should only be regarded as reflecting the recognition that, on some markets, short-run price adjustments are very slow by comparison to what would be needed to assure *permanent* equality between demands and supplies.

Given the prevailing wage and product price and its existing equipment,[11] firm i can define its notional output supply $\tilde{X}_i^s$ and the associated level of notional labour demand $\tilde{L}_i^d$.[12] These are defined as the optimal (profit maximizing) level of operating the plant and the corresponding employment level in the absence of any (perceived) constraint on any market.

The firm is then confronted with an effective demand X_i^d on its product micro market and an effective supply L_i^s on its labour micro market.

Its level of operation will thus be determined by its (profitable) capacity, by demand for its product or by availability of labour. Iwai [1974] shows, in a more formal setting, that profit maximization by the firm leads to the following minimum conditions for the determination of output X_i and employment L_i.

$$X_i = \min (X_i^d, X_i^s)$$

$$X_i = \min [X_i^d, \tilde{X}_i^s, X_i^s(L_i)] \tag{1.10}$$

and similarly

$$L_i = \min (L_i^d, L_i^s)$$

$$L_i = \min [\tilde{L}_i^d, L_i^d(X_i), L_i^s] \tag{1.11}$$

where X_i^d, $\tilde{X}_i^s$, $\tilde{L}_i^d$ and L_i^s are as defined above.

$X_i^s(L_i)$ is the effective output supply, i.e. it is the maximum output the firm manages to produce with amount of labour L_i. This is the short-run efficient production frontier which is quite naturally assumed to satisfy the following conditions:

$$X_i^s(\tilde{L}_i^d) = \tilde{X}_i^s \tag{1.12}$$

$$X_i^{s'}(.) \geqslant 0 \quad \text{with the prime denoting the first derivative} \tag{1.13}$$

$L_i^d(X_i)$ is the effective demand for labour, i.e. the amount of labour the firm decides to employ when its production is at level X_i. This function is quite naturally assumed to satisfy the following conditions:

$$L_i^d(\tilde{X}_i^s) = \tilde{L}_i^d \tag{1.14}$$

$$L_i^{d'}(.) \geqslant 0 \quad \text{with the prime denoting the first derivative} \tag{1.15}$$

If the firm i were to stay permanently on its efficient production frontier, then the two functions $X_i^s(.)$ and $L_i^d(.)$ would coincide. However, confronted with uncertainty surrounding future demand for its product and future supply of labour, and with the costs (hiring and firing costs) linked with short-run adjustments of labour, the profit-maximizing firm is more likely to enhance its

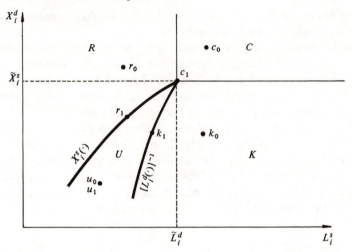

Figure 1.5. Regime definitions for firm i

flexibility[13] by holding excess labour in reserve when demand slackens.

This 'labour hoarding' has been extensively documented as a widely prevailing phenomenon, even at relatively high operating levels (refer to chapter 3 for discussion of some empirical evidence).

The occurrence of labour hoarding forces the $[L_i^d(.)]^{-1}$ function below the efficiency frontier $X_i^s(.)$.

This is expressed as

$$X_i^s[L_i^d(\chi)] \geqslant \chi \qquad \forall \chi \leqslant \tilde{X}_i^s \tag{1.16}$$

It is easily checked that conditions (1.10) to (1.16) yield figure 1.5 in (X_i^d, L_i^s) space.

One can show that firm i can find itself in one of four possible 'regimes', apart from boundary cases.

(1)   In the *classical* case, corresponding to region C in figure 1.5, the firm is confronted with a demand for goods X_i^d and a supply of labour L_i^s which both exceed the firm's notional trade offers. We have

$$X_i = X_i^s(\tilde{L}_i^d) = \tilde{X}_i^s < X_i^d$$

$$L_i = L_i^d(\tilde{X}_i^s) = \tilde{L}_i^d < L_i^s$$

To any point c_0 (with coordinates X_{i,c_0}^d, L_{i,c_0}^s) in region C will correspond point c_1 (with coordinates $\tilde{X}_i^s, \tilde{L}_i^d$) representing the effective output–labour combination.

(2)   In the *Keynesian* case, corresponding to region K in the figure, both

(profitable) capacity $\tilde{X}_i^s$ and labour supply L_i^s are sufficient to meet demand. We have

$$X_i = X_i^d < X_i^s(L_i)$$

$$L_i = L_i^d(X_i) < L_i^s$$

The firm is seen to spillover its 'rationing' on the goods market $(X_i^d < \tilde{X}_i^s)$ to the labour market $(L_i^d < \tilde{L}_i^d)$. To the point k_0 in region K will correspond the effective output–labour combination k_1.

(3)   In the *repressed inflation* case, corresponding to region R, both demand for goods X_i^d and capacity $\tilde{X}_i^s$ are sufficient but labour supply L_i^s is the constraining factor. We have

$$X_i = X_i^s(L_i) < X_i^d$$

$$L_i = L_i^s < L_i^d(X_i)$$

The spillover effect now works itself from the labour market to the goods market. To the point r_0 in region R corresponds the effective output–labour combination r_1.

(4)   In the *underconsumption* case, corresponding to region U inside the 'double wedge' $X_i^s(.) - [L_i^d(.)]^{-1}$, the firm is constrained on both markets. We have

$$X_i = X_i^d < X_i^s(L_i)$$

$$L_i = L_i^s < L_i^d(X_i)$$

The two points u_0 and u_1 coincide in this case.

The existence of the 'underconsumption' regime, which is due to the non-coincidence of the two curves $X_i^s(.)$ and $[L_i^d(.)]^{-1}$, is in this model clearly linked to the 'labour hoarding' phenomenon.

Now that we have a clear description of the various 'regimes' in which a firm may find itself, we may consider the business survey questions relevant to our problem. These questions will be seen to be directly interpretable in the light of the preceding discussion.

Before going further into this discussion, a short remark seems in order. The labels 'Keynesian', 'classical', etc., attributed to the four possible regimes of the firm have been chosen by reference to the received terminology of disequilibrium macro models. Although the terms 'Keynesian' and 'classical' inevitably suggest some policy diagnosis and prescription, they should only be interpreted here as describing the instantaneous situation of the firms on both their labour and goods micro markets. For example, if a majority – say 65% – of the firms are found to be in the 'Keynesian' regime, it only means that 65% of the firms are on their demand curves on both goods and labour micro markets. That is the information which is relevant to us for model building and analysis of policy multiplier effects;[14] further extrapolation of such a statistic to the conclusion that the policy prescriptions linked to the 'classical' school of thought are mostly irrelevant in such a context should only be made with care and should certainly rely on other economic information.

This point will be developed in more detail in subsection 1.2.4; the point we want to make clear is that the 'regime proportions' conveyed by the business survey results are the right statistical information to exploit in connection with the 'theory of aggregation' developed so far.

In the next two subsections, we first describe the business survey and then discuss the interpretation of their results in relation to the (weighted) proportions P_G and P_L of goods and labour micro markets in excess demand.

1.2.2   Description of the survey on the use of capacity

Since the mid 1950s, regular surveys have been conducted by the Belgian National Bank (BNB) within firms of the Belgian manufacturing sector. There are a number of different surveys, whose periodicity varies with the issue at stake, from monthly surveys about short-term market developments with qualitative answers (better, no change, worse), to half-yearly surveys about fixed investment decisions with quantitative answers.

The survey which is of interest to us here, called 'survey on production capacities', has been conducted every quarter[15] since 1963 within a sample of about 1000 firms of all sectors of Belgian manufacturing industry.[16] The firms are asked to fill *one questionnaire per product* (or group of products). Besides some 'qualitative' questions mainly concerned with their prospects, they are asked the following questions which are directly of interest to us.

Question 1. During the month under review, the degree of utilization of our production capacity was, according to our estimation, about ☐ %.

Question 2. During the month under review, did insufficient demand for this product prevent you from producing more?

yes ☐   no ☐

Question 3 is to be answered only by firms which have answered 'no' to question 2.

Question 3. During the month under review, it was impossible for us to meet the existing demand for this product, because we were unable to bring to a higher level the utilization of our production capacity, due to the following reason(s):

- lack of overhead and/or skilled labour ☐
- lack of equipment   ☐
- lack of raw materials   ☐
- other causes   ☐
    (please specify the other causes)

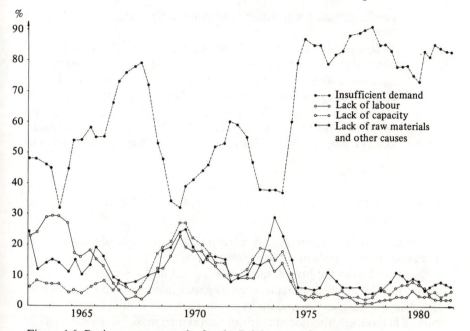

Figure 1.6. Business survey results for the Belgian manufacturing sector

Individual answers are then weighted (first by turnover at a most disaggregated level and then by value added) to yield aggregate results at a subsectoral and sectoral level. Figure 1.6 displays the quarterly data for the Belgian manufacturing sector (excluding food processing, beverage and tobacco, oil refineries and garages) over the period 1963.1 to 1981.4. The data displayed on the figure are the original data as published by the BNB, before any subsequent data management (refer to appendix H for some details about data processing).

Since the interpretation of these data is discussed in the following section, only a few immediate remarks are made here.

–   The formulation of question 3 involves *skilled* labour only since information gathered before the survey started revealed that totally unskilled labour never constituted a bottleneck because of the possibility of attracting immigrant labour.

–   The reporting by firms of several simultaneous bottlenecks happens only infrequently and in these cases mostly involves labour and equipment together, according to information from the research unit of the BNB.

–   Still according to information from that source, the most often mentioned 'other causes' involve lack of storage capacity for finished goods, strikes, strong absenteeism, financial constraints faced by the firms, etc.

–   A last possibility, not explicitly offered to the firms, is the 'no constraint' answer expressed by crossing the 'no' answer to question 2 without mentioning any bottleneck at question 3. It may be interesting to mention that, according to information from the research unit of the BNB, the degree of capacity utilization reported by firms answering that way typically approaches the maximum (always $\geqslant 90\%$). In the next subsection we will say more about this.

1.2.3   Interpretation of the business survey data in relation to the P_G and P_L statistics

Questions 2 and 3 are now directly interpretable in the light of the preceding discussion of the firm's possible regimes.

Question 2 asks the firm if, during the period under review, it has been constrained by insufficient demand on its goods micro market or, otherwise stated, if with a higher demand for its product it would (could) have produced more. This is clearly the case of the firms being either in the 'Keynesian' (K) or the 'underconsumption' (U) regimes.

The other firms, answering 'no' to question 2, were unable to meet existing demand for their product either because of labour constraints (R regime) or because of 'capacity constraints' (C regime).

'Capacity constraints' may be experienced by firms in two different ways, likely to induce two types of answers:

–   either the firm runs short of physical installed capacity in which case it will answer 'no' to question 2 and cross off the 'lack of equipment' item in question 3;

–   or the firm may find itself in a situation as described in note 12 where notional output supply $\tilde{X}_i^s$ is strictly lower than total installed capacity because economically obsolete equipment has not been scrapped immediately. Since the profit-maximizing firm is assumed not to produce beyond its notional output supply $\tilde{X}_i^s$, a firm standing at this point (point c_1 in figure 1.5) is most likely to answer 'no' to question 2 without crossing any of the physical bottlenecks proposed in question 3. The fact that firms answering this way typically approach full installed capacity (see subsection 1.2.2 above) supports this interpretation.

Anyway, either version of the 'capacity constraints' case falls within the 'classical' regime (C) case. Table 1.1, summarizing the preceding discussion,

Table 1.1. *The 'survey on production capacities' and the regime proportions*

Percentage of answers to		Proportion of firms in various regimes
Question 2	yes	$P_K + P_U (= 1 - P_G)$
	no	$P_R + P_C (= P_G)$
Question 3	labour constraints	P_R
	capacity and (other)	P_C
	constraints[17]	

shows the correspondence between the aggregate business survey results and the proportions P_k ($k = K, U, R, C$) of firms in the various regimes.

The sum $P_R + P_C$ (i.e. the percentage of 'no' answers to question 2) gives the proportion of goods micro markets for which $X_i^d > X_i^s$, i.e. which are in excess demand. Since the individual answers to the survey are weighted by output shares (or the best proxies available), we find that *the statistic*

$$P_G = P_w(X_i^d > X_i^s)$$

is directly yielded by the aggregate (weighted) percentage of 'no' answers to question 2.

Unfortunately, the statistic P_L (weighted proportion of labour micro markets in excess demand) is not as readily available from the business survey results as the P_G statistic, basically because firms answering 'yes' to question 2 are no longer asked about their possible constraints on their labour micro market.

It is thus impossible, on the basis of the survey results alone, to discriminate among the firms answering that way between those which are constrained on their labour micro market (proportion P_U) and those which are not (proportion P_K).

Forgetting for a moment the 'weighting factor' aspect (which will be discussed shortly), the proportions P_k of table 1.1 may be written:

$$P_K = \text{Pr.}\,(X_i^d < X_i^s \text{ and } L_i^d < L_i^s)$$

$$P_U = \text{Pr.}\,(X_i^d < X_i^s \text{ and } L_i^d > L_i^s)$$

$$P_R = \text{Pr.}\,(X_i^d > X_i^s \text{ and } L_i^d > L_i^s)$$

$$P_C = \text{Pr.}\,(X_i^d > X_i^s \text{ and } L_i^d < L_i^s)$$

Remembering that the micro demands and supplies on both goods and labour micro markets were assumed (see section 1.1) to be jointly lognormally distributed, it follows that the variables

$$\chi_i = \ln\,(X_i^s / X_i^d)$$

and

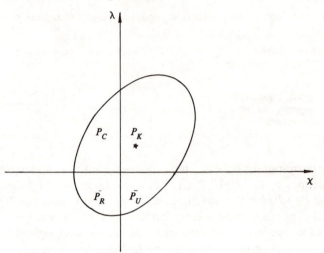

Figure 1.7. Proportions P_k in the χ–λ plane

$$\lambda_i = \ln (L_i^s/L_i^d)$$

are *jointly normally* distributed.

The proportions P_k above are thus the relative frequencies of pairs falling in each quadrant of the χ–λ plane. This is illustrated in figure 1.7.

Our problem is the following: knowing the proportions P_R and $P_G (= P_R + P_C)$, which are directly observable, we want to get an estimate of $P_L (= P_R + P_U)$. Clearly this will depend on the correlation coefficient ρ^* of the bivariate normal distribution.[18]

With $\rho^* = 0$ (independence of χ and λ), the ellipsoid of concentration is circular and we have directly

$$P_L = P_R + P_U = \frac{P_R}{P_R + P_C} = \frac{P_R}{P_G}$$

while $\rho^* > 0$ induces

$$P_L < \frac{P_R}{P_G}$$

What are the a-priori expectations about the sign and size of ρ^*? First, about the sign, both the geographical concentration of activities and the possible specialization of the labour force lead us to expect a *positive* correlation: indeed when geographical concentration of some activities (i.e. of the fabrication of some specific products i) takes place, depressed demand for some products is likely to be accompanied by a similar depressed demand on the local labour markets inducing, with reduced geographical labour mobility, a positive covariance between demand–supply ratios on both markets; similarly if high specialization of the labour force results in some qualifications corresponding closely to some products.

The importance of these phenomena should not however be exaggerated: modern economies are better characterized as an intricate network of activities scattered over a country so that each region is comprised of firms which are present on a diversified spectrum of activities; moreover, even a dominant activity usually covers a variety of diversely demanded products. As for the argument on the specification of the labour force, it should not be given too much strength given the marked 'heterogeneity of the labour structures associated with the fabrication of identical products' (de Falleur [1978]) brought into evidence by labour economists.

The above discussion suggests that, on balance, a positive but weak correlation ρ^* (for the bivariate χ–λ distribution) is to be expected.

Two pieces of empirical evidence support this a-priori expectations. First, empirical results of P. Kooiman [1983] (based on the answers to the corresponding Dutch business survey) in a slightly different but still comparable statistical setting point toward the correlation ρ^* as being weakly positive ($\hat{\rho}^* = 0.17$) but not (statistically) significantly different from zero. However, the most informative piece of evidence on this issue is to be found in a recent paper of Bouissou, Laffont and Vuong [1983]. Using the data provided by the corresponding French business survey, these authors are interested in 'explaining' the probability that a firm finds itself in one of the four regimes, conditionally on its previous situation and other 'exogenous' qualitative variables. Their results, though preliminary, are very interesting but are not the primary reason for our mentioning their paper.

Instead, our interest here stems mainly from some statistical data disclosed in the paper: not only does the French business survey 'on the use of capacities' happen to ask a question similar to our question 2 but *all* firms are also asked about labour constraints,[19] *whatever the firm's answer to question 2.*

Availability of the individual answers to both questions enables the authors to present time series of the (unweighted) proportions P_k of firms in each regime. On the basis of our assumption of a bivariate normal distribution for χ–λ, these proportions P_k yield sufficient information for the inference of ρ^*. Indeed it may be shown (see J. F. Richard [1980]) that an estimate of ρ^* is yielded by

$$\rho^* = \cos\left(\frac{\pi}{1+\sqrt{\psi}}\right)$$

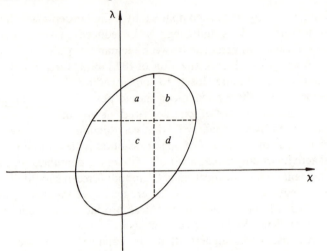

Figure 1.8. Sufficient information for the estimation of the contingency coefficient ψ

where ψ is the contingency (or association) coefficient of the corresponding C-type bivariate normal distribution. A simple estimator of ψ is given by

$$\tilde{\psi} = \frac{b \cdot c}{a \cdot d}$$

where a, b, c and d are the frequency of pairs computed at an arbitrary point of dichotomy in the χ–λ plane as illustrated by figure 1.8. With $(0,0)$ chosen as the point of dichotomy (as on figure 1.7), we may readily compute

$$\tilde{\rho}^* = \cos\left(\frac{\pi}{1 + \sqrt{(P_K P_R / P_U P_C)}}\right) \tag{1.17}$$

Using the reported proportions P_{kt}, we simply calculate $\tilde{\rho}_t^*$ using the above formula. The resulting $\tilde{\rho}_t^*$ statistic suggests two observations.

(i)   The correlation coefficient $\tilde{\rho}^*$ does not appear to be constant during the observation period but instead exhibits *mild* fluctuations (see point (ii) below), increasing in recessions and decreasing with improving general business conditions. In view of the mild character of these fluctuations, it is felt that a constant value of ρ^* may be safely assumed in this first attempt at capturing the heterogeneity of both goods and labour markets.

(ii)   The estimated $\tilde{\rho}_t^*$ exhibits values comprised between 0.15 and 0.30 for the available observation period (1975:1 to 1982:3).[20] Moreover, for reasons discussed by the authors, their proportions P_K are likely to have been somewhat overestimated at the expense of P_C. As formula (1.17) makes clear, this would result in the estimates reported above overestimating somewhat the true correlation ρ^*.

As a conclusion, the available empirical evidence (outside our sample data) also points toward a positive but weak correlation coefficient ρ^*, as was suggested by our theoretical considerations earlier.

For moderate (positive or negative) values of ρ^*, the bivariate normal distribution function $F_{\chi,\lambda}(.,.)$ may be approximated by[21]

$$F_{\chi,\lambda}(x, y) = F_\chi(x) F_\lambda(y) . [1 + \alpha(1 - F_\chi(x)) . (1 - F_\lambda(y))] \quad \text{with } \alpha = (\psi - 1)$$

where $F_\chi(.)$ and $F_\lambda(.)$ are the marginal distribution functions of χ and λ respectively.

With $(x, y) = (0, 0)$, we have

$$P_R = P_G . P_L . [1 + \alpha(1 - P_G)(1 - P_L)] \tag{1.18}$$

Clearly $\alpha = 0$ (implying $\rho^* = 0$) yields $P_L = P_R/P_G$, while $\alpha > 0$ (implying $\rho^* > 0$) yields $P_L < P_R/P_G$.

Expressing P_L as the root of the second-degree equation (1.18), we get a complicated expression of P_L as a function of the observables P_R and P_G and the 'association' coefficient α:

$$P_L = \frac{[P_G(\alpha P_G - \alpha - 1)] + \{[P_G(\alpha P_G - \alpha - 1)]^2 + 4\alpha P_G(P_G - 1)P_R\}^{1/2}}{[2\alpha(P_G - 1)P_G]} \tag{1.19}$$

Denoting by the symbol $\hat{P}_L$ the 'bench-mark' value $\hat{P}_L = P_R/P_G$, it is readily verified that

$$\lim_{\substack{\alpha \to 0 \\ \text{(i.e. } \rho^* \to 0)}} P_L = \hat{P}_L = P_R/P_G$$

while

$$P_L \underset{\substack{\alpha > 0 \\ \text{(i.e. } \rho^* > 0)}}{} < \hat{P}_L = P_R/P_G$$

If, in view of the empirical evidence just reported above, the assumption of a negligible correlation ρ^* seems unacceptably strong, it may be tested (and ρ^* estimated) by substituting the above specification for P_L in the empirical model proposed for estimation. In view of the highly non-linear character of this P_L specification, a grid search over α is likely to be the most appropriate estimation procedure. Refer to chapter 3 for more details and the empirical results.

Another, more tractable, approximate expression for P_L may also be derived. Since in equation (1.18) the second term between brackets is likely to be small, we may approximate equation (1.18) by

$$P_R = P_G \cdot P_L \cdot [1 + \alpha(1 - P_G)(1 - P_L)] \simeq \frac{P_G \cdot P_L}{[1 - \alpha(1 - P_G)(1 - P_L)]}$$

This yields a simpler approximation for P_L as

$$P_L = \frac{P_R}{P_G} \cdot \frac{[1 - \alpha(1 - P_G)]}{\left[1 - \alpha(1 - P_G)\frac{P_R}{P_G}\right]} = \hat{P}_L \frac{[1 - \alpha(1 - P_G)]}{[1 - \alpha(1 - P_G)\hat{P}_L]} \tag{1.20}$$

One can show that here also the 'negligible correlation' assumption $\rho^* = 0$ (hence $\alpha = 0$) yields $P_L = \hat{P}_L = P_R/P_G$, while $\rho^* > 0$ (hence $\alpha > 0$) implies $P_L < \hat{P}_L = P_R/P_G$.

Specification (1.20) may also be substituted for P_L in the empirical application and, since it does not look too complicated, it may be possible to estimate α freely (along with all the other parameters of the model) by FIML methods. Section 4 of chapter 3 will report on this.

Before commenting on the 'regime proportions', two remarks are in order.

The first concerns formula (1.18) and the derived expressions (1.19) and (1.20). Although we use, for ease of exposition, the notation P_G, P_L and P_R (referring to *weighted* proportions), these formulas are, strictly speaking, valid only for the corresponding *unweighted* proportions.

The rigorous derivation of analogous formulas for the *weighted* proportions does not appear self-evident at all. However, since weighted and unweighted proportions turn out to be very close (at least in the relevant range of parameters – see note 22), it seems acceptable for our purposes to adopt formula (1.18) as valid (as an approximation) for weighted proportions also. Expressions (1.19) or (1.20) are then the right formulas to substitute for the (weighted) P_L in the empirical application.

The second remark concerns P_L. In subsection 1.2.2 we said that the available statistics P_G and P_R are weighted by *output* shares. However, to conform to the theoretical expressions derived in appendix A, the weighted proportion P_L has to be weighted by *labour* shares. To achieve this, the best feasible solution appeared to be the following: since P_L is expected (for reasons developed above) not to depart very much from its 'bench-mark' value $\hat{P}_L$, we constructed – and used in the empirical estimation – an appropriately weighted $\hat{P}_L$ statistic.[23]

Regime proportions may easily be computed. Indeed figure 1.7 makes clear that

$$P_C = P_G - P_R$$

$$P_U = P_L - P_R$$

$$P_K = 1 - P_G - P_L + P_R$$

which, combined with equation (1.18), yields the following expressions:

$$P_R = P_G \cdot P_L \cdot [1 + \alpha(1 - P_G)(1 - P_L)]$$

$$P_C = P_G\{1 - P_L[1 + \alpha(1 - P_G)(1 - P_L)]\}$$

$$P_U = (1 - P_G)\{1 - (1 - P_L)[1 + \alpha P_G P_L]\}$$

$$P_K = (1 - P_G)(1 - P_L)[1 + \alpha P_G P_L]$$

These are the (weighted) proportions of firms being respectively in the 'repressed inflation', the 'classical', the 'underconsumption', or the 'Keynesian' regime. The formulas are easily seen to embody – as a particular case – the conventional 'disequilibrium' approach: indeed, it is shown in appendix A that the proportions P_L and P_G tend to 0 or 1 (depending on aggregate excess supply or excess demand in either market) with shrinking distributions at the micro level. In such a case, the regime proportions given by the above formulas reduce to 0 or 1 (only one proportion takes the value 1) and we are back to the conventional aggregate approach.

At the expense of spoiling somewhat the 'suspense' about the numerical estimate of the 'association' parameter α, we can be more specific at this stage about the historical experience of these various 'regime proportions'.

Let us only say here that the value which came out of the estimation procedure is $\alpha = 0$ (hence $\rho^* = 0$) (refer to section 3.4 for more details).

It follows that the (weighted) proportion P_L reduces to its 'bench-mark' value $P_L = P_R/P_G$ while the 'regime proportions' take the simple expressions

$$P_K = (1 - P_G)(1 - P_L)$$

$$P_R = P_G \cdot P_L$$

$$P_C = P_G(1 - P_L)$$

$$P_U = (1 - P_G)P_L$$

The P_G (directly observed) and P_L statistics are displayed in figures 1.9 and 1.10 respectively.[24]

It may be mentioned with interest that the estimated P_L series is in line with conclusions drawn by H. Sneessens [1981] from his estimation of an aggregate disequilibrium model of the Belgian economy. Indeed, from that work, the labour market appears to have been constantly in excess supply, except during the first half of the 1960s where the market was first close to equilibrium and then even in excess demand (in 1964–5 in Sneessens' work). This profile conforms with out P_L series.

The 'regime proportions' for the Belgian manufacturing sector are displayed in figure 1.11 where the observation period is partitioned in subperiods according to their 'dominant' regime. To ease comparison and highlight general accordance with Sneessens' results (but do not forget his

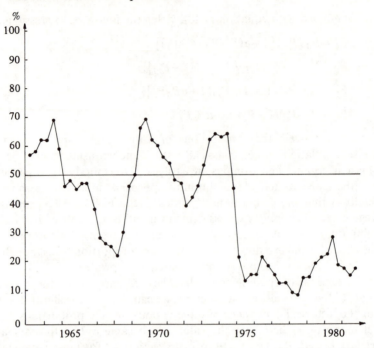

Figure 1.9. P_G, the weighted proportion (in %) of goods micro markets in excess demand in the Belgian manufacturing sector

model was about the whole economy while ours only concerns the manufacturing sector), his partition of regimes (with account being taken of his corrective remark for the period 1969–74) is also reported in the figure.

It is interesting to note that the period 1963–65 is the only one with no clearly dominating regime; here all four regime proportions are close to 25%, which indicates a situation close to equilibrium on both aggregate markets.

The rest of the observation period is characterized by an alternation of 'Keynesian' and 'classical' regimes as the dominating regime, the extent of the 'repressed inflation' and 'underconsumption' regimes being quite moderate in comparison with the other two. From 1975 on, the 'Keynesian' regime appears as the highly dominant one.

The labels 'Keynesian' and 'classical' have been adopted here, in reference to the received terminology of fix-price models, to characterize the instantaneous situation of a firm which may be constrained on either goods or labour micro markets.

However, the straightforward interpretation of the extent of either regime in view of policy diagnosis and/or prescription calls for some caution as will be argued in the next subsection.

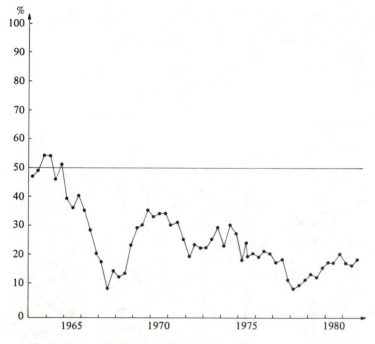

Figure 1.10. P_L, the weighted proportion (in %) of labour micro markets in excess demand in the Belgian manufacturing sector

1.2.4 *Interpretation of the 'Keynesian' situation in a policy perspective*

First of all, a majority of firms finding themselves in the 'Keynesian' regime is not at all incompatible with the main share of unemployment being 'classical' in nature, i.e. being caused by insufficient profitable (at prevailing prices and wages) capacities. This apparent paradox may be easily clarified by examining the following hypothetical extreme case: assume a situation where all firms are operating at full (profitable) capacity with the corresponding level of employment (equal then to the notional demand for labour), which appears, however, insufficient to absorb the whole labour supply. Unemployment is then purely 'classical' in nature (the 'Keynesian' share – i.e. that share of unemployment which could be cured by expansionary policies – being non-existent).

Assume now that all the firms experience a significant drop in demand for their products, which they perceive as purely transitory. In such a situation, the firms are very likely to decrease (temporarily, in their view) their production levels while keeping employed their full labour force (resorting to generalized labour hoarding). With our definitions, all the firms would then

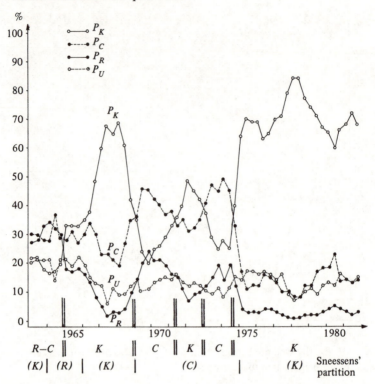

Figure 1.11. The 'regime proportions' for the Belgian manufacturing sector

find themselves in a 'Keynesian' situation ('insufficient demand prevented me from producing more') whereas existing unemployment would remain purely 'classical' in nature. Indeed, given the installed production capacities, an expansionary ('Keynesian type') policy would be totally ineffective in curing existing unemployment. Of course, the example just described is an extreme case, chosen to put into full perspective the difference of interpretation to be attached to the 'regime proportions' and to the nature of prevailing unemployment. The empirical results of chapter 3 will, however, make clear that a similar (but of course less clear-cut) situation characterizes the recent evolution of the Belgian manufacturing sector: the proportion of firms in the 'Keynesian' regime is not considerably higher than it was in the early 1970s while the 'classical' share of unemployment appears to have been increasing steadily since then.

Besides this argument about the conceptual difference between 'regime proportions' and the nature of prevailing unemployment, another reason may be put forward against a too 'mechanistic' interpretation of the estimated 'regime proportions'. This alternative type of argument stems from the consideration of possible price-setting behaviour on behalf of the surveyed firms. Before proceeding to the exposition of this second type of argument, it should be clear however that considering (at least for interpreting some results) endogenous price-setting is by no means contradictory with our adopting the fix-price approach for short-run analysis, as is well illustrated by Benassy's model [1976]. Taking into account the empirical evidence about infrequent price adjustment on one side, and frequent and rapid quantity adjustment on the other side (see for example Kawasaki, McMillan and Zimmerman [1982, 1983]), Benassy retains a process implying *intraperiod* adjustments in quantities and *interperiod* price adjustments, occurring only when a fix-price equilibrium has been established. The economy then evolves through a sequence of fix-price temporary equilibria.

This is precisely the point of view adopted in this work which, aiming to develop appropriate short-run empirical models, concentrates on modelling accurately these fix-price temporary equilibria. The role to be played by the 'regime proportions' in this modelling strategy should be clear: they are (hopefully) correct indicators of the instantaneous situation of firms and provide as such the right information to be used in our models (as further developments – see especially section 2.1 – will make clear). However, as the above short discussion illustrates and as will now be argued from another viewpoint, some qualification has to be introduced to warn against improper interpretations of these statistics in a policy diagnosis perspective.

This clarification made, let us discuss the 'regime proportions' results in connection with (possible) price-setting behaviour of firms.

As is well known, when the aggregate two-market fix-price model is amended to allow for price flexibility (keeping wages rigid), the distinction between the 'Keynesian' and 'classical' regimes becomes irrelevant since both 'Keynesian' (expand aggregate demand) and 'classical' (reduce costs, in particular labour costs) prescriptions are then effective in reducing unemployment[25] (see for example chapter 13 of Benassy [1982] for a formal discussion of this model).

Considering the business survey answers, we will verify that a similar type of conclusion arises for these price-setting firms in the sense that a 'Keynesian answer' may well cover cases where a 'classical type' diagnosis and prescription are, all things considered, most relevant.

The most appropriate framework for analyzing the *short-run* price-setting behaviour of manufacturing firms is thought to be the model of monopolistic competition, as Arrow pointed out in his pioneering work on the theory of price adjustment (K. J. Arrow [1959]). In this model, each firm is assumed to enjoy, at least in the short-run, some market power in the sense that it faces a downward sloping demand curve for its product and sets its price as a function of its 'perceived' demand and its cost conditions.

This view is at variance with the view conveyed by the so-called 'Scandinavian model' (see for example Aukrust [1970]) which assumes the firms of the 'open sector' (to which the manufacturing sector surely belongs) to be simple 'price-takers' of the unique international price set by the large foreign firms.

Empirical evidence, however, induces us to strongly qualify such a simple model.

First of all, a large number of manufacturing firms sell differentiated products whose heterogeneity naturally allows for some market power. Indeed, studies relying on disaggregated data point towards a majority of Belgian manufacturing subsectors as being price-setters instead of price-takers (see for example C. Huveneers [1981] for recent empirical results).

Secondly, even for sectors producing more homogeneous goods and classified as price-takers, the short-run price elasticity of demand appears to be relatively low, which suggests some scope for oligopolistic conduct at least in the short-run, as stressed by A. Kervyn [1979]. This stems partly from the prohibitive information costs the buyers would incur if they were to gather all the information (prices and other selling conditions of all their potential suppliers) to enable them to make at each moment the most profitable (for them) transaction. In view of such information costs, they are most likely to adopt the rational behaviour of acting under incomplete information when they want to purchase a commodity from a firm. Therefore, the firm can raise its price relative to the price of competitors without immediately losing all its customers.

However, longer-term elasticity of demand may be substantially higher than the short-term elasticity of perceived demand in the sense that a policy of above-average prices for a rather homogeneous product will, if maintained for a sufficiently long time, induce a progressive *shift to the left of the short-run demand curve* and a shrinkage of the firm's market share.

If these above-average prices were induced by a particularly unfavourable cost structure (of which the wage is usually a main determinant), then the 'insufficient demand' likely to be reported by the firm (classified then in the K and U regimes) reveals a situation where prescriptions linked to the 'classical' school of thought (reduce costs; for example, stunt real wage growth) may be more to the point than those attached to the 'Keynesian' view.

Although the classification of a specific firm (or a majority of firms in a certain subsector) in the 'Keynesian' (or 'underconsumption') regime undoubtedly catches what it intends to do, namely the instantaneous situation on the goods market, a diagnosis as to the ultimate causes for such a situation calls for a comparison with the situation of direct competitors: are those enjoying more favourable costs in excess demand? A good indicator in this respect may also be the evolution of market shares: a systematic deterioration points toward non-competitive costs. As an example, this seems to be globally the case of the American steel industry which has seen its market share shrink since 1981 and is well known to possess outdated equipment. The same analysis can be applied to Belgian firms manufacturing some textiles which are now produced at much lower cost by Third World producers.

As a conclusion, *diagnosis aiming at policy prescriptions* ought to interpret carefully the business survey answers (in particular the 'insufficient demand' ones) and should exploit this statistical information in combination with other economic information like recent evolution of market shares, of competitivity indexes, of profit ratios, of real wages, etc.

The complexity of this diagnosis helps explain the continuing debate about the nature of the recession that hits most Western industrial economies and about the appropriate way to cure it (see, for example, Basevi *et al.* [1983] for a recent discussion of the appropriate economic policies in this context).

From the point of view of the model builder, who is interested in estimating aggregate demand and supply functions from aggregation of individual components, *the business surveys provide exactly the appropriate information* since they indicate, for each period, the proportion of firms which are constrained by demand and those which are on their supply curve, either because they have met a physical bottleneck or because they have reached their optimal (notional) production level.

Macroeconomic model building along these lines provides a rigorous framework for the integration of business survey data with other pieces of economic information: the potential of this approach for policy analysis will appear from the results presented in the next chapters.

1.3 Contrasting our approach with the conventional 'disequilibrium' empirical models

As already stated in the introduction, there have been so far only a few attempts at estimating small 'disequilibrium' aggregate models: Kooiman and Kloek [1980, 1985] for the Netherlands, Sneessens [1981] for Belgium, Vilares [1981] and Artus, Laroque and Michel [1984] for France. These models have been described above as being mainly 'econometric transpositions' of the canonical Barro–Grossman model, inasmuch as they, like the theoretical prototype, completely overlook aggregation issues. This is of course the crucial difference with our approach which is a first attempt at developing a much needed aggregation theory.

Beyond the theoretical advance of handling aggregation issues in models supposed to provide 'microeconomic foundations to macroeconomics', the immediate practical advantage is to generate models endowed with the same continuity properties as the real world and hence more suitable than the conventional 'discrete switching' models for effective policy analysis. This will perhaps be best illustrated in section 2.1.2 of chapter 2 where short-run policy multipliers as computed from our model are contrasted with those computed from the more conventional models. Also in the absence of complementary information (see later) on the proportions of the economy in the different regimes, such a statistic may be computed by the model to provide a less clear-cut picture of the economy than the conventional models.

This increased 'realism' of the models is however not the only outcome of our explicit aggregation procedure: indeed the models developed along the 'smoothing by aggregation' lines also exhibit a natural ability to – properly – integrate a body of outside information on the extent of disequilibrium on the various markets, namely regular business survey data. Malinvaud [1983] distinguishes two ways – an 'indirect' way and a 'direct' way – towards the identification of disequilibria affecting our economies. What he calls the 'indirect' way is simply the estimation of conventional 'disequilibrium' models which yield as results (hence indirectly) estimates of the direction and extent of the disequilibria affecting the aggregate markets. The 'direct' way, by contrast, is seen as the processing and interpretation of statistical data (originating mainly from business surveys), yielding direct information on the extent of rationing on various markets. Malinvaud then compares the 'direct' statistical information with the results obtained through the 'indirect' way in order to assess the credibility to be attached to the results. Our type of models, providing the appropriate framework for integrating business survey information, may hence be seen as a synthesis between Malinvaud's two disconnected approaches to disequilibrium phenomena. As will be shown in chapter 2, the analytical expressions derived above (in section 1.1) for the proportions P_G and P_L (corresponding to the information provided by the business survey data) may be easily combined with the other equations of the model in order to yield a structural form suitable for estimation with the P_G and P_L statistics showing up everywhere in the model with cross-equation restrictions.

An important remark is to be made here: we have just stressed, as an interesting feature, the natural ability of our model to integrate outside information on 'regime proportions'. It should be clear, however, that the models developed along the 'smoothing by aggregation' lines by no means need such outside information to be estimated: if such information is not available, our models are able to produce it by using the analytical expressions derived above for the 'regime proportions'.

Also our 'regime proportions' are not to be confused (or compared) with the 'regime probabilities' computed from the conventional 'disequilibrium' models. Remember that, in these models, the *whole* economy is assumed to be at each moment in one of a few distinct regimes so that the estimated 'regime probabilities' are to be interpreted as a measure of the degree of confidence to be attached to the obtained results; this is conceptually quite different from our 'regime proportions' which are directly interpretable as *proportions* of the economy in the various regimes.

The business survey data provide direct information on the extent of disequilibrium in the various aggregate markets. It may be worth mentioning at this stage that this role of additional source of information is sometimes played in empirical work by the adjunction of a price/wage adjustment equation of the form

$$\Delta p_t = \gamma(X_\tau^d - X_\tau^s) + u_t$$

where τ is taken to be either t or $t-1$ and where γ may be specified to have different values γ_1, γ_2 according to whether $X^d > X^s$ or $X^d \leqslant X^s$.

In some works, the error term u_t is set to be identically zero, implying known sample separation (between observations in excess demand and excess supply) which may greatly facilitate estimation in the conventional discrete switching model (see Quandt [1982]).

It is to be noted however that, while the business survey data used in this study provide direct information on the extent of disequilibrium in the various markets, the information content about disequilibria provided by the above price equation rests entirely on the postulated theory of price adjustment which is hardly rooted in choice theoretic considerations and has quite an ad hoc nature – hence the (possibly) dubious quality of the information incorporated in the model. It is to be stressed that neither of the above-mentioned disequilibrium empirical macro models makes use of such a device for providing 'outside' information, being all purely fix-price models. Closing this short digression on alternative ways of incorporating additional information on disequilibria, let us return to our critical discussion of contrasting features of our model with respect to the more conventional 'discrete switching' models.

Another outcome of the explicit aggregation procedure behind our structural equations is the possibility of taking into account a type of structural change which is necessarily ignored in conventional rationing models, namely changes of the distribution function of micro supplies and demands on both the goods and the labour markets. With the distributional assumptions discussed at the end of section 1.1, this amounts to possibly endogenizing the ρ_G and ρ_L parameters (corresponding, for the goods market and the labour market respectively, to the parameter ρ_* appearing in formulas (1.5) and (1.6) of section 1.1), reflecting the 'degree of mismatch' between demands vs. supplies at the micro level. Let us illustrate this with a practical example: frictional unemployment is usually (as in this study) defined as the somewhat irreducible component of unemployment, subsisting even when the labour market globally clears, as a result of the mismatch between demands and supplies at the micro level.

It may be shown that, with this definition, the frictional unemployment rate reduces in our framework to a simple function of the sole parameter ρ_L. In the empirical application developed in chapter 3, the constancy of this parameter is rejected by the data so that it has in a sense to be 'endogenized', reflecting a simultaneous increase in frictional and global unemployment.

Conventional models are, in their very essence, unable to handle structural changes in the underlying distributions at the micro level; in the example just referred to, since these models need to exhibit some frictional unemployment in order to reconcile persistently observed unemployment with the possibility of excess demand for labour, they have to resort to rather primitive and ad-hoc specifications for this phenomenon.

The crucial differences between the type of models elaborated and estimated in this work and the more conventional 'disequilibrium' models stem of course from the underlying aggregation procedure. On a number of points, however, our model is comparable to previous works. For example, it embodies simplifications and complications similar to those in the other empirical models, when compared with the theoretical prototype of Barro–Grossman. One simplification common to all these models concerns the labour supply function where the spillover effect arising from possible constraints on the demand for goods has been suppressed (see subsection 2.1.1.1).

Common complications, the precise treatment of which may however vary depending on the model, arise for example from the need to take into account the open character of the economy or the short-run productivity cycle (Okun's law). Instead of comparing at length, for each particular issue, the treatment actually adopted in our empirical model with the one adopted in the other works, we feel that a better overview may be provided by a comparative presentation in concise tabular form, like the one adopted by J. J. Laffont [1983] in his survey of empirical fix-price models. As far as the conventional models are concerned, the table below draws heavily from Laffont's survey.

For each item discussed, after a brief characterization of the treatment given in our model, a cross-reference to the section in this book handling that particular issue is given so that interested readers can refer to a more detailed discussion.

Main features of existing empirical disequilibrium macro models

	Kooiman and Kloek [1980, 1985]	Artus, Laroque and Michel [1984]	Sneessens [1981]	Vilares [1981]	Lambert [1984]
	Annual data The Netherlands 1952–78	Quarterly data France 1963–78	Annual data Belgium 1953–78	Annual data France 1952–78 Portugal 1953–79	Annual data Belgium 1963–80
					Aggregation issues are explicitly dealt with (section 1.1)
					Statistical information coming from business surveys may be readily incorporated in the model (section 1.2)
	The *whole* economy in one of 4 distinct regimes	The *whole* economy in one of 4 distinct regimes	The *whole* economy in one of 3 distinct regimes	The *whole* economy in one of 3 distinct regimes	The economy characterized by the *proportion* of firms in the 4 distinct regimes (section 1.2)
	Maddala–Nelson (MN) stochastic specification	MN stochastic specification	Ginsburgh–Tishler–Zang (GTZ) stochastic specification	GTZ stochastic specification	MN stochastic specification (remark (f) in subsection 2.1.1.1)
	Coherency ensured by linear spillover effects	Coherency checked numerically for some range of values for parameters	Coherency ensured by checking the (estimated) slopes of the effective trade offers	Coherency ensured by making the model recursive (by replacing the endogenous variable demand by the exogenous expected demand)	Coherency ensured by checking the parameter estimates of log-linear spillover effects (discussion of sufficient conditions in subsection 2.1.1.2 and of empirical estimates in section 3.5)

(*continued*)

Table (cont.)

Kooiman and Kloek [1980, 1985]	Artus, Laroque and Michel [1984]	Sneessens [1981]	Vilares [1981]	Lambert [1984]
Clay–Clay vintage technology (Den Hartog–Tjan)	Cobb–Douglas production function with technical progress + explicit formulation of adjustment costs of labour and output	Cobb–Douglas production function with technical progress for the long-run + little substitution possible in the short-run	Clay–Clay vintage technology; slow adjustment of labour	CES production function for the aggregate long-run production function but little substitution possible in the short-run (cf. Sneessens). Adopted functional forms are compatible with the aggregation of elementary production units (section 2.2)
Frictional unemployment is a time-varying linear function of (employed + registered unemployed)	(cf. Kooiman and Kloek)	Supply of labour is a constant fraction of exogenous labour force (employed + registered unemployed)	Rosen–Quandt formulation of labour supply + treatment of emigrants from Portugal	Frictional unemployment is defined as the residual unemployment when global equilibrium is achieved on the labour market; is endogenized (section 1.1 and section 3.6)
Hendry–Von Ungern Sternberg consumption function	Borrowed from French quarterly model		(cf. Kooiman and Kloek)	Aggregate demand for domestic goods is of the 'reduced form' type (section 3.3)
When demand for domestic goods is constrained, some rationing of exports and consumption take place; then imports complete demand	(cf. Kooiman and Kloek)	Exports exogenous. Imports complete demand when excess demand	Imports complete demand when excess demand. Some rationing of exports when close to full capacity	Demand for domestic goods is always rationed (to varying degrees however). The specification adopted is compatible with whatever rationing scheme is at work between consumption, exports and imports (section 3.3)

Maximum likelihood estimation	Maximum likelihood	Maximum likelihood estimation. Single equation estimation technique	Single equation estimation technique	Full information maximum likelihood estimation of a fairly 'large' model (5 stochastic equations) by the standards of these 'disequilibrium' models (section 3.6)
Difficulties in the optimization of the likelihood function are reported (multiple maxima)			No difficulties reported	No difficulties reported; model appears well conditioned (section 3.6)

2

The macro model: econometric formulation and the production function derived by aggregation of elementary production units in the presence of rationing

2.1 The aggregate model

2.1.1 The macro model and its econometric formulation

It has been shown in section 1.1 that, in our framework, aggregate transactions always fall short of both aggregate demand and aggregate supply on both markets (giving rise to the simultaneous appearance of unemployment and unfilled vacancies in the labour market or undesired idle capacities and unfilled orders in the goods market). Since at any time there will be some firms constrained on the goods market while others are constrained on the labour market, and similarly for the workers–consumers, the spillover effects will always be operative and *effective* trade offers will always depart from *notional* trade offers in the aggregate.

Let the symbol 'tilde' distinguish the notional from the effective trade offers so that for example X^d and $\tilde{X}^d$ denote respectively the effective and the notional demand for goods; similarly for X^s and $\tilde{X}^s$, L^d and $\tilde{L}^d$, L^s and $\tilde{L}^s$.

Notional demands and supplies are those which would arise in the absence of any rationing experienced by domestic producers and/or workers-consumers, so that we may define:

$\tilde{X}^d$ = notional demand for domestic goods

$\quad = f_{\tilde{X}^d}$ (active population, real wage rate, budgetary policy, relative import prices, level of world demand, relative export prices, degree of utilization of capacities abroad,...)

$\tilde{X}^s$ = notional supply of domestic goods

> = $f_{\tilde{X}^s}$ (existing capital stock, price level of goods relative to wage rate and cost of use of capital, technical progress, ...)

$\tilde{L}^d$ = notional demand for labour

> = $f_{\tilde{L}^d}$ (same determinants as for $\tilde{X}^s$ since inverted production function, ...)

$\tilde{L}^s$ = notional supply of labour

> = $f_{\tilde{L}^s}$ (population in age of work, sex structure, level of real wages, ...).

If we adopt log-linear specifications, this may be expressed as

$$\ln \tilde{X}^d = \beta^d \ln \mathcal{X}^d + u_{XD}$$
$$\ln \tilde{X}^s = \beta^s \ln \mathcal{X}^s + u_{XS}$$
$$\ln \tilde{L}^d = \lambda^d \ln \mathcal{L}^d + u_{LD}$$
$$\ln \tilde{L}^s = \lambda^s \ln \mathcal{L}^s + u_{LS}$$

$$(2.1)$$

where $\mathcal{X}$ and $\mathcal{L}$ represent vectors of exogenous variables, β and λ represent vectors of parameters, and $u_{XD}, u_{XS}, u_{LD}, u_{LS}$ represent stochastic error terms which are assumed to be jointly normally distributed.

If we assume log-linear aggregate spillover terms (see section 2.2 below for the justification of this), we still face the choice between alternative specifications of the effective trade offers. Indeed, in the absence of an empirically relevant general theory explaining how perceptions of rationing are formed and translated into effective demands and supplies, various a-priori admissible specifications of effective trade offers have been proposed for empirical macroeconometric applications. Portes [1977] analyzed the following specifications:[1]

(1) Barro and Grossman [1976]/Gouriéroux, Laffont and Montfort [1980a]

$$\ln X^d = \begin{cases} \ln \tilde{X}^d & \text{if } L = L^s \\ \ln \tilde{X}^d + \gamma_{XD}(\ln L - \ln \tilde{L}^s) & \text{otherwise} \end{cases}$$

$$\ln X^s = \begin{cases} \ln \tilde{X}^s & \text{if } L = L^d \\ \ln \tilde{X}^s + \gamma_{XS}(\ln L - \ln \tilde{L}^d) & \text{otherwise} \end{cases}$$

$$\ln L^d = \begin{cases} \ln \tilde{L}^d & \text{if } X = X^s \\ \ln \tilde{L}^d + \gamma_{LD}(\ln X - \ln \tilde{X}^s) & \text{otherwise} \end{cases}$$

$$\ln L^s = \begin{cases} \ln \tilde{L}^s & \text{if } X = X^d \\ \ln \tilde{L}^s + \gamma_{LS}(\ln X - \ln \tilde{X}^d) & \text{otherwise} \end{cases}$$

with all the spillover coefficients γ being positive.

(2) Ito [1980]

$$\ln X^d = \ln \tilde{X}^d + \gamma_{XD}(\ln L - \ln \tilde{L}^s)$$

$$\ln X^s = \ln \tilde{X}^s + \gamma_{XS}(\ln L - \ln \tilde{L}^d)$$

$$\ln L^d = \ln \tilde{L}^d + \gamma_{LD}(\ln X - \ln \tilde{X}^s)$$

$$\ln L^s = \ln \tilde{L}^s + \gamma_{LS}(\ln X - \ln \tilde{X}^d)$$

(3) Portes [1977]/Benassy

$$\ln X^d = \ln \tilde{X}^d + \gamma_{XD}(\ln L - \ln L^s)$$

$$\ln X^s = \ln \tilde{X}^s + \gamma_{XS}(\ln L - \ln L^d)$$

$$\ln L^d = \ln \tilde{L}^d + \gamma_{LD}(\ln X - \ln X^s)$$

$$\ln L^s = \ln \tilde{L}^s + \gamma_{LS}(\ln X - \ln X^d)$$

In our framework only the last two specifications may be relevant[2] since, as explained above, aggregate transactions always depart from the effective trade offers. Both models assume the spillover effect to be proportional to the difference between (the logarithms of) actual transactions and demand or supply in the other market but that demand and supply is to be the notional one for Ito and the effective one for Portes–Benassy.[3] As stated by Quandt [1982] in his survey of econometric disequilibrium models, 'it is not easy to see how any of the above formulations could claim preeminence on theoretical grounds', which makes him advocate further research on micro behaviour in the presence of rationing. In order to distinguish empirically, Portes suggested that the various specifications should be tried in empirical applications.[4] To our knowledge, this suggestion has not yet been taken up. It will be shown below that this type of empirical comparison may be performed relatively easily within our framework due to the basic similarity of the final structural forms suitable for estimation.

The full model will now be presented and commented upon, after which the structural form suitable for estimation purposes will be derived. For clarity of exposition, this will be done for Portes' specification and then for Ito's specification. A few a-priori considerations on some advantages of Ito's formulation will close the subsection.

2.1.1.1 Portes' specification. Bringing together Portes' specification of the effective trade offers and the specifications derived in chapter 1, the full model is then specified as:

$$\ln X^d = \ln \tilde{X}^d + \gamma_{XD}(\ln L - \ln L^s) \quad \gamma_{XD} \geqslant 0$$

$$\ln X^s = \ln \tilde{X}^s + \gamma_{XS}(\ln L - \ln L^d) \quad \gamma_{XS} \geqslant 0$$

$$\ln L^d = \ln \tilde{L}^d + \gamma_{LD}(\ln X - \ln X^s) \quad \gamma_{LD} \geqslant 0$$

$$\ln L^s = \ln \tilde{L}^s$$

$$X = [(X^d)^{-\rho_G} + (X^s)^{-\rho_G}]^{-1/\rho_G}$$

$$P_G = \left[1 + \left(\frac{X^d}{X^s}\right)^{-\rho_G}\right]^{-1} \tag{2.2}$$

$$\text{DUC} = \frac{X}{\tilde{X}^s}$$

$$L = [(L^d)^{-\rho_L} + (L^s)^{-\rho_L}]^{-1/\rho_L}$$

$$P_L = \left[1 + \left(\frac{L^d}{L^s}\right)^{-\rho_L}\right]^{-1}$$

$$\text{UNR} = \frac{L}{L^s}$$

where $\tilde{X}^d, \tilde{X}^s, \tilde{L}^d, \tilde{L}^s$ are the notional trade offers whose specifications are given in system (2.1); X^d, X^s, L^d, L^s are 'latent' variables; and X, P_G, DUC, L and P_L are the *observed endogenous variables.*[5]

A few remarks may be in order at this stage:

(a)   The households may be rationed in their demand for *domestic* goods but, because of the largely open character of the small Belgian economy and the great substitution possibilities among goods, they never expect to be rationed on the goods market seriously enough and for a sufficiently prolonged period to induce them to alter their labour supply. This explains the absence of the spillover term in the labour supply equation.

(b) ρ_G and ρ_L are the 'dispersion parameters' on the goods market and the labour market whose significance has been explained in chapter 1. It was said there that in some cases, the 'constancy' assumption might not hold and that the dispersions had then to be endogenized. However, the ρ parameters are written here as constants for ease of exposition.

(c)   Although the degree of capacity utilization DUC is equal by definition to $X/\tilde{X}^s$, this concept does not correspond exactly to the statistics DUC_{obs} yielded by the business surveys (question 1); this explains our positing a stochastic specification for DUC_{obs}

$$\text{DUC}_{\text{obs}} = \alpha_{\text{DUC}} \cdot \frac{X}{\tilde{X}^s} \cdot \exp(u_{\text{DUC}}) \qquad\qquad (2.3)$$

instead of an identity. Much more will be said on this point when the empirical application is presented in chapter 3.

(d)   For symmetry of the system of equations (2.2), we write down the identity defining the unemployment rate UNR, which appears as the counterpart on the labour market of the statistics DUC on the goods market. However, since no UNR statistics are available for the Belgian manufacturing sector which is to be modelled, this identity is not considered in the following discussion.

(e)   For ease of exposition, the model presented here is static. Of course, for the empirical application, the existence of adjustment costs, of adaptive expectations, etc. ought to entail dynamic specifications.

(f)   The variables P_G and P_L, although stochastic, are assumed to be observed without error. The inclusion of additional error terms would complicate things extremely, as may be seen from the non-linear expressions for P_G and P_L in the structural form suitable for estimation which will be derived below.

(g)   This statistical model adopts the Maddala–Nelson [1974] (henceforth MN) stochastic specification as opposed to the Ginsburgh–Tishler–Zang [1980] (henceforth GTZ) specification.

The MN approach first specifies the joint distribution of the notional variables (as in system (2.1) above) and then derives the joint distribution of the observed variables, while the GTZ approach directly specifies the joint distribution of the observed variables.

In conventional aggregate disequilibrium models, this issue amounts to the location of stochastic disturbance terms inside (MN) or outside (GTZ) the *min* condition, the GTZ specification

$$X = \min(D, S) + u_X$$

appearing however as the particular case of the MN specification

$$X = \min(D + u_D, S + u_S)$$

where $u_D = u_S = u_X$.
The most general specification mixing the two approaches reduces to the MN case with correlated error terms.

In our framework, the aggregate *min* has been replaced by the smooth CES-type transaction function but the same choice basically remains between the MN specification

$$X = [(D \cdot e^{u_D})^{-\rho_G} + (S \cdot e^{u_S})^{-\rho_G}]^{-1/\rho_G}$$

and the GTZ specification

$$X = [(D)^{-\rho_G} + (S)^{-\rho_G}]^{-1/\rho_G} \cdot e^{u_X}$$

with MN again reducing to GTZ when $u_D = u_S = u_X$.

The relative merits of alternative approaches from the point of view of both economic interpretation and statistical tractability have been extensively discussed in Sneessens [1981, 1985], Quandt [1982], and Richard [1980, 1982]. Since no decisive argument seems to have emerged in favour of either specification, the best strategy should be to choose the most general stochastic specification compatible with estimation of the particular model at hand.

It will be shown that the MN specification, which has been adopted here, allows an easy derivation of a structural form suitable for estimation purposes, i.e. where the unobservable variables have been eliminated.

Combining the equations of X and P_G, we may write

$$X = [(X^d)^{-\rho_G} + (X^s)^{-\rho_G}]^{-1/\rho_G}$$

$$= X^s \left[1 + \left(\frac{X^d}{X^s} \right)^{-\rho_G} \right]^{-1/\rho_G}$$

$$= X^s \cdot (P_G)^{1/\rho_G}$$

Proceeding similarly for X^d, L^s and L^d, we have the following system:

$$X^d = X \cdot (1 - P_G)^{-1/\rho_G}$$

$$X^s = X \cdot (P_G)^{-1/\rho_G}$$

$$L^d = L \cdot (1 - P_L)^{-1/\rho_L} \tag{2.4}$$

$$L^s = L \cdot (P_L)^{-1/\rho_L}$$

where the 'latent variables' are expressed in terms of observables only.

Combining these expressions with the specifications of the effective trade offers (the first four equations of system (2.2)), we write for the X^d specification (for example):

$$\ln X^d = \ln X - \frac{1}{\rho_G} \ln (1 - P_G) = \ln \tilde{X}^d + \gamma_{XD}(\ln L - \ln L^s)$$

$$= \ln \tilde{X}^d + \frac{\gamma_{XD}}{\rho_L} \ln (P_L)$$

Substituting the notional goods demand $\tilde{X}^d$ by its specification from system (2.1), we write finally

$$\ln X = \frac{1}{\rho_G} \ln (1 - P_G) + \frac{\gamma_{XD}}{\rho_L} \ln (P_L) + \beta^d \ln \mathcal{X}^d + u_{XD}$$

One readily verifies that, since ρ_G, ρ_L and γ_{XD} are positive,

$$X = [(1 - P_G)^{1/\rho_G} \cdot P_L^{\gamma_{XD}/\rho_L}] \tilde{X}^d \leqslant \tilde{X}^d$$

as expected.

Proceeding similarly for all four effective trade offers equations plus the DUC equation, we finally get the following *structural form suitable for estimation*, which involves only the observable variables:

$$\ln X = \frac{1}{\rho_G} \ln (1 - P_G) + \frac{\gamma_{XD}}{\rho_L} \ln (P_L) + \beta^d \ln \mathcal{X}^d + u_{XD} \qquad (2.5.1)$$

$$\ln X = \frac{1}{\rho_G} \ln (P_G) + \frac{\gamma_{XS}}{\rho_L} \ln (1 - P_L) + \beta^s \ln \mathcal{X}^s + u_{XS} \qquad (2.5.2)$$

$$\ln \mathrm{DUC}_{\mathrm{obs}} = \ln \alpha_{\mathrm{DUC}} + \frac{1}{\rho_G} \ln P_G + \frac{\gamma_{XS}}{\rho_L} \ln (1 - P_L) + u_{\mathrm{DUC}} \qquad (2.5.3)$$

$$\ln L = \frac{1}{\rho_L} \ln (1 - P_L) + \frac{\gamma_{LD}}{\rho_G} \ln (P_G) + \lambda^d \ln \mathcal{L}^d + u_{LD} \qquad (2.5.4)$$

$$\ln L = \frac{1}{\rho_L} \ln (P_L) \qquad\qquad + \lambda^s \ln \mathcal{L}^s + u_{LS} \qquad (2.5.5)$$

with the error terms assumed to be jointly normally distributed $u_t \sim N(0, \Sigma^2)$.

We finish with a simultaneous model (five equations; five endogenous variables $X, P_G, \mathrm{DUC}_{\mathrm{obs}}, L, P_L$) where the 'tension indicators' P_G and P_L show up non-linearly as expected, but where the log-linear form of the equations looks rather attractive from the estimation point of view.

The system of equations (2.5) is the structural form of our (static) model[6] *with Portes' specification of the spillover effects.* It will now be shown that Ito's specification allows a similar structural form to be derived.

2.1.1.2 Ito's specification. Bringing together Ito's specification of the effective trade offers and the specifications derived in chapter 1, the full model is specified as

$$\ln X^d = \ln \tilde{X}^d + \gamma_{XD}(\ln L - \ln \tilde{L}^s) \quad \gamma_{XD} \geqslant 0$$

$$\ln X^s = \ln \tilde{X}^s + \gamma_{XS}(\ln L - \ln \tilde{L}^d) \quad \gamma_{XS} \geqslant 0$$

$$\ln L^d = \ln \tilde{L}^d + \gamma_{LD}(\ln X - \ln \tilde{X}^s) \quad \gamma_{LD} \geqslant 0$$

$$\ln L^s = \ln \tilde{L}^s$$

$$X = \left[(X^d)^{-\rho_G} + (X^s)^{-\rho_G} \right]^{-1/\rho_G}$$

$$P_G = \left[1 + \left(\frac{X^d}{X^s} \right)^{-\rho_G} \right]^{-1} \tag{2.6}$$

$$\mathrm{DUC} = \frac{X}{\tilde{X}^s}$$

$$L = \left[(L^d)^{-\rho_L} + (L^s)^{-\rho_L} \right]^{-1/\rho_L}$$

$$P_L = \left[1 + \left(\frac{L^d}{L^s} \right)^{-\rho_L} \right]^{-1}$$

$$\mathrm{UNR} = \frac{L}{L^s}$$

with X^d, X^s, L^d, L^s the 'latent' variables; and X, P_G, DUC, L and P_L the *observed endogenous variables*.

Remarks (a) to (g) in subsection 2.1.1.1 about 'Portes' version' are also valid for 'Ito's version' of this model.

Here also, with the assumed Maddala–Nelson stochastic specification, we can easily derive a structural form suitable for estimation purposes, which will appear very similar to that derived for Portes' version.

First of all, let us remark that the system of equations (2.4) still remains valid whatever the precise specification adopted for the effective trade offers.

Then, let us rewrite the spillover terms in order to express them as functions of the observed regime proportions P_G and P_L as was done in Portes' version.

Taking the effective supply of goods X^s as an example, its spillover term may be rewritten, by substituting appropriately the trade offers' definitions, as

$$\begin{aligned}
(\ln L - \ln \tilde{L}^d) &= (\ln L - \ln L^d) + (\ln L^d - \ln \tilde{L}^d) \\
&= (\ln L - \ln L^d) + \gamma_{LD}(\ln X - \ln \tilde{X}^s) \\
&= (\ln L - \ln L^d) + \gamma_{LD}\left[(\ln X - \ln X^s) + (\ln X^s - \ln \tilde{X}^s)\right] \\
&= (\ln L - \ln L^d) + \gamma_{LD}(\ln X - \ln X^s) \\
&\qquad + \gamma_{LD}\gamma_{XS}(\ln L - \ln \tilde{L}^d) \\
&= \frac{1}{1 - \gamma_{LD}\gamma_{XS}} \left[(\ln L - \ln L^d) + \gamma_{LD}(\ln X - \ln X^s) \right]
\end{aligned}$$

The effective supply of goods is then

$$\ln X^s = \ln \tilde{X}^s + \frac{1}{1-\gamma_{LD}\gamma_{XS}}(\ln L - \ln L^d) + \frac{\gamma_{XS}\gamma_{LD}}{1-\gamma_{XS}\gamma_{LD}}(\ln X - \ln X^s)$$

which, in view of the equations of system (2.4), may be rewritten

$$\ln X^s = \ln \tilde{X}^s + \left(\frac{\gamma_{XS}}{1-\gamma_{LD}\gamma_{XS}}\right)\cdot\frac{1}{\rho_L}\ln(1-P_L) + \left(\frac{\gamma_{XS}\gamma_{LD}}{1-\gamma_{LD}\gamma_{XS}}\right)\cdot\frac{1}{\rho_G}\ln(P_G)$$

Using again the equation which relates X to X^s (from 2.4) and substituting the notional supply of goods $\tilde{X}^s$ by its specification from system (2.1), we write finally

$$\ln X = \frac{1}{\rho_G}\frac{1}{(1-\gamma_{LD}\gamma_{XS})}\ln(P_G) + \frac{1}{\rho_L}\frac{\gamma_{XS}}{(1-\gamma_{LD}\gamma_{XS})}\ln(1-P_L)$$
$$+ \beta^s \ln \mathscr{X}^s + u_{XS}$$

One readily verifies that, with ρ_G, ρ_L and γ_{XS} positive and $\gamma_{LD}\gamma_{XS} < 1$ (see below for comments on this last restriction),

$$X = \{[P_G]^{1/\rho_G}(1-P_L)^{\gamma_{XS}/\rho_L}]^{1/(1-\gamma_{LD}\gamma_{XS})}\}\tilde{X}^s \leqslant \tilde{X}^s$$

as expected.

Proceeding similarly for all four effective trade offers equations plus the DUC equation, we finally get the following *structural form suitable for estimation*, which involves only the observable variables:

$$\ln X = \frac{1}{\rho_G}\ln(1-P_G) + \frac{\gamma_{XD}}{\rho_L}\ln(P_L) + \beta^d \ln \mathscr{X}^d + u_{XD} \tag{2.7.1}$$

$$\ln X = \frac{1}{\rho_G}\frac{1}{(1-\gamma_{LD}\gamma_{XS})}\ln(P_G) + \frac{1}{\rho_L}\frac{\gamma_{XS}}{(1-\gamma_{LD}\gamma_{XS})}\ln(1-P_L)$$
$$+ \beta^s \ln \mathscr{X}^s + u_{XS} \tag{2.7.2}$$

$$\ln \text{DUC}_{\text{obs}} = \ln \alpha_{\text{DUC}} + \frac{1}{\rho_G}\frac{1}{(1-\gamma_{XS}\gamma_{LD})}\ln(P_G)$$

$$+ \frac{1}{\rho_L}\frac{\gamma_{XS}}{(1-\gamma_{XS}\gamma_{LD})}\ln(1-P_L) + u_{\text{DUC}} \tag{2.7.3}$$

$$\ln L = \frac{1}{\rho_L}\frac{1}{(1-\gamma_{XS}\gamma_{LD})}\ln(1-P_L) + \frac{1}{\rho_G}\frac{\gamma_{LD}}{(1-\gamma_{LD}\gamma_{XS})}\ln(P_G)$$

$$+ \lambda^d \ln \mathscr{L}^d + u_{LD} \tag{2.7.4}$$

$$\ln L = \frac{1}{\rho_L}\ln(P_L) \qquad\qquad + \lambda^s \ln \mathscr{L}^s + u_{LS} \tag{2.7.5}$$

with the error terms assumed to be jointly normally distributed $u_t \sim N(0, \Sigma^2)$.

This structural form of our (static) model with Ito's specification of the spillover effects looks very similar to the final structural form of Portes' version but involves different cross-equation restrictions among the spillover and 'dispersion' parameters. The close resemblance of these final structural forms facilitates of course their parallel estimation which is handled in chapter 3 along with the discussion of the empirical results. Although both models are non-nested, in the sense that neither can be obtained as a special case of the other, it is still possible to resort to the hypothesis-testing approach by embedding these competing models within a general model by means of a Box–Cox-type procedure.

This is done most easily in our case: the general model looks like system of equations (2.7) but with the expression $(1 - \gamma_{XS}\gamma_{LD})$ replaced everywhere by $(1 - \theta\gamma_{XS}\gamma_{LD})$. It is readily seen that with $\theta = 1$ this general model reduces to Ito's model while $\theta = 0$ yields Portes' model. This suggests estimating freely the parameter θ within the general model in order to discriminate between the two restricted models, remembering however that values of θ differing from 0 or 1 yield a model for which the theoretical interpretation is unclear. More comments will be given on this with the empirical results in chapter 3.

Before considering the a-priori respective merits of Ito's vs. Portes' formulations, it is worth commenting briefly on the *restrictions imposed on the spillover coefficients*. In the absence of a spillover effect from the goods market to the supply of labour (see remark (a) in subsection 2.1.1.1 above), there are only two restrictions, namely $\gamma_{XD}\gamma_{LD} < 1$ and $\gamma_{XS}\gamma_{LD} < 1$. As will be shown from the multiplier analysis developed in the next subsection (and in appendix D), these restrictions on the spillover coefficients correspond to *stability conditions* for both Portes' and Ito's versions of our non-linear model. The same stability conditions were derived by Muellbauer and Portes [1978] in their analysis of the aggregate discrete switching model.

These restrictions also correspond to the necessary and sufficient conditions ensuring the existence and uniqueness of an equilibrium point (hence guaranteeing the existence of a well-defined reduced form) for the conventional piecewise-linear models (see Gouriéroux, Laffont and Monfort [1980 b] and Ito [1980]). It is to be remembered that the piecewise-linear case arises as a particular (extreme) case of our non-linear model for the 'dispersion' parameters ρ_G and ρ_L tending to infinity.

For finite values of ρ_G and ρ_L, our model becomes totally non-linear (which complicates the formal analysis of existence and uniqueness conditions), but it may be graphically shown that the above *conditions* are still sufficient *to ensure the existence and uniqueness of equilibrium*.

The determination of the traded quantities can be represented diagrammatically in (X, L) space with the 'double wedge' apparatus developed in Muellbauer and Portes [1978].

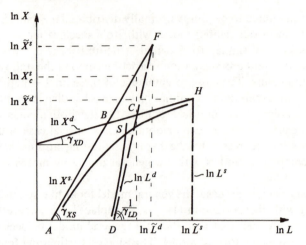

Figure 2.1. Diagrammatic representation of the non-linear disequilibrium model

This is illustrated for Ito's model in figure 2.1.

For households, we start from the notional position ($\ln \tilde{X}^d, \ln \tilde{L}^s$), labelled H, and draw $\ln X^d$ and $\ln L^s$ extending 'southwest' from H. Similarly for firms, whose effective trade offers $\ln X^s$ and $\ln L^d$ extend 'southwest' from their notional position ($\ln \tilde{X}^s, \ln \tilde{L}^d$), labelled F. In the conventional piecewise-linear models, the *min* condition prevails on both aggregate markets, yielding the locus ABH (for the goods market) and the locus DF (for the labour market). The conditions for the two loci to have only one intersection point (i.e. the existence and uniqueness sufficient conditions) are that the slope $1/\gamma_{LD}$ be greater than γ_{XS} and γ_{XD} or equivalently that $\gamma_{LD}\gamma_{XS} < 1$ and $\gamma_{LD}\gamma_{XD} < 1$.

However, when the 'dispersion' parameters ρ_G and ρ_L have finite values, we depart from the conventional piecewise-linear model: the two loci to consider are no longer kinked line segments but smooth curves having the former line segments as their asymptotes. These curves are drawn on figure 2.1 and intersect at point S. It is readily verified that the conditions for such curves to have only one intersection point amount to conditions on the slopes of their asymptotes which are the same as those already derived for the piecewise-linear case, namely that $\gamma_{XD}\gamma_{LD} < 1$ and $\gamma_{XS}\gamma_{LD} < 1$.

In the empirical applications, the parameters γ_{XD}, γ_{XS} and γ_{LD} will be estimated freely (i.e. without imposing the a-priori restrictions in the estimation procedure) but it is of course expected that the resulting estimates satisfy the above restrictions. Refer to chapter 3 for the empirical results and their comments.

Although we rely mostly on the empirical results to 'discriminate' between

Portes' and Ito's versions, as explained above, some a-priori considerations may be given on the respective merits of both versions.

One important difference between Portes' and Ito's versions, already commented on by Portes [1977] and Ito [1980], is that Portes' effective trade offers do not define a feasible trade while this is never the case for Ito's effective trade offers.

This is most clearly illustrated by the following extreme example: suppose the economy is in a situation characterized by general excess supply on both aggregate markets, in the sense that all firms i find themselves in the Keynesian regime, i.e. with $X_i = X_i^d < X_i^s$ and $L_i = L_i^d < L_i^s$, $\forall i$. Aggregate output is then equal to $X = X^d$ and aggregate labour to $L = L^d$. This situation is represented by point C on figure 2.1.[7]

Under Ito's specification, the firms announce as their effective goods supply their maximum feasible output *taking account of their presently available labour force*. At the aggregate level, we have

$$\begin{cases} \ln X^s = \ln \tilde{X}^s + \gamma_{XS}(\ln L - \ln \tilde{L}^d) \\ \ln L = \ln L^d = \ln \tilde{L}^d + \gamma_{LD}(\ln X - \ln \tilde{X}^s) \end{cases}$$

On figure 2.1, $\ln X_c^s$ on the production frontier is the level of Ito's effective output supply corresponding to equilibrium point C.[8]

On the other hand, according to Portes' specification, when firms do not experience any constraint on their demand for labour (which in the extreme example considered here is the case of all firms), they express their notional supply of goods as their effective supply, *irrespective of their presently available labour force*.

Indeed, in our case where $L = L^d$, Portes' specification of the producers' aggregate behaviour is easily seen to reduce to

$$\begin{cases} \ln X^s = \ln \tilde{X}^s \\ \ln L = \ln L^d = \ln \tilde{L}^d + \gamma_{LD}(\ln X - \ln \tilde{X}^s) \end{cases}$$

Clearly, since actual $L < \tilde{L}^d$, the effective supply of goods corresponding to Portes' definition is not technically feasible.

For clarity of exposition, this feature of Portes' model has been illustrated in the extreme case of a purely Keynesian regime ($P_G = 0$ and $P_L = 0$) but it still characterizes more general situations (i.e. when $0 < P_G < 1$ and $0 < P_L < 1$). This is easily seen by reexpressing Portes' effective goods supply after some manipulations:

$$\begin{aligned} \ln X_{\text{Portes}}^s &= \ln \tilde{X}^s + \gamma_{XS}[\ln L - \ln L_{\text{Portes}}^d] \\ &= \ln \tilde{X}^s + \gamma_{XS}[\ln L - (\ln \tilde{L}^d + \gamma_{LD}(\ln X - \ln X_{\text{Portes}}^s))] \\ &= [\ln \tilde{X}^s + \gamma_{XS}(\ln L - \ln \tilde{L}^d)] + \gamma_{XS}\gamma_{LD}(\ln X_{\text{Portes}}^s - \ln X) \end{aligned}$$

The first term between brackets is precisely Ito's definition of the effective goods supply, so we have finally

$$\ln X^s_{\text{Portes}} = \ln X^s_{\text{Ito}} + \gamma_{XS}\gamma_{LD}(\ln X^s_{\text{Portes}} - \ln X)$$

Since, by definition (remember the CES-type transaction curve), $X \leqslant X^s_{\text{Portes}}$, it follows that $X^s_{\text{Portes}} \geqslant X^s_{\text{Ito}}$ and thus X^s_{Portes} is always above the feasible output supply (with the labour force actually available)[9].

Since Portes' effective trade offers do not define feasible trades, we should be cautious when using them as a measure of the size of disequilibrium, as Grandmont [1977] has observed. Since reliable estimates of the size of disequilibrium on various markets are however thought to be an interesting by-product of empirical disequilibrium models, particularly in view of their prospective role for studying the dynamics of such models, the 'unfeasibility' of Portes' effective trade offers implies an a-priori advantage of Ito's model over Portes' one, before any confrontation with empirical data. Since moreover, as will appear in chapter 3, Ito's version proves empirically superior, this explains our giving some sort of preeminence to Ito's model in the following discussion of certain issues, relegating the parallel discussion for Portes' model to an appendix.

Before going to chapter 3 for the empirical application, two interesting points will be discussed: the first, which is the subject of the next subsection, concerns economic policy multipliers in this type of model; the second, which is discussed in section 2.2, concerns the likely form of the aggregate short-run production function obtained from aggregation over micro production units in a rationing context.

2.1.2   *Economic policy multipliers*

It was claimed in the introduction that conventional aggregate disequilibrium models are not very appropriate for economic policy analysis since, as a consequence of the discrete switches, these models imply that economic policy multipliers jump at some dates between a limited number of different values. The real world, however, exhibits much more continuity: the effect of any economic policy measure is likely to vary continuously with business conditions,[10] depending on the proportions of the goods and labour micro markets in various disequilibria. Since it rests on explicit aggregation over micro markets in disequilibrium, our approach naturally involves multipliers endowed with the same continuity properties. This will be illustrated here for the case of the autonomous demand multiplier (exogenous increase in demand for exports, for example) in the framework of Ito's model.[11]

Starting from the structural form (2.6) in subsection 2.1.1.2, and remembering that (see chapter 1)

$$\frac{\partial \ln X}{\partial \ln X^d} = (1 - P_G) \qquad \frac{\partial \ln L}{\partial \ln L^d} = (1 - P_L)$$

$$\frac{\partial \ln X}{\partial \ln X^s} = P_G \qquad \frac{\partial \ln L}{\partial \ln L^s} = P_L$$

we obtain

$$\frac{\partial \ln X}{\partial \ln \tilde{X}^d} = \frac{\partial \ln X}{\partial \ln X^d} \cdot \frac{\partial \ln X^d}{\partial \ln \tilde{X}^d} + \frac{\partial \ln X}{\partial \ln X^s} \cdot \frac{\partial \ln X^s}{\partial \ln \tilde{X}^d}$$

$$= (1 - P_G) \cdot \frac{\partial \ln X^d}{\partial \ln \tilde{X}^d} + (P_G) \cdot \frac{\partial \ln X^s}{\partial \ln \tilde{X}^d}$$

The definitions of notional trade offers and their specification in implicit form sketched in section 2.1.1 make it clear that

$$\frac{\partial \ln \tilde{X}^s}{\partial \ln \tilde{X}^d} = 0$$

$$\frac{\partial \ln \tilde{L}^d}{\partial \ln \tilde{X}^d} = 0$$

$$\frac{\partial \ln \tilde{L}^s}{\partial \ln \tilde{X}^d} = 0$$

so that, from the specifications of Ito's effective trade offers, we derive

$$\frac{\partial \ln X^d}{\partial \ln \tilde{X}^d} = 1 + \gamma_{XD} \frac{\partial \ln L}{\partial \ln \tilde{X}^d}$$

and

$$\frac{\partial \ln X^s}{\partial \ln \tilde{X}^d} = \gamma_{XS} \cdot \frac{\partial \ln L}{\partial \ln \tilde{X}^d}$$

Substituting these two expressions in the equation above, we write

$$\frac{\partial \ln X}{\partial \ln \tilde{X}^d} = (1 - P_G) + [\gamma_{XD}(1 - P_G) + \gamma_{XS}(P_G)] \frac{\partial \ln L}{\partial \ln \tilde{X}^d} \tag{2.8}$$

This expression still contains the elasticity $\partial \ln L / \partial \ln \tilde{X}^d$ which has similarly to be expressed as a function of the regime proportions and the spillover coefficients:

$$\frac{\partial \ln L}{\partial \ln \tilde{X}^d} = \frac{\partial \ln L}{\partial \ln L^d} \cdot \frac{\partial \ln L^d}{\partial \ln \tilde{X}^d} + \frac{\partial \ln L}{\partial \ln L^s} \cdot \frac{\partial \ln L^s}{\partial \ln \tilde{X}^d}$$

$$= (1-P_L)\frac{\partial \ln L^d}{\partial \ln \tilde{X}^d} + (P_L)\frac{\partial \ln L^s}{\partial \ln \tilde{X}^d}$$

$$= (1-P_L)\left[\gamma_{LD}\frac{\partial \ln X}{\partial \ln \tilde{X}^d}\right] + (P_L)\cdot 0 \tag{2.9}$$

By combining equations (2.8) and (2.9), we obtain the final expression for the autonomous demand multiplier (in elasticity form)

$$\frac{d \ln X}{d \ln \tilde{X}^d} = \frac{(1-P_G)}{1-\{[\gamma_{XD}(1-P_G)+\gamma_{XS}(P_G)]\gamma_{LD}(1-P_L)\}}$$

A first remark, linked with the discussion of a preceding paragraph, concerns the stability conditions: with $0 \leqslant P_G \leqslant 1$ and $0 \leqslant P_L \leqslant 1$, the conditions on the spillover parameters to ensure positive and finite multipliers for whatever values of P_G and P_L are readily seen to be $\gamma_{XD}\gamma_{LD} < 1$ and $\gamma_{XS}\gamma_{LD} < 1$. Refer to the preceding subsection for more comments about these conditions.

We observe that, as expected, the precise value of the multiplier will depend on the 'regime proportions' P_G and P_L and will vary continuously as P_G and P_L themselves evolve continuously between 0 and 1. This continuous multiplier may be contrasted with the discrete 'four-tier' multiplier of the conventional disequilibrium model. That model may be considered as the limiting case of ours for the dispersion parameters ρ_G and ρ_L tending to infinity: in that case the proportions P_G and P_L only take the value 0 and 1 and by substituting the four possible combinations into the above formula, we get

$$\left.\begin{array}{l}P_G=0\\P_L=0\end{array}\right\}P_K=1 \ \textit{pure Keynesian regime} \qquad \frac{d \ln X}{d \ln \tilde{X}^d} = \frac{1}{1-\gamma_{XD}\gamma_{LD}}$$

$$\left.\begin{array}{l}P_G=1\\P_L=0\end{array}\right\}P_C=1 \ \textit{pure classical unemployment regime} \qquad \frac{d \ln X}{d \ln \tilde{X}^d} = 0$$

$$\left.\begin{array}{l}P_G=1\\P_L=1\end{array}\right\}P_R=1 \ \textit{pure repressed inflation regime} \qquad \frac{d \ln X}{d \ln \tilde{X}^d} = 0$$

$$\left.\begin{array}{l}P_G=0\\P_L=1\end{array}\right\}P_U=1 \ \textit{pure underconsumption regime} \qquad \frac{d \ln X}{d \ln \tilde{X}^d} = 1$$

The multiplier in the pure Keynesian regime conforms to the traditional textbook formula: $\gamma_{XD}\gamma_{LD}$ represents the traditional 'consumption' demand response to increased output consisting of the consumption demand response to sales of labour (γ_{XD}) and the labour demand response to sales of goods (γ_{LD}). In the pure classical unemployment and pure repressed inflation regimes, the multiplier is zero since there is no spare capacity ($P_G = 1$) to meet the autonomous demand increase. And in the pure underconsumption regime (which could be viewed as the situation where all firms are in excess supply on the goods market but, due to generalized labour hoarding, are facing labour markets which are at full employment), the multiplier only equals 1 (impact effect) since no further multiplier effect arises from the derived labour demand.

While the conventional disequilibrium approach constrains the multiplier to jump discretely between the three values 0, 1 and $1/(1 - \gamma_{XD}\gamma_{LD})$, our approach implies a multiplier being a continuous function of P_G and P_L defined over the whole range $[0, 1/(1 - \gamma_{XD}\gamma_{LD})]$, which makes it more appropriate for empirical policy analysis.

It may be readily verified by differentiation of the above formula (we leave it to the reader) that, if the stability conditions are verified, the above multiplier is a decreasing function of both P_G and P_L.

This means that the extent of the rationing on both markets (goods and labour) concur in reducing the multiplier effect of an autonomous increase in the demand for goods. Considering first the case where $P_G = 0$ (in that case $X = X^d$ which makes X^s appear as irrelevant or 'infinite') but $0 < P_L < 1$ (so that the individual firms may find themselves either in the Keynesian regime or the underconsumption regime), the expression for the multiplier reduces to $1/(1 - \gamma_{XD}\gamma_{LD}(1 - P_L))$ which makes clear that labour constraints (or, equivalently, the presence of firms in the underconsumption regime) reduce the multiplier effect working itself through induced labour demand. When, moreover, P_G departs from zero (X^s appearing now as a limiting constraint as well), the multiplier effect is further reduced due to the inability of the firms already in excess demand to meet any increase (either direct or derived) in demand for goods; the last term of the denominator (effective only for $P_G \neq 0$, i.e. 'finite' X^s) represents a positive supply effect (weaker however than the negative effect just described above) originating from increased labour.

The variation of multiplier effects along the business cycle is illustrated in figure 2.2 where it has been estimated for the Belgian manufacturing sector on the basis of the historical observations for P_G and P_L and the parameter estimates of chapter 3. For the sake of comparability with traditional multiplier estimates, the figure reports our estimate no longer in elasticity form but as $dX/d\tilde{X}^d$.[12] This is seen to be varying widely depending on the prevailing mix of regimes (refer to figure 1.8 in chapter 1). Sneessens' [1981] partition of regimes has also been reported on the figure (although Sneessens' work concerned the whole Belgian economy while this only concerns the Belgian manufacturing sector): this clearly brings into evidence that traditional budgetary policy (increase in public spending) is most effective in a situation characterized by a (dominant) Keynesian regime and less effective when repressed inflation or classical unemployment prevails.

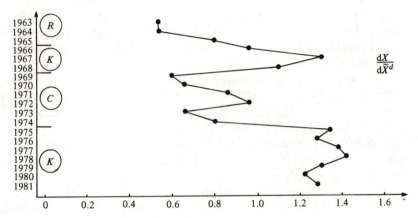

Figure 2.2. Variable multiplier of autonomous demand increase on manufacturing output

2.2   Aggregation of micro production units in a rationing context and the aggregate production function

In the adopted framework, each aggregate sector is viewed as consisting of a huge number of goods micro markets and labour micro markets in very diverse disequilibrium situations and on which the *min* condition is taken to hold.

Since a macro sector no longer appears as a homogeneous entity in this theoretical setting, this heterogeneity should naturally characterize the production structure also and it seems difficult to maintain the fiction of N strictly identical firms.

Empirical observation (as reported by L. Johansen [1972], K. Sato [1975] and W. Hildenbrand [1981] for example) has highlighted the great disparity of firms belonging to the same production sector (even narrowly defined) with respect to their production factors' efficiencies. This raises the question of the short-run and long-run aggregate function which will be discussed in this section.

2.2.1   *The aggregate short-run production function*

This is the most difficult question. It may be stated like this: the production sector of interest consisting of a large number of elementary production units (firms, machines, ... according to the chosen level of disaggregation) whose production functions as well as the stock and the characteristics of the capital are given in the short-term, does an aggregate production function $Q = Q(L)$ exist and is this function likely to be represented by one of the commonly adopted functional forms?

This problem has been handled by several authors (H. S. Houthakker [1955–56]; D. Levhari [1968]; L. Johansen [1972]; K. Sato [1975]; W. Hildenbrand [1981], a.o.), but always in a perfectly competitive equilibrium framework. Let us briefly recall their main conclusions before considering a rationing framework.

Let the micro production function be represented by

$$q_i = f(\alpha_i k_i, \beta_i l_i)$$

with the function f being common to all production units but with the 'efficiency parameters' α_i and β_i varying among the micro units. These differences reflect the heterogeneity of the capital stock. For each production unit, k_i is fixed in the short-term and associated to the pair (α_i, β_i) while output is varying with l_i. Typically, the micro production function could be a Leontieff function

$$q_i = \min (\alpha_i k_i, \beta_i l_i)$$

or a CES function with weak short-term elasticity of substitution ($\sigma \ll 1$)

$$q_i = [(\alpha_i k_i)^{-\rho} + (\beta_i l_i)^{-\rho}]^{-1/\rho} \qquad \sigma = 1/(1+\rho)$$

One can show that in both cases

$$\lim_{l_i \to \infty} q_i = \alpha_i k_i$$

and so $\alpha_i k_i$ is the maximum productive capacity of micro unit i.

Let us now define the 'capacity density function'

$$\Phi(\beta) = \int_\alpha \alpha k(\alpha, \beta) \, d\alpha \geqslant 0$$

which is the total productive capacity of 'firms'[13] with a labour efficiency level of β.

Assuming Leontieff production functions at the micro level, for a given real wage rate w, producers will engage in production so long as their quasi-rents are non-negative, i.e.

$$q_i - wl_i = q_i\left(1 - \frac{w}{\beta_i}\right) \geqslant 0 \quad \text{or} \quad \beta_i \geqslant w$$

In the framework of perfect competition, nobody is ever rationed at prevailing prices and wages. In particular, the producers produce and sell exactly the amount of goods they like and similarly hire all the labour they want.

In that case, the total output of the industry is

$$Q(w) = \int_w^{\beta_0} \Phi(\beta) \, d\beta \tag{2.10}$$

and total employment

$$L(w) = \int_w^{\beta_0} \frac{\Phi(\beta)}{\beta} \, d\beta \tag{2.11}$$

where β_0 is the supremum of the labour efficiency β. By eliminating w from these two equations, we get the aggregate short-run production function $Q = Q(L)$. K. Sato [1975] shows in a more general setting (where the micro production functions are not restricted to the sole Leontieff case) that the properties of the 'capacity density function' $\Phi(\beta)$ condition the short-run aggregate production function $Q = Q(L)$:

– $Q(L)$ exists if $\Phi(\beta)$ is a non-negative, continuous and differentiable function;
– $Q(L)$ is invariant with time if $\Phi(\beta)$ keeps its basic form while shifting.

Moreover, K. Sato shows that $\sigma_{aggr.} > \sigma_{min}$, i.e. that the elasticity of substitution of the aggregate function is strictly greater than the minimum value of the micro elasticities of substitution (which are not necessarily constant in the most general case). More precisely, micro units exhibiting a Leontieff technology ($\sigma_{min} = \sigma_i = 0$, $\forall i$) do not generate an aggregate Leontieff production function (since $\sigma_{aggr.} > \sigma_{min} = 0$) because the dispersion of the micro efficiencies allows units which are more or less 'labour intensive' to be incorporated.

The precise functional form of the aggregate function $Q(L)$ will of course depend on both the specification of the micro functions and on the capacity density function $\Phi(\beta)$. But even in the simple case of Leontieff-type micro production functions, the empirical distributions $\Phi(\beta)$ observed by K. Sato and others do not seem likely to generate the simplest functional forms for the aggregate short-run production function.[14] In particular, the aggregate elasticity of substitution should not be taken to be constant even in the case of σ_{micro} constant. As a consequence, a CES specification (and *a fortiori* a Leontieff specification) for the short-run macro production function should only be useful as a local approximation of a more general function (like a VES function).

The above analysis is valid in a perfectly competitive framework where, at prevailing prices and wages, no rationing ever takes place either on the goods market or on the labour market. This is indeed the condition for equations like (2.10) and (2.11) to hold. Moreover, it only assumes a static optimizing behaviour (short-term equilibrium defined by the marginal conditions) while, in the real world, firms are confronted by adjustment costs of all types which entail dynamic optimizing behaviour even for short-run decisions. The 'labour hoarding' phenomenon is one of the best-known and most important examples of such behaviour.

We would like to show now that, even in a rationing context and in the presence of labour hoarding, it is still possible to aggregate micro production functions into a short-run macro production function. We will then show that the resulting production function is in line with the specification presented in section 2.1 for the aggregate model.

A typical firm may be viewed as the aggregation of elementary production units (machines, processes, . . .) which, if defined at a sufficiently low level of disaggregation, may without loss of generality be taken to exhibit a Leontieff technology $q_i = \min(\alpha_i k_i, \beta_i l_i)$.

In a perfectly competitive framework like the one considered above, we always have

$$\beta_i l_i = 0 \qquad \text{if quasi-rent} \leqslant 0$$

$$= \alpha_i k_i \quad \text{if quasi-rent} > 0$$

so that the ratios $\beta_i l_i / \alpha_i k_i$ take the values 0 or 1 only.

But if we introduce quantity rationing on both the goods and the labour markets and take labour hoarding into consideration, the ratio $\beta_i l_i / \alpha_i k_i$ is likely to take a large range of values from 0 to much over 1:

- the difficulty of finding qualified workers for some equipment may entail $\beta_i l_i < \alpha_i k_i$;
- insufficient demand for some goods may induce producers to produce at a moderate rate with reduced labour and hence $\beta_i l_i < \alpha_i k_i$;
- but in the face of adjustment costs (hiring and firing costs) and the uncertainty about the duration and severity of the reduction in demand, the most commonly adopted solution will be labour hoarding. This is a most general phenomenon even in periods of high activity, as R. Fair [1969] noted for example.

Labour hoarding amounts to a reduction in production without reduction (or with a less than proportional reduction) of labour. This may be represented in our framework by an inefficient allocation of labour among micro production units, implying a fairly large dispersion of the ratios $\beta_i l_i / \alpha_i k_i$. Let us illustrate this by the simple example of the firm consisting of two identical micro production units

$$q = q_1 + q_2$$
$$= \min(\alpha_1 k_1, \beta_1 l_1) + \min(\alpha_2 k_2, \beta_2 l_2)$$

Let us assume the following numerical values:

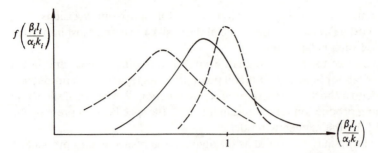

Figure 2.3. Distribution of the ratios $\beta_i l_i / \alpha_i k_i$ of the elementary production units

$$k_1 = k_2 = 5$$

$$\alpha_1 = \alpha_2 = 1$$

$$\beta_1 = \beta_2 = 1$$

If the producer wants to produce at full capacity to meet a sustained demand, it has to put 5 workers on each machine in order to produce 10. In that case the ratios $\beta_1 l_1 / \alpha_1 k_1$ and $\beta_2 l_2 / \alpha_2 k_2$ both equal 1.

In the case of a reduction in demand perceived as temporary, the producer might choose to keep its full labour force (10) while producing less than full capacity (let us take 8 for the example). This behaviour may be viewed as an inefficient allocation of the labour force: indeed, it amounts to allocating 3 workers to one machine and 7 to the other one as may be readily verified:

$$8 = \min (1 * 5, 1 * 3) + \min (1 * 5, 1 * 7) \qquad .$$

This inefficient allocation of labour implies an increased dispersion of the ratios $\beta_i l_i / \alpha_i k_i$ since we now have $\beta_1 l_1 / \alpha_1 k_1 = 3/5$ and $\beta_2 l_2 / \alpha_2 k_2 = 7/5$.

In an aggregate sector comprising a large number of diversely demanded products and made up of a huge number of elementary production units, the ratios $\beta_i l_i / \alpha_i k_i$ are likely to exhibit a continuous distribution as in figure 2.3. If we assume the $\beta_i l_i$ and $\alpha_i k_i$ to be jointly lognormally distributed, which is a reasonable assumption in view of the evidence on the size distribution of economic variables (see section 1.1 for more comments on this distributional assumption), then we face a problem formally similar to the one handled in chapter 1 for the derivation of the aggregate transaction curve since aggregate output is equal to

$$X = \sum_i \min (\alpha_i k_i, \beta_i l_i)$$

Aggregating by integration over the elementary production units (as was done in chapter 1 over the micro markets) yields similarly an aggregate CES-type production function

$$X = [(\bar{\alpha}K)^{-\rho} + (\bar{\beta}L)^{-\rho}]^{-1/\rho} \tag{2.12}$$

with $\bar{\alpha}$ and $\bar{\beta}$ being the weighted averages of the α_i and β_i

$$\bar{\alpha} = \sum_i \frac{k_i}{(\sum_i k_i)} \alpha_i$$

$$\bar{\beta} = \sum_i \frac{k_i}{(\sum_i k_i)} \beta_i$$

and the parameter ρ being a (negatively sloped) function of the dispersion of the $\beta_i l_i / \alpha_i k_i$.

This dispersion is however likely to vary along the business cycle since a reduction (resp. a pick-up) of the aggregate demand for goods will normally induce a combination of reduction (resp. increase) of total labour force together with an augmented (resp. diminished) recourse to labour hoarding. This is represented on figure 2.3 by the combination of a shift in the distribution of the $\beta_i l_i / \alpha_i k_i$ together with a variation of the dispersion.

Since the parameter ρ of expression (2.12) is a function of the dispersion of the $\beta_i l_i / \alpha_i k_i$ ratios and since the aggregate elasticity of substitution $\sigma = 1/(1+\rho)$, we end up with a variable elasticity of substitution production function (VES).

Moreover, since ρ is always greater than or equal to 0, σ is always less than or equal to 1.

Now that we have shown that aggregation over elementary production units in a rationing framework leads to a short-run production function of the VES type, let us show that the specification of our aggregate model presented in section 2.1 effectively implies such a production function.

Taking the VES production function proposed by Lu and Fletcher [1968], the demand for labour may be derived as

$$\ln L = c_0 + c_1 T - \sigma_1 \ln\left(\frac{w}{p}\right) + \left(1 - \frac{\sigma_1}{\sigma_2}\right) \ln K + \frac{\sigma_1}{\sigma_2} \ln X \tag{2.13}$$

where L, K, X, T, p, w denote respectively the labour, the stock of fixed capital, the output, a time trend, and the prices of goods and labour. It may be noticed that the particular case $\sigma_1 = \sigma_2 = \sigma$ brings us back to the CES case with no capital stock term showing up in the labour demand equation.

Since the equation (2.13) is derived in a framework without labour constraints, let us compare it to the corresponding equation of our model in the same conditions, i.e. when $L \simeq L^d <<< L^s$.

In that case, it may be easily derived from the equations of model (2.2) (or (2.6)) that

$$\ln L = \ln \tilde{L}^d + \gamma_{LD}(\ln X - \ln \tilde{X}^s) \tag{2.14}$$

where $\tilde{L}^d$ and $\tilde{X}^s$ are respectively the notional demand for labour and the notional supply of goods, i.e. corresponding to full capacity utilization. These notional trade offers are determined by the aggregate long-run production function for which any conventional neo-classical production function may be assumed, as will be discussed in subsection 2.2.2. Assuming a CES long-run production function, we obtain for the technical coefficients (see chapter 3 for the derivation):

$$\ln\left(\frac{\tilde{X}^s}{K}\right) = \text{const.} + c_1^* T - \sigma \ln\left(\frac{p}{r}\right)$$

$$\ln\left(\frac{\tilde{L}^d}{K}\right) = \text{const.} + c_2^* T - \sigma \ln\left(\frac{w}{r}\right)$$

where r, σ designate the price of capital and the long-run elasticity of substitution.

Substituting these specifications for $\tilde{X}^s$ and $\tilde{L}^d$ into equation (2.14), we obtain finally

$$\ln L = c^{te} + c^* T - \sigma\left[\ln\left(\frac{w}{r}\right) - \gamma_{LD}\ln\left(\frac{p}{r}\right)\right]$$

$$+ (1 - \gamma_{LD})\ln K + \gamma_{LD}\ln X \tag{2.15}$$

which relates short-run variations in labour and output. It is easy to check the similarity between this equation and equation (2.13) derived from Lu and Fletcher's VES production function. Here also the case $\gamma_{LD} = 1$ brings us back to the CES case.

Intuitively, we understand that if the possibility of rationing on the labour market is allowed, the aggregate short-term elasticity of substitution (which measures the ease with which labour may be substituted with capital in the short-run) will also be a function of the 'tension' prevailing on the labour market, accentuating the 'VES character' of our aggregate short-run production function.

Let us briefly summarize the preceding discussion: contrary to previous works which were concerned with a perfectly competitive environment without adjustment costs, our analysis examined the aggregation of micro production functions in a framework characterized by quantity rationing and labour hoarding.

It has been shown that explicit aggregation is feasible and results in a short-run production function of the VES type (with elasticity of substitution lower than unity). It was then shown that the specification of our aggregate model effectively implied such a short-run production function. Let us now consider the distinct issue of the aggregate long-run production function.

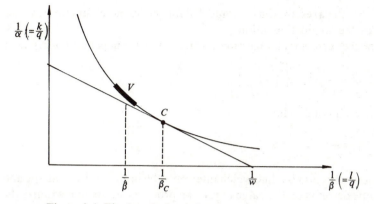

Figure 2.4. The 'ex-ante' unit isoquant

2.2.2 *The aggregate long-run production function*

This question, which differs widely from the preceding one, may be stated in the following terms:

A macro production sector consists of a large number of elementary production units characterized by a great diversity in their production factors' efficiencies. At the moment of the choice of an investment, all firms have access to the same technology ('best practice technology') and consequently face the same 'ex-ante' micro production function. Once a specific technique is chosen, the 'ex-post' substitution possibilities at the micro level are however very limited. The *aggregate long-run production function* is the locus of full capacity points when the (heterogeneous) stock of capital evolves and when the distribution of the micro efficiencies shifts with technical progress and relative prices. It will be shown that this aggregate long-run production function exhibits the same form as the 'ex-ante' micro production function and hence may be represented by any neo-classical production function.

The following discussion closely follows the presentation of K. Sato [1975].

Let us first examine the role of the 'ex-ante' micro production function and why producers, all behaving rationally and confronting the same function, may however be led to different choices.

Let the 'ex-ante' micro production function be represented by figure 2.4.

Let us suppose the putty–clay model is a good approximation of reality at the level of the elementary production unit (machine, equipment, ...): any technique (pair α_i, β_i) may be chosen along the 'ex-ante' production frontier but, once the investment has been embodied into physical capital, the technical coefficients are fixed and the 'ex-post' production function for this equipment is a Leontieff

$$q_i = \min(\alpha_i k_i, \beta_i l_i)$$

In figure 2.4, the axes are thus $1/\alpha$ and $1/\beta$ for the 'ex-ante' function and k/q and l/q for the 'ex-post' function.

Let w be the current real wage rate. Then, the quasi-rent per unit of capital is

$$r = \left(\frac{q - wl}{k}\right) = \alpha\left[1 - \left(\frac{w}{\beta}\right)\right]$$

in the current period. Thus

$$\frac{r}{\alpha} + \frac{w}{\beta} = 1$$

The above equation is a line which intercepts the horizontal axis at $1/w$ and whose slope depends on the value of r. If the producer wants to maximize the quasi-rent of the current period, he will choose the technique $C(\alpha_C, \beta_C)$ at the point of tangency between the straight line and the 'ex-ante' production frontier. However, as capital goods are durable, the point C is likely to be suboptimal for maximizing quasi-rents over the lifetime of the capital stock embodying the technique. Indeed, if w is expected to keep increasing in the future, the quasi-rents coming from the equipment (α_C, β_C) will progressively decrease to zero, at which moment the equipment reaches the end of its economic life.

Let us state the problem in a more formal way. Assume that the producer anticipates the real wage to increase at the rate ω so that

$$w_{t+v} = w_t e^{\omega v} \qquad \omega > 0, \quad v \geqslant 0$$

Capital goods depreciate over time (wear of some pieces of equipment, increasing maintenance work with age, ...) which may be represented by a deterioration of the efficiency parameters α and β at the rates of μ and γ respectively. The equipment k embodying the technique (α, β) at time t will earn a quasi-rent

$$k\alpha e^{-\mu v}\left[1 - \frac{w_t e^{\omega v}}{\beta e^{-\gamma v}}\right]$$

at time $t + v$.

Let the discount rate be ρ. The goal of the producer is to maximize the present discounted value of the stream of quasi-rents

$$V = \int_0^T k\alpha e^{-\mu v}\left[1 - \frac{w_t}{\beta} e^{(\omega + \gamma)v}\right] e^{-\rho v}\, dv$$

where T the (anticipated) economic life of this equipment is determined by the quasi-rent becoming zero so that $e^{-(\omega + \gamma)v} = w_t/\beta$. This maximization is performed with respect to α and β under the constraint of the 'ex-ante' production function. It may be shown (see K. Sato [1975] for the detailed

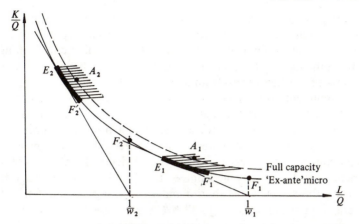

Figure 2.5. 'Ex-ante' micro and full capacity macro production functions

derivation) that the optimal technique depends on the form of the production function and on the value of $\lambda = (\omega + \gamma)/(\rho + \mu)$. More precisely, the optimal technique $(\hat{\alpha}, \hat{\beta})$ will be defined by a point V to the left of the point C on the 'ex-ante' isoquant and the distance between V and C will be a positive function of λ.

The choice of the technique $(\hat{\alpha}, \hat{\beta})$ thus depends on the producer's expectations about each element ω, γ, μ and ρ. Since it is most likely that different producers will have different expectations of these elements, the optimum $(\hat{\alpha}, \hat{\beta})$ will vary from one firm to the other. In other words, the techniques chosen by a number of rational producers facing the same 'ex-ante' production function may display a sizeable dispersion along the isoquant. This is illustrated in figure 2.4 by the 'thickening' of the isoquant in the region of point V.

Let us now show that the locus of full capacity points exhibits the same form as the 'ex-ante' micro production function.

Figure 2.5 shows again the 'ex-ante' micro production function. This may be any neo-classical production function with a significant elasticity of substitution (since it represents an 'ex-ante' choice possibility). Before commenting on this figure, a preliminary remark must be made: for clarity of exposition, technical progress (implying a shift of the 'ex-ante' micro isoquant) will be ignored in the following discussion. Due to this shift, the distribution of the micro efficiencies is not only concentrated along the isoquant but also in a neighbouring region above and to the right of the isoquant (the shaded region in the figure). If however the efficiency distribution keeps its basic form while shifting (constant technical progress, ...), there is no need to modify the analysis hereafter and the fundamental conclusion remains valid.

For the real wage w_1, producers are led to choose (as has been shown above) production techniques distributed around the point E_1 for their new equipment. Older equipment embodies techniques distributed along the isoquant to the right of the point E_1. These techniques become less and less profitable the more they depart from point E_1. So the points to the right of the point F_1 represent techniques with a negative quasi-rent ($l/q > 1/w$, thus $q - wl < 0$) which are thus eliminated; in fact producers not only ask for a positive quasi-rent but instead for a positive net profit (i.e. account being taken of provision for capital depreciation) in order to keep equipment active. As a consequence, for a real wage w_1, the efficiency distribution of active equipment spreads for example from E_1 to F'_1. When the real wage rate is raised to w_2, the efficiency distribution moves up along the isoquant to $E_2F'_2$. The average aggregate ratios L/Q and K/Q are represented by points like A_1 and A_2 (slightly above the 'ex-ante' micro isoquant because of the well-known properties of averages). The locus of these full capacity points is the dotted line: obviously, if the efficiency distribution keeps a stable form when shifting, the full capacity isoquant is a replica of the 'ex-ante' micro production function. Consequently, any conventional neo-classical specification may be assumed for the aggregate long-run production function (corresponding to the notional supply of goods $\tilde{X}^s$ and demand for labour $\tilde{L}^d$ in our notation). A CES specification will be adopted in the empirical application which will be the subject of the next chapter.

3

Empirical estimation of a macro sectoral model of the Belgian manufacturing industry based on business survey data

To illustrate the practicability and the potential of the 'aggregation by integration' approach for empirical macroeconomics, we present in this chapter an econometric application for the Belgian manufacturing industry.[1]

Our model is an annual model estimated on the period 1965–80. Both the frequency and the estimation period were dictated by data availability.[2]

Data definitions and sources are given in appendix H.

Let us first recall the structural form which was derived in section 2.1:

$$\ln X = \frac{1}{\rho_G}\ln(1-P_G) + \frac{\gamma_{XD}}{\rho_L}\ln(P_L) + \beta^d \ln \mathscr{X}^d + u_{XD} \qquad (3.1.1)$$

$$\ln X = \frac{1}{\rho_G}\cdot\frac{1}{(1-\theta\,\gamma_{LD}\gamma_{XS})}\ln P_G + \frac{1}{\rho_L}\cdot\frac{\gamma_{XS}}{(1-\theta\,\gamma_{LD}\gamma_{XS})}\ln(1-P_L)$$
$$+ \beta^s \ln \mathscr{X}^s + u_{XS} \qquad (3.1.2)$$

$$\ln \mathrm{DUC_{obs}} = \ln \alpha_{\mathrm{DUC}} + \frac{1}{\rho_G}\cdot\frac{1}{(1-\theta\,\gamma_{XS}\gamma_{LD})}\ln(P_G)$$
$$+ \frac{1}{\rho_L}\cdot\frac{\gamma_{XS}}{(1-\theta\,\gamma_{XS}\gamma_{LD})}\ln(1-P_L) + u_{\mathrm{DUC}} \qquad (3.1.3)$$

$$\ln L = \frac{1}{\rho_L}\cdot\frac{1}{(1-\theta\,\gamma_{XS}\gamma_{LD})}\ln(1-P_L) + \frac{1}{\rho_G}\cdot\frac{\gamma_{LD}}{(1-\theta\,\gamma_{LD}\gamma_{XS})}\ln(P_G)$$
$$+ \lambda^d \ln \mathscr{L}^d + u_{LD} \qquad (3.1.4)$$

$$\ln L = \frac{1}{\rho_L}\ln(P_L) + \lambda^s \ln \mathscr{L}^s + u_{LS} \qquad (3.1.5)$$

with the error terms assumed to be jointly normally distributed $u_t \sim N(0, \Sigma^2)$. This simultaneous model (five equations; five endogenous variables X, P_G, DUC_{obs}, L, P_L) is written here in a form suitable for estimation with only observable variables in the equations. As was shown in chapter 2, this general form encompasses two different models depending on the value taken by the parameter θ: $\theta = 0$ implies Portes' model, while Ito's model is obtained for $\theta = 1$. The difference between these two models arises from alternative specifications of the aggregate spillover effect; on the other hand, both models share the same definitions of the notional trade offers. Appropriate specifications for these notional trade offers – represented in the above equations by the '$\beta \ln \mathscr{X}$' and the '$\lambda \ln \mathscr{L}$' – will be proposed and discussed in the next three sections. Once fully specified, the model will be estimated by the FIML method and empirical results will be the subject of the following sections.

Section 3.4 reports the empirical results of the specification of P_L, an issue which was discussed in chapter 1. Section 3.5 is devoted to another issue which was discussed at length in chapter 2, namely the choice between Ito's and Portes' specifications of the spillover effect: empirical evidence reported there favours Ito's specification. As a consequence, the last section presents all types of empirical estimates (parameter estimates, effective excess demand ratios, effective and notional supplies and demands for both aggregate markets, . . .) obtained on the basis of Ito's model while the counterparts for Portes' model are relegated to appendix E.

3.1   The long-run production function and the notional supply of goods and demand for labour

In the preceding chapter, we showed that the long-run aggregate production function (corresponding to the locus of full capacity points) could be represented by any conventional neo-classical specification and we suggested the CES specification. Under this technological assumption, we now derive the specification of the notional supply of goods[3] $\tilde{X}^s$ and the notional demand for labour $\tilde{L}^d$ (corresponding to these points of full capacity) appearing in equation (3.1.2) and (3.1.4) respectively.

A static model will first be derived and then dynamic adjustment will be introduced.

Given the desired production capacity $\tilde{X}^s$, the firms choose to combine labour and capital so as to minimize costs:

$$\min_{\tilde{L}^d, K} w\tilde{L}^d + rK$$

subject to the long-run technological constraint[4]

$$\tilde{X}^s = \gamma[\delta(e^{\gamma_1 T} . \tilde{L}^d)^{-\rho} + (1-\delta)(e^{\gamma_2 T} . K)^{-\rho}]^{-1/\rho}$$

where $\tilde{L}^d$ = notional labour demand (labour at full capacity)
$\quad\quad K$ = total stock of fixed capital
$\quad\quad w$ = wage cost
$\quad\quad r$ = cost of use of capital
$\quad\quad T$ = time trend
$\quad\quad \gamma_1, \gamma_2$ = rates of factor augmenting technical progress
$\quad\quad \sigma = (1+\rho)^{-1}$ = long-run elasticity of substitution

First-order conditions are readily shown to be

$$w = \Lambda(\tilde{X}^s)^{1+\rho} \gamma^{-\rho} \delta(e^{\gamma_1 T} \tilde{L}^d)^{-1-\rho} e^{\gamma_1 T}$$

$$r = \Lambda(\tilde{X}^s)^{1+\rho} \gamma^{-\rho} (1-\delta)(e^{\gamma_2 T} K)^{-1-\rho} e^{\gamma_2 T}$$

where Λ is the Lagrangean multiplier. The latter is easily shown to be equal to average cost. This may be done by multiplying the two equations by $\tilde{L}^d$ and K respectively, adding them up and dividing the sum by $\tilde{X}^s$.

If we make the conventional assumption that, in the long run, prices are set equal to a constant mark-up m over long-run average costs,[5] then after substituting p/m for Λ in the above first-order conditions, we obtain two equations defining the technical coefficients. Indeed, taking logarithms, rearranging terms and introducing stochastic disturbance terms, we get

$$\ln\left(\frac{\tilde{X}^s}{K}\right) = c_{0K} + (1-\sigma)\gamma_2 T + \sigma \ln\left(\frac{r}{p}\right) + u_{XS} \tag{3.2}$$

$$\ln\left(\frac{\tilde{L}^d}{K}\right) = c_{0L} + (1-\sigma)(\gamma_2 - \gamma_1)T + \sigma \ln\left(\frac{r}{w}\right) + u_{LD} \tag{3.3}$$

These two equations provide the stochastic specifications of the notional supply of goods $\tilde{X}^s$ and the notional demand for labour $\tilde{L}^d$ represented in the equations (3.1.2) and (3.1.4) respectively by the terms $\beta^s \ln \mathscr{X}^s + u_{XS}$ and $\lambda^d \ln \mathscr{L}^d + u_{LD}$.

Hence combining the above specifications of $\tilde{X}^s$ and $\tilde{L}^d$ with equations (3.1.2) and (3.1.4) (which basically express these latent variables as functions of observables only) yields completely specified *static* equations for the structural form intended for estimation.

It is clear that in a framework where the whole production structure is viewed as the aggregation of elementary production units whose efficiencies are relatively rigid ex post (refer to section 2.2.2), the aggregate technical coefficients will only adjust slowly to new optimal values. Since this adjustment is mostly performed through formation of new fixed capital (along with the scrapping of obsolete equipment), the speed of this adjustment will crucially depend on the rate of investment. A most attractive approach would call for endogenizing manufacturing investment; this is, however, not an easy task since investment itself is known to be sensitive to the extent of rationing on various markets without the appropriate specification for catching these effects being at all evident.[6]

To simplify this first attempt at specifying and estimating 'continuous type' rationing models, we leave investment (and hence the capital stock K) exogenous and take a short-cut by postulating directly a flexible dynamic adjustment process for the aggregate technical coefficients. An interesting dynamic specification which allows for a differentiated treatment of short-run transitory effects vs. longer-run determinants has been shown to be the ECM[7] ('error correction mechanism'). Assuming a dynamic adjustment of the ECM type, equations (3.2) and (3.3) may be replaced by

$$\Delta \ln \left(\frac{\tilde{X}^s}{K}\right)_t = c_{0K} + \delta_{0K}\sigma\Delta \ln \left(\frac{r}{p}\right)_t$$

$$+ (1 - \delta_{2K})\left[(1-\sigma)\gamma_2 T + \sigma \ln \left(\frac{r}{p}\right)_{t-1} - \ln \left(\frac{\tilde{X}^s}{K}\right)_{t-1}\right] + u_{XSt} \quad (3.4)$$

and

$$\Delta \ln \left(\frac{\tilde{L}^d}{K}\right)_t = c_{0L} + \delta_{0L}\sigma\Delta \ln \left(\frac{r}{w}\right)_t$$

$$+ (1 - \delta_{2L})\left[(1-\sigma)(\gamma_2 - \gamma_1)T + \sigma \ln \left(\frac{r}{w}\right)_{t-1} - \ln \left(\frac{\tilde{L}^d}{K}\right)_{t-1}\right] + u_{LDt}$$

$$\text{(with } 0 < \frac{\delta_{0L}}{\delta_{0K}} \quad \text{and} \quad -1 \leqslant \frac{1-\delta_{2K}}{1-\delta_{2L}} \leqslant 1) \quad (3.5)$$

which both reduce to partial adjustment (PA) mechanisms for $\delta_{0K} = 1 - \delta_{2K}$ and $\delta_{0L} = 1 - \delta_{2L}$ and to the static case for $\delta_{0K} = 1 - \delta_{2K} = 1$ and $\delta_{0L} = 1 - \delta_{2L} = 1$.

Substituting the latent variables $\tilde{X}^s$ and $\tilde{L}^d$ in equations (3.4) and (3.5) by their expressions as functions of observables only (given by (3.1.2) and (3.1.4)) results in the final expressions:

$$\Delta \ln X_t = c_{0XS} + \Delta \ln K_t + \frac{1}{\rho_G}\cdot\frac{1}{(1-\theta\gamma_{XS}\gamma_{LD})}\Delta \ln (P_{Gt})$$

$$+ \frac{1}{\rho_L}\cdot\frac{\gamma_{XS}}{(1-\theta\gamma_{XS}\gamma_{LD})}\Delta \ln (1-P_{Lt}) + \delta_{0K}\sigma\Delta \ln \left(\frac{r}{p}\right)_t$$

$$+ (1-\delta_{2K})\left\{(1-\sigma)\gamma_2 T + \sigma \ln \left(\frac{r}{p}\right)_{t-1} - \ln \left(\frac{X}{K}\right)_{t-1}\right.$$

$$+ \frac{1}{\rho_G}\cdot\frac{1}{(1-\theta\gamma_{XS}\gamma_{LD})}\ln (P_{Gt-1}) + \frac{1}{\rho_L}\cdot\frac{\gamma_{XS}}{(1-\theta\gamma_{XS}\gamma_{LD})}\ln (1-P_{Lt-1})\right\}$$

$$+ u_{XSt} \quad (3.6)$$

and

$$\Delta \ln L_t = c_{OLD} + \Delta \ln K_t + \frac{1}{\rho_L} \cdot \frac{1}{(1-\theta\gamma_{XS}\gamma_{LD})} \Delta \ln(1-P_{Lt})$$

$$+ \frac{1}{\rho_G} \cdot \frac{\gamma_{LD}}{(1-\theta\gamma_{XS}\gamma_{LD})} \Delta \ln(P_{Gt}) + \delta_{0L}\sigma\Delta\ln\left(\frac{r}{w}\right)_t$$

$$+ (1-\delta_{2L})\left\{(1-\sigma)(\gamma_2-\gamma_1)T + \sigma\ln\left(\frac{r}{w}\right)_{t-1} - \ln\left(\frac{L}{K}\right)_{t-1}\right.$$

$$\left. + \frac{1}{\rho_L} \cdot \frac{1}{(1-\theta\gamma_{XS}\gamma_{LD})} \ln(1-P_{Lt-1}) + \frac{1}{\rho_G} \cdot \frac{\gamma_{LD}}{(1-\theta\gamma_{XS}\gamma_{LD})} \ln(P_{Gt-1})\right\}$$

$$+ u_{LDt} \tag{3.7}$$

which are the dynamic counterparts[8] of static equations (3.1.2) and (3.1.4). In the spirit of the ECM dynamic specifications, variables exerting only short-run transitory effects may be added (in variations or growth rates) to the first part of the equation without, however, being included in the 'error correction term' (the bracketed term multiplied by $1-\delta_2$) which corrects deviations from the long-run steady-state growth path.

Among the most natural candidates for exerting short-run transitory effects on notional output supply are the variations in profitability induced by short-run changes in relative prices (real wages) relative to labour productivity. This phenomenon is most naturally captured in vintage production models by short-run variations of the 'profitable capacity extensive margin' (age of the oldest profitable equipment) which do not necessarily imply immediate and definitive physical scrapping but may possibly imply maintaining temporarily idle some equipment which is (in the prevailing conditions) no longer profitable.[9] Since our production model is not of the 'vintage-type', we suggest capturing these transitory variations of the 'profitability extensive margin' by allowing notional output supply $\tilde{X}^s$ to be sensitive to short-run fluctuations of a profitability index:

$$\ln \tilde{X}_t^s = (\text{longer-run determinants}) + \alpha_1 \cdot \ln \text{PROFIT}_t$$

with PROFIT_t being defined as[10,11]

$$\text{PROFIT}_t = \left(\frac{p_t \cdot X_t}{w_t \cdot L_t}\right) \Bigg/ \left(\frac{p_{t-1} \cdot X_{t-1}}{w_{t-1} \cdot L_{t-1}}\right)$$

A temporary worsening of profitability, reflected by a negative value of

$$\ln \text{PROFIT}_t = \dot{p}_t - [\dot{w}_t - (\text{labour productivity})_t]$$

will then induce a slight contraction (the parameter α_1 is expected to be positive) of notional output supply with respect to the value of $\tilde{X}^s$ implied by the sole longer-term determinants, and conversely of course for an improvement of profitability.

Since equation (3.6) implies the expression $\Delta \ln \tilde{X}^s$ (as can be readily verified from equation (3.4) from which it is derived), the term to be added in order to represent these short-run effects will be of the form $\alpha_1 . \Delta \ln (\text{PROFIT}_t)$. This short-run 'profitability effect', which will also come into play in the DUC equation (see below), will empirically be found to be (statistically) significant.[12]

Before concluding this section, a few comments have to be given on the specification adopted for the cost of use of capital r_t appearing in equations (3.6) and (3.7). This variable is defined in the usual way (see for example Bischoff [1971]) as

$$r_t = \text{PI}_t (i_t^e + \delta) \pi_t$$

where PI_t = price of investment goods
$\quad i_t^e$ = anticipated real rate of interest
$\quad \delta$ = depreciation rate
$\quad \pi_t$ = index of business income taxation

Due to lack of sufficient information about the evolution of the business taxation regime, the corresponding index has been assumed constant $\pi_t = \pi$ for the whole estimation period. The main uncertainty concerns the proper specification of the anticipated real rate of interest, or equivalently, the proper specification of the expected long-run rate of inflation since i_t^e is defined as

$$i_t^e = (\text{LI}_t - \dot{p}_t^e)$$

where LI_t = long-term nominal interest rate
$\quad \dot{p}_t^e$ = expected long-run rate of inflation (in terms of output prices)

In view of the uncertainty surrounding these expectations, several specifications of i_t^e (and hence of r_t) were tried for the empirical estimation, namely:

(a) $\qquad\qquad i_t^e = i^e$

The anticipated long-run real rate of interest is perceived as constant during the whole period. This specification was selected by Sneessens [1981] for yielding the most satisfactory results. In that case, one has $\ln r_t = \ln \text{PI}_t$ plus a constant which disappears in the constant term of the equations.

(b) $\qquad\qquad i_t^e = \left(\text{LI}_t - \sum_{i=0}^{2} w_i \dot{p}_{t-i} \right)$

The expected long-run rate of inflation is computed as the weighted sum of the rates of inflation of the last three years. Various weights w_i have been tried.

(c) $i_t^e = (LI_t - \dot{p})$

The expected long-run rate of inflation is constant (and set equal to the average rate experienced) over the whole period.

Due most probably to the excessive 'volatility' of its implied long-run rate of inflation, specification (b) turned out to yield only deceptive results compared with those obtained under specifications (a) or (c). Hence only these latter specifications will be compared in the following. The short discussion below is not intended to present final estimation results, which will be the subject of section 3.6, but in a sense to 'clear the way' for section 3.6 by explaining how and why the finally adopted specification was chosen.

Some general features emerged from the empirical estimation:

(i)   The estimates of the dynamic parameters (δ_{0K}, δ_{0L}, δ_{2K}, δ_{2L}) turned out to be fairly (in some cases highly) sensitive to the choice of either specification of r_t so that the 'dynamics issue' has to be discussed together with the question of the proper specification of the user's cost of capital.

(ii)   Since both issues discussed here (the specification of r_t and the dynamic adjustment of the aggregate technical coefficients) concern the *notional* supply of goods and demand for labour, it could be expected *a priori* that qualitative results about these issues would be insensitive to the precise specification (Portes or Ito) adopted for the *effective* trade offers. This was indeed confirmed by empirical estimation: the (qualitative) results which will be reported now were found to hold under either Portes' or Ito's specifications. Hence, when empirical estimates are reported in this subsection in order to illustrate the discussion, they all refer to the same model (actually Ito's model).

(iii)   The model turns out to be robust with respect to this 'dynamics issue', in the sense that the estimates of the key parameters of interest appear to be quite insensitive to the precise dynamics adopted for the adjustment of the technical coefficients.[13] This suggests that, unless some dynamic specification turns out to 'outperform' the others, the cost of adopting a most restricted dynamic specification (remember we only have 16 observations!) might not be too heavy.

We now examine in more detail the empirical results, starting from the most general dynamic specification.

As is expected, the maximum value attained by the likelihood function decreases with the increasing number of restrictions imposed on the dynamic parameters.[14]

Moreover, as is readily verified from the estimation results reported in note 14, the differences of the maximum likelihood values are such that the restricted models would all be rejected for a more general one (ECM1 and PA2 rejected for ECM2, and PA1 rejected for both ECM1 and PA2) by a LR test. However, as will be argued below, the maximum likelihood value need not be the sole criterion for the assessment of a particular specification. This is clearly illustrated in the case of the most general dynamic scheme ECM2: the speed of adjustment implied by the estimates of the dynamic parameters turns out to be excessively *high* with definition (a) of r_t while it turns out to be particularly *low* with definition (c) of r_t.[15] In view of the uncertainty about the appropriate specification of r_t (i.e. the proper specification of long-run anticipations of the rate of inflation) and since specifications (a) and (c) appear equally acceptable *a priori*, it was felt that a desirable property of the dynamic scheme to be adopted was robustness[16] with respect to these two specifications. Since this robustness property is obviously not guaranteed under the ECM2 dynamic scheme, more restricted dynamic schemes had to be considered.

The results obtained under the dynamic scheme ECM1 turn out to be basically the same as those just commented for upon ECM2: excessively high speed of adjustment (93% of the total adjustment performed in the current period) with definition (a) of r_t, but extremely slow adjustment with definition (c) of r_t (actually $\delta_{0K} = \delta_{0L} = \delta_0$ again falls below zero but assuming $\delta_0 \simeq 0$, one gets about 3.9 years for only 50% of the adjustment to be completed).

Turning away from the ECM1 scheme for lack of 'robustness' (in the sense of note 16), let us examine the results obtained under the PA2 scheme. This scheme yielded acceptable and interesting results but only with definition (a) of r_t; failure of the optimization algorithm to converge after a great number of iterations with definition (c) of r_t[17] induced us to abandon the PA2 scheme for lack of robustness so that we ended with the most restricted dynamic scheme PA1. This appeared to be the most robust dynamic specification in the sense that it entails adjustment lags (for the aggregate technical coefficients) which are truly reasonable (although different) for both specifications of r_t.

The final choice between both definitions of r_t was in favour of definition (a) because it yielded a higher maximum likelihood value (184.1 against 180.4) than definition (c) (this was moreover the case for all dynamic schemes envisaged except ECM2). Also the implied adjustment lag is closer to that obtained in previous works (as for example Sneessens [1981]; Lubrano and Sneessens [1981]; the French model METRIC [1977]). The final empirical results are reported and commented upon in section 3.6.

The next section will now handle the specification of equation (3.1.3), the 'DUC equation'.

3.2 · The DUC equation

The degree of capacity utilization DUC_{obs} is defined as the ratio of current production on installed production capacity; the latter concept refers to[18] the maximum output that can be produced using existing plants and equipment, in the absence of any constraint on the markets for (variable) inputs. This concept of capacity corresponds closely to what may be called the 'engineering' concept of capacity (maximum feasible output given existing equipment) which is not identical to our concept of notional output supply $\tilde{X}^s$ where economic considerations also come into play (maximum output producers would like to produce given existing equipment and prevailing prices). These two concepts correspond to the distinction which is drawn in vintage production models between the 'capacity extensive margin' (age of the oldest installed equipment) and the 'profitability extensive margin'[19] (age of the oldest profitable equipment).

This distinction suggests that firms might keep equipment – and report it in their measure of capacity – which is no longer profitable in the prevailing prices and costs conditions. The existence of such behaviour receives support from the findings of studies devoted to critical comparison between various empirical measures of capacity (utilization).[20] Among the reasons for such behaviour on the behalf of producers, Christiano [1981] mentions: (i) fluctuations in (relative) input prices may make it economical to maintain idle plant capacity for periods of time. Rising output prices, for example, might induce a reactivation of previously economically obsolete equipment; (ii) the possibility of a wind-fall demand (not necessarily accompanied by an increase in output prices) may make it rational for producers to maintain spare capacity so that they do not lose customers to competitors in periods of peak demand.

Another type of argument refers to the use of excess capacity as a means of preventing entry into monopolistic or oligopolistic markets (see, for example, Dixit [1980] or Eaton and Lipsey [1979] for models examining such a strategic behaviour).

Denoting by X^s_{obs} the 'engineering' concept of capacity underlying the business survey answers to the DUC question, we may write as a first approximation

$$\tilde{X}^s = \alpha_0 \cdot X^s_{obs} \cdot e^{u_{DUC}}$$

implying a constant share (equal to $1 - \alpha_0$) of economically obsolete equipment at the extensive margin. This is however a rather crude specification since it may be expected (as was suggested in section 3.1) that the share of economically obsolete equipment in total capacity fluctuates with prevailing prices and costs, depending on the short-run variations of profitability conditions. Introducing our profitability index (see section 3.1) we refine the above specification:

$$\tilde{X}^s = \alpha_{DUC} \cdot PROFIT^{\alpha_1} \cdot X^s_{obs} \cdot e^{u_{DUC}} \qquad \text{with } \alpha_1 \geqslant 0$$

Since the DUC_{obs} statistics yielded by the business surveys is defined as $DUC_{obs} = X/X^s_{obs}$ we have

$$DUC_{obs} = \frac{X}{X^s_{obs}} = \alpha_{DUC} \cdot PROFIT^{\alpha_1} \cdot \frac{X}{\tilde{X}^s} \cdot e^{u_{DUC}}$$

Substituting $X/\tilde{X}^s$ by its expression as a function of the observed regime proportions (as was done to get equation (3.1.3)) and taking logarithms, we get the final expression:

$$\ln DUC_{obs_t} = \ln \alpha_{DUC} + \alpha_1 \ln PROFIT_t + \frac{1}{\rho_G} \frac{1}{(1 - \theta \gamma_{XS} \gamma_{LD})} \ln (P_{Gt})$$

$$+ \frac{1}{\rho_L} \frac{\gamma_{XS}}{(1 - \theta \gamma_{XS} \gamma_{LD})} \ln (1 - P_{Lt}) + u_{DUC_t}$$

The share of economically obsolete equipment in installed capacity is equal to $(1 - \alpha_{DUC} \cdot PROFIT^{\alpha_1}_t)$ and will be computed in section 3.6 from estimation results.

3.3   The demand for goods and the supply of labour

The specification of the *demand for goods*[21] (more precisely: for domestically produced manufactures) is provided by equation (3.1.1):

$$\ln X = \frac{1}{\rho_G} \ln (1 - P_G) + \frac{\gamma_{XD}}{\rho_L} \ln (P_L) + \beta^d \ln \mathscr{X}^d + u_{XD}$$

This becomes more evident when presented slightly differently: by transferring one spillover term to the other side of the equality sign, one gets:

$$\ln X - \frac{1}{\rho_G} \ln (1 - P_G) = \ln X^d = \frac{\gamma_{XD}}{\rho_L} \ln (P_L) + \beta^d \ln \mathscr{X}^d + u_{XD}$$

The term $\beta^d \ln \mathscr{X}^d$ represents the specification of the notional demand for domestically produced manufactures and the term $(\gamma_{XD}/\rho_L) \ln (P_L)$ represents the spillover effect arising from the labour market. However, in this context of a sectoral model, notional demand for goods refers to the demand which would be expressed in the absence of any constraint (experienced by the suppliers of labour) on the sole sectoral labour market but taking into account – since exogenous to this sectoral model – the effect of unemployment in all the other labour markets. Similarly the 'spillover term' only refers to the negative effect on demand for manufactures arising from constraints (unemployment) on the sole sectoral labour market.

It will be argued that this is not the most appropriate specification in this context. Indeed in the case of our (restricted)[22] manufacturing sector, whose outward looking character is a most typical feature, private domestic consumption only accounts for a small part (about 15% according to the I/O tables) of its deliveries to final demand while exports constitute by far the largest part (about 70% according to the I/O tables) of the final demand outlets. Moreover, manufacturing labour[22] only accounts for 20%–25% of the Belgian active population. This ratio may be considered as a close proxy for the ratio in terms of households (the economic decision making unit) which should in full rigour be considered but is unavailable. As a consequence the spillover effect from the *sectoral* labour market on the demand for domestically produced manufactured goods is expected to be fairly weak; more importantly, in view of the small sample size (16 observations) and the coincident fluctuations of labour in different sectors, this 'own labour market' spillover effect is likely to be statistically indistinguishable from the spillover effect arising from all the other labour markets.

Since the measure of this 'own labour market' spillover effect is not thought to be of particular interest here, it seems more appropriate to specify equation (3.1.1) in the following form:

$$\ln X = \frac{1}{\rho_G} \ln (1 - P_G) + \beta^d \ln \mathscr{X}^d + u_{XD}$$

where the term $\beta^d \ln \mathscr{X}^d$ now represents the specification – to be discussed now – of the effective demand for domestic manufactures.

The proposed specification, which involves the main potential determinants in a reduced form-type equation, reads in its static version:

$$\ln X^d = c_{0XD} + c_{1XD} \ln \text{DOMDEM} + c_{2XD} \ln \text{FORDEM}$$

$$+ c_{3XD} \ln \frac{\text{PW}}{\text{PX}} + c_{4XD} \ln \frac{\text{PM}}{\text{P}_{\text{dom}}} + u_{XD}$$

where DOMDEM represents an indicator of domestic demand

      FORDEM represents an appropriately weighted index of foreign demand for manufacturing output

      PW is an appropriately weighted index of our competitors' prices on foreign markets

PX   is the export price index of Belgian manufacturers
PM   is the import price index of manufactured goods
P_{dom} is the production price index in the Belgian manufacturing industry.
(see appendix H for detailed definitions and sources; the price indexes have of course been converted into common currency)

and with c_{1XD}, c_{2XD}, c_{3XD}, c_{4XD} expected to be positive.

Among the various possible indicators of domestic demand, the best results were obtained with the contemporaneous real disposable income of households YDH/PCH (current disposable income deflated by the consumer price index) which for simplicity is treated as exogenous in estimation.[23] Since demand is known to adjust only slowly to changes in relative prices, experiments were made with various lag structures for the price ratios PW/PX and PM/P_{dom}. Due to multicollinearity problems the index PM/P_{dom} never yielded significant results and consequently was dropped from the equation. The remaining price ratio PW/PX is hence believed to capture both effects (through increased export demand and decreased import demand) of an improvement in price competitivity. Keeping for PW/PX the lag structure which performed best, the final specification of equation (3.1.1) is

$$\ln X_t = c_{0XD} + \frac{1}{\rho_G} \ln (1 - P_{Gt}) + c_{1XD} \ln \left(\frac{YDH}{PCH}\right)_t + c_{2XD} \ln FORDEM_t$$
$$+ c_{3XD}\left[0.5 \ln \left(\frac{PW}{PX}\right)_t + 0.3 \ln \left(\frac{PW}{PX}\right)_{t-1} + 0.2 \ln \left(\frac{PW}{PX}\right)_{t-2}\right]$$
$$+ u_{XDt}$$

Since, in this type of model, aggregate output falls short of both aggregate supply and aggregate demand ($X < X^s$ and $X < X^d$), *some* rationing of the demand for domestically produced manufactured goods will always prevail. However, compensation may come from increased imports. The issue of whether compensation is complete (in the case of an infinitely elastic supply of imports which is sometimes assumed for a 'small open economy' like Belgium) or only partial (more likely for larger economies), inducing then a rationing of some components of final demand (in the form of increased delivery lags), is not addressed here and is not relevant to the above equation. In other words, this equation is compatible with whatever rationing scheme – if any – is at work between the components of final demand.

From a theoretical point of view, one notices that the inclusion in the equation of an indicator of foreign demand (the variable FORDEM) is of course at odds with the extreme 'small open economy' assumption according to which the economy can buy or sell as much of the tradable goods (such as the manufacturing products considered here) as it wishes. Such an extreme assumption was first adopted for example in the single-good fix-price model developed by Dixit [1978]. With this extreme assumption, the Keynesian situation is automatically ruled out, which does not correspond to observation, even for small economies. Later works then proposed more realistic and elaborate models by introducing the distinction between tradables and non-tradables (Neary [1980]) and/or between importables (most frequently assumed to be in infinitely elastic supply) and exportables (assumed to face a downward sloping curve) (Cuddington [1980]; Steigum [1980]). The specifications adopted in this empirical work (absence of spillover effect from the demand for goods to the supply of labour and foreign demand showing up in the demand for goods equation) suggest that our view is closest to the one adopted in these latter models.

The reader interested in a comprehensive theoretical treatment of open economies macroeconomics in a 'disequilibrium' context is urged to refer to the recent book by Cuddington, Johansson and Löfgren [1984].

The specification to be provided of sectoral (manufacturing) *labour supply* is represented by the term $\lambda^s \ln \mathscr{L}^s$ in equation (3.1.5):

$$\ln L = \frac{1}{\rho_L} \ln (P_L) + \lambda^s \ln \mathscr{L}^s + u_{LS}$$

Let us first remember (see the justification in section 2.1) that, in this model, effective supply of labour was set equal to notional supply.

Despite this conventional simplifying assumption, some difficulties subsist concerning the precise definition – and hence specification – of a sectoral labour supply. Indeed, since labour supply, of any category, is defined as the sum of workers already at work and those searching for jobs, it is usually computed by summing up the numbers of employed and unemployed workers of the relevant category (sometimes reduced by a constant factor to account for the share of very unskilled people in the relevant labour force).

In the majority of cases (aggregate labour supply, labour supply by sex, age, region, qualification, . . .) the concept is unambiguous and the computation of the relevant statistic is straightforward, but things are not so simple for *sectoral* labour supply. Indeed, on which basis should one allocate the existing unemployed labour force between the different sectors?

In the absence of any ready-made answer, a simple and most 'neutral' solution would be to consider the share of sectoral labour in aggregate labour as a measure of the sectoral 'attraction potential' on unemployed workers.

Denoting by UN (resp. by UNR) the number of unemployed workers (resp. the unemployment rate) and using the subscript 'tot' for aggregate by opposition to sectoral (no subscript), this is expressed as:

$$\frac{UN}{UN_{tot}} = \frac{L}{L_{tot}}$$

which of course implies

$$\frac{L^s}{L^s_{tot}} = \frac{L}{L_{tot}}$$

and hence

$$UNR = UNR_{tot}$$

Adding a stochastic error term, we finally get the following specification for the sectoral labour supply:

$$L^s = L \cdot \frac{L^s_{tot}}{L_{tot}} e^{u_{LS}} = \frac{L}{(1 - UNR_{tot})} e^{u_{LS}}$$

Substituting this specification of L^s in equation (3.1.5) we have

$$\ln L_t = \frac{1}{\rho_L} \ln (P_{Lt}) + \ln L_t - \ln (1 - UNR_{tot_t}) + u_{LSt}$$

which simplifies into the final solution

$$\ln (P_{Lt}) = \rho_L \ln (1 - UNR_{tot_t}) + u_{LSt} \qquad (3.8)$$

The above specification of sectoral labour supply L^s is the one that is adopted in the subsequent empirical work so that equation (3.8) holds for equation (3.1.5) in the model subjected to empirical estimation.[24]

Further refinement of specification (3.8) in the light of first empirical results will be extensively discussed in a moment; however, before that point, a few comments have to be given on an alternative specification of sectoral labour supply which is most frequently adopted in empirical works (see a.o. Muellbauer and Winter [1980] or Pissarides [1978]): according to this alternative specification, sectoral labour supply is defined as sectoral labour plus 'sectoral unemployed', i.e. the unemployed workers whose last employment was in the sector under consideration.[25]

For the manufacturing sector, which is the sector of interest here, one would expect *a priori* both definitions to imply highly divergent labour supply figures: for example, the steep decline in manufacturing employment since 1975, which results in a shrinking share of manufacturing employment in total employment, induces one to expect the manufacturing unemployment rate to have increased considerably in recent years relative to the aggregate unemployment rate (remember the former definition of sectoral labour supply implies the sectoral unemployment rate to be identical to the aggregate unemployment rate). In that case, the choice of one or the other specification for sectoral labour supply could be of (possibly) serious consequence to the overall model performance and empirical parameter estimates.

This issue is examined in detail in appendix F along with some sensitivity analysis of the empirical results to the sectoral labour supply specification. This examination points toward the following conclusions:

–   Contrary to initial beliefs, the manufacturing unemployment rate (as computed on the basis of the ONEM statistics) appears to be extremely close to the aggregate unemployment rate so that the choice of the alternative specification of manufacturing labour supply – instead of the one adopted above – is seen to be of no consequence to the empirical results.

–   Moreover, the structural parameters (with the exception of ρ_L and, to a much lesser extent, ρ_G) appear to be fairly insensitive to alternative specifications tried for sectoral labour supply.

Comforted by these findings, we feel authorized to proceed with some confidence with the adopted specification and we return to the discussion of equation (3.8).

The parameter ρ_L, although showing up in almost all the equations of the model, could be expected to be strongly determined by the above equation, since it is the equation's sole parameter. This is indeed the case as can be verified by comparison of the estimates obtained by FIML of the entire model with those obtained by LI estimation (instrumental variables) of the sole 'labour supply' equation.

Estimation of the above equation (either within a FIML procedure or by LI estimation) yields a highly significant estimate of ρ_L but the profile of the residuals makes clear that ρ_L may not be assumed to stay constant during the whole observation period; instead the pattern of residuals suggest it to decline steadily – slowly during the 1960s, much faster during the 1970s – implying an increasing 'mismatch' of demands vs. supplies at the micro level (remember that the ρ's are inversely related to the dispersion of the micro demand/supply ratios).

Similar findings were reported by Kooiman and Kloek [1979] in their application of the 'aggregation by integration' approach to the Dutch labour market: their corresponding 'dispersion' parameter exhibited the same pattern as described above. Interpreting this increasing 'mismatch' of labour demands vs. supplies at the micro level as related to the accelerating rate of technical innovation, Kooiman and Kloek propose to specify the 'dispersion' parameter as depending on long-run increases in labour productivity. This specification is shown to improve the fit and the pattern of residuals but only for the period up to 1973: for the years after 1973 (marked by a huge increase in unemployment) the pattern of the residuals still reveals a very strong increasing 'dispersion' not accounted for by the labour productivity gains variable. As a conclusion, while the phenomenon of accelerating technical innovation (reflected by long-run trends in labour productivity) might play some role in increasing the 'mismatch' in labour micro markets, it does not seem to provide a satisfying explanation to the strong increase in the 'dispersion' witnessed during the 1970s.

Some effort was thus devoted in this work to the search for a more appropriate specification of ρ_L to provide an explanation for both the mild increase in the 1960s and the pick-up in the 1970s of the dispersion parameter.

Among the large number of trials (with various underlying explanatory hypotheses), the following specification proved to be the most satisfactory:

$$\frac{1}{\rho_{Lt}}=\sigma_0+\sigma_1 \cdot \text{UNR}_t \qquad \sigma_1 \geqslant 0$$

The dispersion of the demand vs. supply ratios on the labour micro markets is seen to increase with the level of aggregate unemployment, suggesting an explanation in the line of theories on the 'selectivity mechanism of unemployment'.

This issue is dealt with more formally in appendix B in a model incorporating intertemporal spillover effects at the micro market level: it is shown that the 'dispersion' of micro demands vs. micro supplies is a negative function of the 'mobility' of both demanders and suppliers on the labour micro markets.

It is then argued that this 'mobility' should not be regarded as constant parameters but should depend, as a result of optimizing behaviour, on prevailing economic conditions in the labour market. Refer to appendix B for more elaboration on this.

Substituting the above specification of ρ_L in the 'sectoral labour supply equation', we write

$$\ln (P_{Lt})=\frac{1}{\sigma_0+\sigma_1 \, \text{UNR}_t} \ln (1-\text{UNR}_t)+u_{LSt}$$

Of course, the same specification (with UNR lagged when appropriate) has to be substituted for ρ_L wherever this parameter appears in all the other equations of the model.

To ease the further presentation and discussion of the estimation results, we rewrite below the full model as it is proposed for estimation.

The stochastic equations are presented here in the same order as they are in system (3.1).

$$\ln X_t = c_{0XD}+\frac{1}{\rho_G} \ln (1-P_{Gt})+c_{1XD} \ln \left(\frac{\text{YDH}}{\text{PCH}}\right)_t +c_{2XD} \ln \text{FORDEM}_t$$

$$+c_{3XD}\left[0.5\ln\left(\frac{\text{PW}}{\text{PX}}\right)_t +0.3\ln\left(\frac{\text{PW}}{\text{PX}}\right)_{t-1} +0.2\ln\left(\frac{\text{PW}}{\text{PX}}\right)_{t-2}\right]+u_{XDt}$$

$$(3.9.1)$$

$$\Delta \ln X_t = c_{0XS} + \alpha_1 \Delta \ln \text{PROFIT}_t + \Delta \ln K_t + \frac{1}{\rho_G} \frac{1}{(1 - \theta \gamma_{XS} \gamma_{LD})} \Delta \ln (P_{Gt})$$

$$+ \frac{\gamma_{XS}}{(1 - \theta \gamma_{XS} \gamma_{LD})} [(\sigma_0 + \sigma_1 \, \text{UNR}_t) \ln (1 - P_{Lt})$$

$$- (\sigma_0 + \sigma_1 \, \text{UNR}_{t-1}) \ln (1 - P_{Lt-1})]$$

$$+ \delta_0 \left\{ \sigma \ln \left(\frac{r}{p} \right)_t + (1 - \sigma) \gamma_2 T - \ln \left(\frac{X}{K} \right)_{t-1} \right.$$

$$+ \frac{1}{\rho_G} \frac{1}{(1 - \theta \gamma_{XS} \gamma_{LD})} \ln (P_{Gt-1})$$

$$+ \frac{\gamma_{XS}(\sigma_0 + \sigma_1 \, \text{UNR}_{t-1})}{(1 - \theta \gamma_{XS} \gamma_{LD})} \ln (1 - P_{Lt-1}) \right\} + u_{XSt} \quad (3.9.2)$$

$$\ln \text{DUC}_{obst} = \ln \alpha_{\text{DUC}} + \alpha_1 \ln \text{PROFIT}_t + \frac{1}{\rho_G} \frac{1}{(1 - \theta \gamma_{XS} \gamma_{LD})} \ln (P_{Gt})$$

$$+ \frac{\gamma_{XS}}{(1 - \theta \gamma_{XS} \gamma_{LD})} (\sigma_0 + \sigma_1 \, \text{UNR}_t) \ln (1 - P_{Lt}) + u_{\text{DUC}t}$$
$$(3.9.3)$$

$$\Delta \ln L_t = c_{0LD} + \Delta \ln K_t$$

$$+ \frac{1}{(1 - \theta \gamma_{XS} \gamma_{LD})} [(\sigma_0 + \sigma_1 \, \text{UNR}_t) \ln (1 - P_{Lt})$$

$$- (\sigma_0 + \sigma_1 \, \text{UNR}_{t-1}) \ln (1 - P_{Lt-1})]$$

$$+ \frac{1}{\rho_G} \frac{\gamma_{LD}}{(1 - \theta \gamma_{XS} \gamma_{LD})} \Delta \ln (P_{Gt})$$

$$+ \delta_0 \left\{ \sigma \ln \left(\frac{r}{w} \right)_t + (1 - \sigma)(\gamma_2 - \gamma_1) T - \ln \left(\frac{L}{K} \right)_{t-1} \right.$$

$$+ \frac{(\sigma_0 + \sigma_1 \, \text{UNR}_{t-1})}{(1 - \theta \gamma_{XS} \gamma_{LD})} \ln (1 - P_{Lt-1})$$

$$+ \frac{1}{\rho_G} \frac{\gamma_{LD}}{(1 - \theta \gamma_{XS} \gamma_{LD})} \ln (P_{Gt-1}) \right\} + u_{LDt} \quad (3.9.4)$$

$$\ln (P_{Lt}) = \frac{1}{(\sigma_0 + \sigma_1 \, \text{UNR}_t)} \ln (1 - \text{UNR}_t) + u_{LSt} \quad (3.9.5)$$

$$\text{PROFIT}_t = \left(\frac{p_t X_t}{w_t L_t} \right) \bigg/ \left(\frac{p_{t-1} X_{t-1}}{w_{t-1} L_{t-1}} \right) \quad (3.9.6)$$

$$\text{UNR}_t = 1 - \frac{\text{LEXO}_t + \text{L}_t}{\text{LSEXO}_t} \quad (3.9.7)$$

where   LEXO = labour at work in the rest of the economy
            LSEXO = total Belgian active population

Before presenting and discussing (in sections 3.5 and 3.6) the general empirical results, we will report on the empirical results about the specification of P_L, an issue which was discussed theoretically in chapter 1. This will be the subject of the next section.

3.4   The specification of P_L

As was discussed in detail in chapter 1, the (weighted) proportion of labour micro markets in excess demand P_L is not directly observable; instead, in system of equations (3.9), P_L stands for its specification as a function of observables and an 'association' parameter α.

It was shown in chapter 1 how, on the basis of an assumption of 'weak correlation' (of the bivariate distribution of the micro demands/micro supplies ratios on both markets), strongly supported by the available 'empirical evidence', the following specification of P_L could be derived:

$$P_L = \frac{[P_G(\alpha P_G - \alpha - 1)] + \{[P_G(\alpha P_G - \alpha - 1)] + 4\alpha P_G(P_G - 1)P_R\}^{1/2}}{[2\alpha P_G(P_G - 1)]} \tag{3.10}$$

An approximation, hopefully more easily estimable, to the preceding specification was also proposed:

$$P_L = \hat{P}_L \cdot \frac{[1 - \alpha(1 - P_G)]}{[1 - \alpha(1 - P_G)\hat{P}_L]} = \frac{P_R}{P_G} \cdot \frac{[1 - \alpha(1 - P_G)]}{\left[1 - \alpha(1 - P_G)\dfrac{P_R}{P_G}\right]} \tag{3.11}$$

where $\hat{P}_L$ is the observed 'bench-mark' value of P_L (see chapter 1) and $P_R \underset{\text{def}}{=} \hat{P}_L \cdot P_G$.

Both specifications of P_L appeared to produce, qualitatively, equivalent results which are now reported and commented upon.

First, after substituting specification (3.10) for P_L in the system of equations (3.9), FIML estimation[26] of the whole model[27] was performed conditionally on a number of values for the 'association parameter' α. This was done for Ito's version of the model (θ fixed at the value 1) and for Portes' version ($\theta = 0$). For *both* versions, the grid search over α in the range $[-1, 1]$ resulted in the maximum likelihood being attained for negative values of α (more precisely for $\alpha = -0.29$, i.e. $\rho = \cos\{\pi/[1 + \sqrt{(1 + \alpha)}]\} = -0.14$, in Ito's version and $\alpha = -0.57$, i.e. $\rho = -0.32$, in Portes' version).

These negative values for α are in clear contradiction to the *a-priori* expectations derived both from economic reasoning and from the available empirical evidence (see chapter 1). However, the likelihood function appears to be very flat along the α direction and, for both Ito's and Portes' models, the LR test clearly fails to reject the null hypothesis $\alpha = 0$.[28]

The same basic conclusion is obtained by substituting the simpler – but approximate – specification (3.11) for P_L and estimating freely all the parameters (including α) by FIML estimation of the whole model. Indeed the ML estimate of α is (with standard errors in parentheses):

for Ito's model: $\alpha = -0.24$
$$(0.72)$$

for Portes' model: $\alpha = -0.79$
$$(0.86)$$

The conclusion to be drawn from these estimations is clear: the sample at hand is insufficiently informative on this correlation issue. Negative values of α being neither (economically) sensible nor (statistically) significant, the value $\alpha = 0$ will be assumed in subsequent estimation. In that case, P_L reduces to its 'bench-mark' value $P_L = \hat{P}_L = P_R / P_G$. Empirical analysis will now be pursued with $P_L = \hat{P}_L$ as the observed endogenous variable.

3.5   Ito's vs. Portes' specification of the spillover effect

As was developed in chapter 2, Ito's and Portes' specifications of the spillover effect lead to testable structural forms with different cross-equation restrictions among the parameters. However, it was shown that the two competing models could be embedded within a general one (represented by system of equations (3.9)) which reduces to either Ito's or Portes' version depending on the value (1 or 0) given to the parameter θ. This suggests estimating freely the parameter θ (along with all the other parameters) within the general model in order to possibly discriminate between the two restricted models, remembering that values of θ differing from 0 or 1 yield a model without a clear theoretical interpretation.

FIML estimation of the general model (system (3.9)) yields the following estimate for our parameter of interest (with standard error in parentheses):

$$\theta = 0.418$$

$$(0.414)$$

This intermediate value between 0 and 1 with such a large standard error is clearly inconclusive with respect to the issue at stake.

The lack of a definite conclusion is also reflected by the outcome of likelihood ratio tests (LR) of each restricted model against the general one. The maximum values of the likelihood functions under the various hypotheses on θ are:

$\ln L_{(\theta\,\text{free})} = 184.322$

$\ln L_{(\theta = 1)} = 184.104$ (Ito's specification)

$\ln L_{(\theta = 0)} = 183.970$ (Portes' specification)

Since the LR statistics

$$LR = 2 \ln L_{(\theta\,\text{free})} - 2 \ln L_{(\theta\,\text{restricted})}$$

are asymptotically distributed as χ_1^2 under alternative null hypotheses, it is readily verified that both restricted models fail to be rejected.

This rather deceptive conclusion need not be our final one on this issue since the maximized log-likelihood functions are not the only results brought about by our FIML estimations.

Indeed the parameter estimates also provide indications that one model is more appropriate than the other. Although the parameter estimates usually do not differ significantly between the models (see next section and appendix E for the detailed values), one crucial feature strongly distinguishes them both. Since Ito's and Portes' models only depart on their specification of the spillover effect, it could be expected that their difference would be mainly reflected in the estimates of the spillover coefficients.

Estimation yields the following results for these coefficients:

Ito's model	Portes' model
$\gamma_{XS} = 1.446$	$\gamma_{XS} = 5.191$
(0.222)	(1.230)
$\gamma_{LD} = 0.480$	$\gamma_{LD} = 0.431$
(0.091)	(0.073)

While the estimates of γ_{LD} in both models are very close to each other, the estimates of γ_{XS} differ considerably.

However, the crucial difference between both models does not so much lie in the value of γ_{XS} as in the value of the product $\gamma_{XS} \cdot \gamma_{LD}$. Indeed it was shown in chapter 2 that stability and existence–uniqueness conditions required that[29]

$$\gamma_{XS} \cdot \gamma_{LD} < 1$$

This statistic is reported below (with its standard error) for both models:

Ito's model	Portes' model
$\gamma_{XS} \cdot \gamma_{LD} = 0.694$	$\gamma_{XS} \cdot \gamma_{LD} = 2.237$
(0.069)	(0.56)

Clearly the estimates in Ito's model spontaneously satisfy the above restriction while Portes' counterparts violate it.

Of course, it could be argued that γ_{XS} is only very weakly determined in Portes' version (this is easily understandable: $\gamma_{XS(\text{Portes})}$ translates the impact on the supply of goods of constraints facing the producers on the labour markets which are known from the P_L statistics to have been significant only in 1963–65 and in 1969–70) and indeed it can be shown that using the value $\gamma_{XS} = 1.45$ results only in a slightly reduced maximized log-likelihood value[30] and minor changes in the other parameters. In particular the product of the spillover coefficients now becomes

$$\gamma_{XS} \cdot \gamma_{LD} = 1.45 \times 0.451 = 0.654$$
$$(*) \quad (0.073) \quad (0.106)$$

which satisfies the stability and existence–uniqueness conditions.

However, the simultaneous occurrence of both a higher log-likelihood value and the spontaneous satisfying of theoretical constraints strongly points towards the choice of Ito's model against its competitor.

Since moreover, as was developed in chapter 2, *a-priori* theoretical considerations also pointed in favour of Ito's model, a clear advantage seems to be given, both theoretically and empirically, to Ito's model against Portes' one. As a consequence, the following discussion will focus on the empirical results of Ito's model, while the results obtained with Portes' model will be presented more succinctly in appendix E.

3.6 Empirical results of Ito's model

Before discussing in detail the empirical results, mention has to be made of a parameter constraint which had to be imposed due to strong multicollinearity problems.

Indeed, two variables $\ln(r/w)_t$ and T (trend) appearing in the 'error correction term' of equation (3.9.4) happen to be strongly correlated (their simple correlation coefficient being equal to -0.997) so that their freely estimated coefficients are weakly determined with excessively large standard errors. In order to get sufficient precision on the estimate of σ (the long-run elasticity of substitution) which is considered a parameter of interest, it was decided to impose the constraint $\gamma_1 = \gamma_2 = \gamma$, hence postulating 'neutral technical change' in the Hicks sense.

This restriction is moreover not rejected by the sample at hand as may be easily verified by a LR test of the restricted model (with $\gamma_1 = \gamma_2$) against the unrestricted one (with γ_1 and γ_2 free)[31].

The FIML estimates of the parameters (with standard errors in

Table 3.1. *FIML estimates of the parameters of Ito's model*

Parameters	Estimates		Parameters	Estimates	
$\ln(\alpha_{DUC})$	−0.075	(0.018)	γ_{LD}	0.480	(0.091)
α_1	0.235	(0.050)	γ_{XS}	1.446	(0.22)
σ	0.538	(0.048)	c_{1XD}	0.484	(0.189)
γ	0.066	(0.007)	c_{2XD}	0.601	(0.112)
δ_0	0.292	(0.055)	c_{3XD}	2.180	(0.281)
$1/\rho_G$	0.029	(0.007)	c_{0XD}	2.487	(1.40)
σ_0	0.014	(0.003)	c_{0XS}	−0.170	(0.03)
σ_1	0.386	(0.042)	c_{0LD}	0.118	(0.031)

Table 3.2. *'Goodness of fit' statistics of the FIML estimation*

Equation		RMSE (fit) in %	R^2	DW
(3.9.1)	(X^d)	2.56	0.989	1.79
(3.9.2)	(X^s)	1.8	0.995	1.14
(3.9.3)	(DUC)	1.4	0.945	1.19
(3.9.4)	(L^d)	1.34	0.975	1.54
(3.9.5)	(L^s)	1.0	0.921	1.23

parentheses) are reported in table 3.1 while table 3.2 presents some summary statistics of the estimation.

The model appears to be well conditioned since starting the optimization procedure from a number of points within a fairly large domain around the ML point estimates, always ends up quite rapidly (in 15 to 25 iterations) to the same global maximum.

The *parameter* α_{DUC} was introduced in the discussion of the DUC equation in section 3.2: as it was shown there, $(1 - \alpha_{DUC})$ was meant to provide a measure of the average share of economically obsolete equipment in total installed capacity. This average share is estimated here at about 7% (more precisely, 7.2%) of total installed capacity. It was also argued that this share was likely to fluctuate with short-run variations of profitability conditions: this hypothesis receives heavy support, judging from the strong statistical significance of the *parameter* α_1 which is intended to capture such short-run effect. The share of economically obsolete equipment in total installed capacity (computed as $(1 - \alpha_{DUC} \cdot \text{PROFIT}^{\alpha_1})$) is hence estimated to vary between about 6% (in 1970 and 1973) and about 9–10% (in 1975 and 1980).

The estimate of the *long-run elasticity of substitution* σ is equal to 0.538 and is significantly different from 1, which discards the Cobb–Douglas production function as a suitable long-run production function for the Belgian manufacturing industry. It is interesting to note that our estimate is very close to the results obtained for the manufacturing sector in other works: the French model METRIC retained for σ an estimate of 0.61 while Artus and Bismut [1980] studying long-run substitution possibilities in the French manufacturing industry obtained an estimate of $\sigma = 0.54$.

The rate of *Hicks neutral technical change* is estimated at 6.6% a year: this is about the order of magnitude currently reported for labour augmenting technical progress in the manufacturing industry (see, for example, Raoul and Rouchet [1980]).

Estimates of the capital augmenting technical progress are typically lower but it should be added that their estimates are usually affected by a great imprecision and are often fixed in empirical works; moreover the equality $\gamma_1 = \gamma_2$ was in our case not rejected by the sample as was just reported above.

The value of 0.292 for the *dynamic parameter* δ_0 implies that the adjustment of the technical coefficients to changes in the relative prices of labour and capital is realized for 50% within the first two years and for 75% within the first four years. A commonly reported summary statistic for dynamic processes is the median lag: it gives the number of time periods it takes for 50% of the total adjustment to be completed. This median lag was just seen to be 2 years in our application. It may be interesting to compare this estimate with the implied median lags obtained for the adjustment of technical coefficients in other works:

–   for the whole Belgian economy (Sneessens [1981]), median lag = 1.61 years
–   for the French manufacturing sector (Lubrano and Sneessens [1982]), median lag (with a non-informative prior) = 2.16 years

The speed of the adjustment process in our model seems in line with previous findings.

It is interesting to note that the *dispersion parameter on the goods market,* $1/\rho_G$, is significantly different from zero: indeed, as was shown in chapter 1, our CES-type transaction curve converged towards the aggregate discrete *min* condition for $\rho_G \to \infty$.

It was also shown in chapter 1 that ρ_G provides a measure of the 'inefficiency at equilibrium' on the goods macro market. Indeed, at equilibrium on the goods macro market $(X^d = X^s = X^*)$, we have $X/X^* = 2^{-1/\rho_G}$ such that a measure of the 'inefficiency at equilibrium' may be defined as

$$\frac{X^* - X}{X^*} = 1 - \frac{X}{X^*} = 1 - 2^{-1/\rho_G}$$

With $1/\rho_G = 0.029$, this gives $1 - (X/X^*) = 0.020$.

Thus when aggregate demand equals aggregate supply on the market for domestic goods, about 2% of demand for domestic goods is rationed, inducing possible compensation (total or only partial?) through imports.

We discussed at length in section 3.3 why the *dispersion parameter on the labour market* $1/\rho_L$ could not be assumed to stay constant. The best performing specification was found to be

$$\frac{1}{\rho_{Lt}} = \sigma_0 + \sigma_1 \, \mathrm{UNR}_t$$

This hypothesis of an endogenous variation of the distribution of micro demands and micro supplies on the labour market receives ample support from the estimation results since σ_1 appears to be highly significant.

Here, also, a measure of the 'inefficiency at equilibrium' may be computed: indeed, when $L^d = L^s = L^*$, we have $L/L^* = 2^{-1/\rho_{Lt}}$. Since $L/L^* = 1 - \mathrm{UNR}^*$, we may write

$$\ln\,(1 - \mathrm{UNR}^*) = -\frac{1}{\rho_{Lt}} \, (\ln 2) = (-\sigma_0 - \sigma_1 \mathrm{UNR}^*)(\ln 2)$$

Since $\ln\,(1 - \mathrm{UNR}^*) \simeq -\mathrm{UNR}^*$ for the relevant values of UNR^*, we have

$$\mathrm{UNR}^* = (\sigma_0 + \sigma_1 \, \mathrm{UNR}^*)(\ln 2)$$

and finally

$$\mathrm{UNR}^* = \frac{\sigma_0(\ln 2)}{1 - \sigma_1(\ln 2)}$$

With the estimates of σ_0 and σ_1, we compute the 'equilibrium unemployment rate' to be

$$\mathrm{UNR}^* = 0.014$$

It is interesting to note that this figure is very close to the UNR statistic (unemployment rate as a percentage of the active population) recorded during the mid 1960s, which appears in this work (devoted to the manufacturing sector) as well as in Sneessens' work [1981] (devoted to the whole Belgian economy) as characterized by a near-equilibrium on the labour market. Indeed, the aggregate UNR for the years 1963, 1964, 1965 were respectively 1.5%, 1.3% and 1.6%.

The *spillover coefficients* γ_{XS} and γ_{LD} have already been discussed in the preceding section in relation to the Ito vs. Portes issue. The parameter γ_{LD} is the short-run elasticity of the demand for manufacturing labour with respect to manufacturing output[32] (the long-run elasticity corresponding to the long-run production function being equal to 1).

It is interesting to mention that our estimate of the short-run elasticity of employment is greater than usually reported estimates (which cluster around

0.3) obtained in traditional (non-rationing) models[33] but smaller than the estimate (0.68) recently reported by Sneessens [1981] from his quantity rationing model. Those results, however, should only be taken as indicative; they are not fully comparable to ours since they concern the whole Belgian economy and not just the manufacturing sector.

The parameter γ_{XS} is the short-run elasticity of manufacturing output supply with respect to manufacturing employment, *when this sector is on its efficient production frontier* (i.e. on the line segment AF in figure 2.1 of section 2.1.1). The value greater than unity obtained for γ_{XS} is thus *not* attributable to possible labour hoarding which arises when the economy is *off* its efficient production function. Neither does this value above unity necessarily imply increasing returns to scale (which were not assumed in the theoretical derivation); this value can even be compatible with a vintage-type representation of the production sector (where labour productivity is assumed to decrease with increasing age of the installed equipment and where the oldest – and hence less profitable equipment – is the first to be made temporarily idle in recessions) provided due account be taken of the existence of overhead labour which is of a quasi-fixed nature. A value significantly greater than unity for γ_{XS} receives direct support from the results of a French quarterly business survey.[34]

The possibility of *labour hoarding*, i.e. for the sector as a whole to be off its production frontier, arises from the inequality $\gamma_{XS}\gamma_{LD} < 1$ as was explained in section 2.1.1 and illustrated by figure 2.1. In our framework, where aggregate X is always assumed to be strictly lower than both X^s and X^d and similarly for aggregate L, the situation of the economy is typically depicted by a point (like point S) *inside* the double wedge AFD in figure 2.1. Since S is off the production frontier AF, labour hoarding (i.e. inefficient use of labour) is taking place. Within such a framework, labour hoarding appears as a *permanent* phenomenon, whose intensity, however, varies with prevailing business conditions. This permanent character of the labour hoarding phenomenon (at the aggregate level) receives direct support from the answers to question (1) of the French business survey described in note 34.

It is striking to verify that the (aggregate) reported margin, however fluctuating widely along the business cycle, is always significantly positive even in the peaks of 1969 and 1973. This stems from the fact that even in these peak periods, some firms are in excess supply and hence are using labour 'inefficiently'.

The conventional way of taking into account the labour hoarding phenomenon in empirical models is through the introduction of the following partial adjustment-type equation:

$$\Delta \ln L_t = \varphi(\ln L_t^* - \ln L_{t-1}) \qquad 0 \leqslant \varphi \leqslant 1$$

where L_t^* denotes the desired (and technically efficient) level of employment. It is easily seen that, with such a specification, labour hoarding is only assumed to occur during the periods characterized by a decrease in the observed labour force; on the contrary, during the periods of increasing employment, the economy is assumed to be on its production frontier with observed employment being equal to the efficient one. Since such a picture is clearly contradicted by the empirical evidence just reported above, it is felt that the specification adopted here, treating labour hoarding as a permanent – but of varying intensity – phenomenon, may be better suited than the conventional partial adjustment-type specification.[35]

An estimate of the extent of the labour hoarding phenomenon during the observation period will be provided below.

The parameters c_{1XD}, c_{2XD} and c_{3XD} are the *parameters of the 'effective demand for domestic manufactured goods'* which is expressed in equation (3.9.1).

The elasticity with respect to the foreign demand indicator (c_{2XD}) is seen to be higher than the elasticity with respect to the domestic demand indicator (c_{1XD}) which was to be expected due to the larger share taken by exports in the total deliveries of the Belgian manufacturing industry.

However, the estimated value of c_{2XD} is somewhat lower than the share of exports (as given by I/O tables) in the deliveries of the Belgian manufacturing sector, which suggests a lower than unity elasticity of the demand for Belgian products with respect to the total foreign demand for manufactured goods, and hence a tendency towards declining market shares. This last phenomenon has been widely documented (see BNB [1980] for a recent detailed study) and seems to be attributable both to an unfavourable specialization (in product as well as geographically) and to a deterioration in competitivity (mostly during the 1970s).

Conversely, the estimated value of c_{1XD} is larger than the share of domestic outlets in total deliveries which suggests (with some caution due to the relatively large imprecision of the estimate) a larger than unity elasticity of the demand for Belgian manufacturing products with respect to domestic disposable income. This could be explained by invoking the 'accelerating principle' since deliveries to fixed investment constitute a substantial share of the deliveries to final domestic demand.

The parameter c_{3XD} is the *long-run* elasticity with respect to foreign prices; the estimate may seem to be high at first sight, but do not forget that it represents the cumulated effects of both increased exports and decreased imports due to foreign prices rising faster than domestic prices. In view of the largely open character of the Belgian manufacturing sector, the estimate of c_{3XD} does not appear to be exaggerated.

Commenting briefly on the *summary statistics* of table 3.2, the RMSE (which, with variables expressed in logarithms, gives an average percentage discrepancy between observed and fitted values) and R^2 statistics indicate a pretty good fit for the manufacturing sector (whose output and employment are characterized by greater fluctuations than the other sectors of the economy). Some low values for the DW statistics could reveal a possible lack of dynamics in some specifications but it is to be remembered that we had to keep parsimonious (we already have 16 structural parameters) since we only have 16 observations at our disposal.

Estimates of some *latent variables* may also be computed. Indeed, expressions of the latent variables (effective and notional trade offers on both aggregate markets) as functions of the observables were derived in chapter 2 and were shown to provide the framework of the structural model finally proposed for estimation (system of equations (3.1) of chapter 3).

We are now in the position of computing these latent variables conditionally on the observations and the parameter estimates. This will be done first for the goods market, then for the labour market.

For the goods market, we have the following expressions (refer to chapter 2 for the derivations):[36]

$$\left(\frac{X^d}{X}\right)_t = (1 - P_{Gt})^{-1/\rho_G}$$

$$\left(\frac{X^s}{X}\right)_t = (P_{Gt})^{-1/\rho_G}$$

$$\left(\frac{\tilde{X}^s}{X}\right)_t = (P_{Gt})^{(-1/\rho_G)(1/(1-\gamma_{XS}\gamma_{LD}))} \cdot (1 - P_{Lt})^{(-\gamma_{XS}/\rho_{LT})(1/(1-\gamma_{XS}\gamma_{LD}))}$$

Conditionally on the estimated values of the parameters $\rho_G, \sigma_0, \sigma_1, \gamma_{XS}$ and γ_{LD} we may then easily compute the following statistics.

$$\left(\frac{X^d}{X}\right)_t - 1 \qquad \text{percentage excess demand on the goods market}$$

$$\left(\frac{X^s}{X}\right)_t - 1 \qquad \text{percentage excess supply on the goods market}$$

$$\left(\frac{\tilde{X}^s}{X}\right)_t - 1 \qquad \text{percentage margin of profitable capacity}$$

These are reported in table 3.3 for the observation period.

It can be shown that, in our approach, strictly positive excess demands *and* excess supplies coexist at any moment. Excess demand for goods is estimated to fluctuate between 0.35 % (of existing output) in the most depressed year of

Table 3.3. *Estimates (in %) of excess demand (supply) on the goods market*

	$[(X^d/X)_t - 1]$ in %	$[(X^s/X)_t - 1]$ in %	$[(\tilde{X}^s/X)_t - 1]$ in %
1963	2.68	1.53	14.2
1964	2.84	1.43	12.5
1965	1.85	2.27	13.5
1966	1.59	2.60	12.6
1967	0.86	4.13	16.2
1968	1.32	3.02	13.5
1969	2.96	1.36	10.1
1970	2.61	1.58	10.6
1971	1.90	2.21	11.6
1972	1.70	2.46	11.7
1973	2.79	1.46	9.0
1974	2.18	1.93	11.0
1975	0.50	5.60	24.4
1976	0.58	5.15	23.8
1977	0.39	6.32	26.8
1978	0.35	6.65	26.8
1979	0.63	4.93	21.7
1980	0.73	4.53	22.1

the sample period (1978) and about 3.0% at the highest peak of the activity (1969).

If all the excess demand for domestically produced goods were to be compensated by increased imports (assuming an infinitely elastic supply of foreign goods facing the 'small open economy') and remembering that imports of manufactured goods amount to about 50% of domestic manufacturing output (54% in the 1970 I/O tables), this would entail compensating 'cyclical' imports amounting to about 6% of total imports in periods of peak demand: this order of magnitude for cyclical imports is about the same as the corresponding estimate in Sneessens [1981] (refer to figure 3.10, on p. 128 of Sneessens' book).

Excess supply of goods (what the firms could produce in excess of current output with their existing equipment and present labour force) is estimated to vary between 1.4% (of existing output) in the most pronounced boom of the sample period (1969) and 6.7% in the most depressed year (1978). This phenomenon (related to labour hoarding) is estimated to be now (i.e. at the end of the sample period) at intensity levels never experienced before 1975 (with the possible exception of the 1967–68 recession). In our framework, observed output and employment are *never* assumed to lie on the efficient production frontier, which is in agreement with the empirical evidence reported in note 34.

The margin of profitable capacity (notional output supply in excess over output) is estimated to vary between 9% in the boom of 1973 and 27% in the

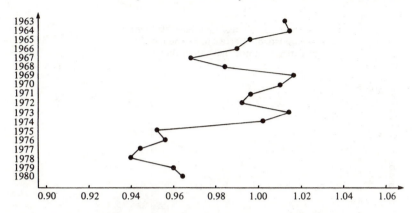

Figure 3.1. The estimated demand–supply ratio on the goods market

worst of the recession in 1977. Notice that the highest margin of profitable capacity is recorded in 1977 while the reported statistic on the degree of (installed) capacity utilization DUC was the lowest in 1975: this apparent discrepancy stems from the role of short-run profitability developments (which were particularly adverse in 1975) which may affect the share of profitable equipment in idle installed capacity.

The estimated ratio $(X^d/X^s)_t$ is reported in figure 3.1. The contrast between two parts of the observation period is most striking: the first part (1963–74) is characterized by a quasi-equality, on average, between effective demand and supply

$$\frac{\sum_{t=1963}^{1974} (X^d/X^s)_t}{12} \simeq 1$$

while the second part (1975–80) is marked by the persistence of insufficient demand.

It may be interesting to notice that the estimated percentages of (positive or negative) excess demands are of the same order of magnitude (on average) as the corresponding estimates in Kooiman and Kloek [1981] for the Dutch manufacturing sector or in Artus, Laroque and Michel [1984] for the French economy.

Figure 3.2 shows the observed series X (output in value added terms) together with the estimates of effective and notional output supply X^s and $\tilde{X}^s$. To preserve the figure's readability, the effective demand for goods X^d has not been drawn; its curve fluctuates closely around the curve X^s during the period 1963–74 and stands very close to curve X from 1975.

The notional output supply $\tilde{X}^s$ of Belgian manufactured products increases steadily during most of the observation period but reaches a ceiling in 1977–78

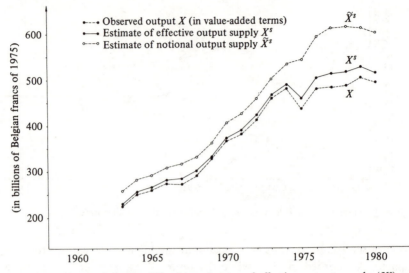

Figure 3.2. Observed output (X) with estimates of effective output supply (X^s) and notional output supply ($\tilde{X}^s$)

and then begins to decline. This evolution is mainly determined by the evolution of the capital stock: capital growth is significantly positive – but to varying extents – throughout the observation period until 1975 when it begins to slow down severely and even becomes negative from 1977. During the two recessions of 1967–68 and 1971–72 a temporary slow down in the rate of growth of capital was recorded, the impact of which on the growth of $\tilde{X}^s$ is visible on the chart. In 1975, the negative impact of the reduced growth in capital is aggravated by particularly adverse developments in profitability as mentioned above.

The distance between the two curves X and X^s, reflecting the labour hoarding phenomenon, is clearly seen to increase in recessions (1967–68; 1971–72; 1975–...) and to reduce in booms (1963–64; 1969–70 and 1973).

The same analysis can be applied to the *labour market*. We have the following expressions (refer to chapter 2 for the derivations):[36]

$$\left(\frac{L^d}{L}\right)_t = (1 - P_{Lt})^{-1/\rho_{Lt}}$$

$$\left(\frac{L^s}{L}\right)_t = (P_{Lt})^{-1/\rho_{Lt}}$$

$$\left(\frac{\tilde{L}^d}{L}\right)_t = (1 - P_{Lt})^{(-1/\rho_{Lt})(1/(1 - \gamma XS\gamma LD))} \cdot (P_{Gt})^{(-1/\rho_G)(\gamma LD/(1 - \gamma XS\gamma LD))}$$

Here also conditionally on the observations and the estimated values of the parameters ρ_G, σ_0, σ_1, γ_{XS} and γ_{LD}, we may easily compute the following statistics:

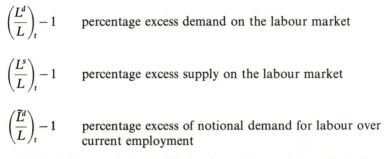

$$\left(\frac{L^d}{L}\right)_t - 1 \qquad \text{percentage excess demand on the labour market}$$

$$\left(\frac{L^s}{L}\right)_t - 1 \qquad \text{percentage excess supply on the labour market}$$

$$\left(\frac{\tilde{L}^d}{L}\right)_t - 1 \qquad \text{percentage excess of notional demand for labour over current employment}$$

A remark should be made immediately about the statistics relating to manufacturing labour supply. The concept of sectoral labour supply has been discussed extensively in section 3.3 and in appendix F where it was shown that no unquestioned definition could emerge. It was also shown (in appendix F) that our specification turned out to be empirically equivalent to a definition most frequently adopted in empirical works, namely the sum of workers actually employed in the manufacturing sector plus the unemployed whose previous job was in the manufacturing sector. This reminder is meant to help assess the significance of the percentages of excess labour supply computed in the following tables.

The statistic $[(\tilde{L}^d/L)_t - 1]$ yields the increase (in %) of the current labour force that would be needed to produce at full (profitable) capacity. It is more-or-less equivalent to the TES statistic[37] (see note 34) collected by the French business surveys (but unfortunately not by Belgian surveys).

The statistics defined above are reported in table 3.4.

Excess demand for labour appears to have been moderate throughout the observation period, culminating in the first part of the sixties (1963–64) with about 1.8% of unsatisfied demands, and falling to its lowest levels in the recessions of 1967–68 (about 0.4% of unsatisfied demands) and 1977–78 (about 0.6% of unsatisfied demands).

An estimate of the number of unfilled vacancies is obtained as $[(L^d/L) - 1] . L$: this number may be seen to vary between about 17 000 in periods of high tension on the labour market (precisely 17 100 in 1963) and about 4000 in periods of slack demand for labour (precisely 3600 in 1967 and 4700 in 1978). The number of unfilled vacancies is estimated at about 9200 at the end of the observation period (1980).

Comparing our estimates with the statistics of unfilled vacancies *for the whole Belgian economy* published by the ONEM (Belgian National Labour Office) raises the following issues:

Table 3.4. *Estimates (in %) of excess demand (supply) on the labour market*

	$[(L^d/L)_t - 1]$ in %	$[(L^s/L)_t - 1]$ in %	$[(\tilde{L}^d/L)_t - 1]$ in %
1963	1.78	1.68	8.5
1964	1.53	1.66	7.4
1965	1.13	2.31	7.5
1966	0.73	3.43	6.6
1967	0.38	6.13	7.9
1968	0.62	5.61	6.9
1969	1.10	3.32	5.9
1970	1.06	2.88	6.1
1971	0.82	3.36	6.3
1972	0.67	4.28	6.2
1973	0.83	3.95	5.1
1974	0.90	4.08	6.1
1975	0.86	6.85	12.0
1976	1.05	8.02	11.9
1977	0.80	10.7	13.0
1978	0.57	13.4	12.7
1979	0.84	11.8	10.8
1980	1.18	10.8	11.4

–   Although our statistic only concerns the manufacturing sector while the ONEM statistic concerns the whole economy, the *levels* of both statistics are comparable: this need not be worrying since it is well known that the ONEM statistics underestimate strongly (for a number of reasons) the true level of unfilled vacancies.

–   The profiles of both statistics are very similar which, to the extent that the above mentioned bias of the ONEM statistic barely affects the fluctuations,[38] gives some indication of the reliability of our statistic.

The percentage excess of notional demand for labour over current employment is estimated to vary between 5.1% in the boom of 1973 and 13% in the worst of the recession of 1977.

In terms of the number of jobs still available (were the level of activity X suddenly pushed to its feasible upper bound $\tilde{X}^s$), this means a figure about 51 000 in 1973 and as much as 112 000 in 1977 (113 000 in 1975). The number of (profitable) jobs still available at the end of the sample period is estimated to be about 89 000.

The estimated ratio (L^d/L^s) is reported in figure 3.3.

Excess supply is easily seen to have been predominant throughout the whole observation period except at the start when the aggregate labour market was near equilibrium. For comparison, let us mention that Artus, Laroque and Michel [1984] estimate the excess supply of labour in the French economy to have also been predominant throughout the whole period 1963–

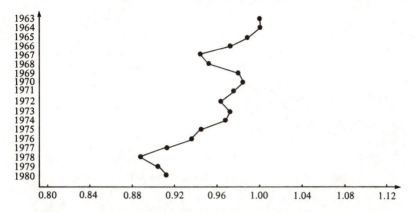

Figure 3.3. The estimated demand–supply ratio on the labour market

78 with the sole exceptions of the years 1964 and 1970 for which excess demand is estimated at 0.1% and 0.2% respectively.

Coming back to figure 3.3, the impact of the two recessions of 1967–68 and (less severely) of 1971–72 are clearly distinguishable as well as the drift from 1975 on. The slight upsurge in demand for labour in 1979–80, which seems surprising at first sight, receives some support from the ONEM statistic which records a marked increase in the unfilled vacancies for these two years (this upsurge in the demand for labour slackened rapidly by 1981 judging from the ONEM statistics).

We report in figure 3.4 the observed series L together with the estimates of effective and notional labour demand L^d and $\tilde{L}^d$.

We also report a series of 'manufacturing labour supply' L^s which has been computed as follows: to the observed employment L, we add the number of unemployed workers whose previous job was in the manufacturing sector plus a share[39] of the unemployed people who arrived on the labour market without previous professional experience.

Since most comments suggested by figure 3.4 refer to results presented in table 3.4, we limit ourselves here to the following observations:

– The margin of available jobs $[(\tilde{L}^d/L) - 1]$ is seen to be smaller and less fluctuating than the margin of profitable capacity $[(\tilde{X}^s/X) - 1]$ in figure 3.2. This phenomenon is supported by the empirical evidence provided by the French business survey presented in note 34.

– Although the definition of sectoral labour supply behind the curve L^s is inevitably conventional, the estimated pattern for the gap between L^s and $\tilde{L}^d$ strongly points towards a phenomenon already stressed by Sneessens [1981] (in his case, for the whole Belgian economy): the

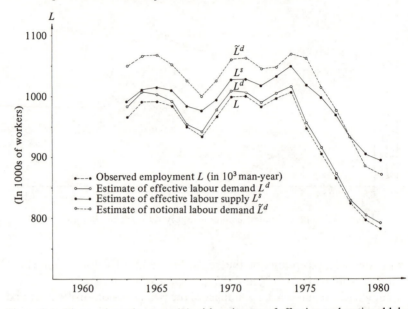

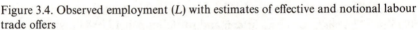

Figure 3.4. Observed employment (L) with estimates of effective and notional labour trade offers

decreasing rate of capital formation in the manufacturing sector inexorably leads towards a situation where this sector would be unable to (re)absorb its previously fired workers plus its quota of new arrivals on the labour market. According to the above estimates, the years 1977–78 usher in a period characterized by a 'deficit' of available jobs. The results presented in figure 3.4 clearly illustrate the upward trend of the 'classical' share of unemployment, a tendency which seems to have started in the early 1970s (refer also to the discussion at the beginning of section 1.2.4 of chapter 1 to put this result into perspective with the 'regime proportions' result).

The temporary reductions in the rate of growth of capital in the recessions of 1967–68 and 1971–72 were seen above to have had only a slow-down effect on the growth of notional output supply $\tilde{X}^s$, due mainly to the strong effects of factor augmenting technical progress. The negative effect on notional labour demand $\tilde{L}^d$ is much more pronounced (as may be verified from figure 3.4) since the positive effect of technical progress is here replaced by the negative effect of the continuing substitution between capital and labour. When this negative substitution effect is combined with a *decreasing* stock of capital, as is the case from 1977, the collapse of $\tilde{L}^d$ becomes irresistible.

Table 3.5. *Estimates of the 'excess labour' in % of the current labour force*

	$[1-(L_{\text{eff}}/L)_t]$ in %
1963	1.05
1964	0.98
1965	1.54
1966	1.76
1967	2.76
1968	2.04
1969	0.93
1970	1.08
1971	1.50
1972	1.66
1973	1.00
1974	1.31
1975	3.70
1976	3.41
1977	4.15
1978	4.36
1979	3.27
1980	3.01

Two more statistics may be of interest. The first one is directly related to the labour hoarding phenomenon. In the same way as we compute the level of output X^s which could be obtained by using current labour efficiently (i.e. a point (X^s, L) on the line segment AF in figure 2.1), we can also compute the *level of employment* L_{eff} which would be technically needed to produce the current output X (i.e. another point (X, L_{eff}) also on the line segment AF but to the left of the point (X^s, L)).

Since both points are situated on the efficient production frontier, we write

$$\ln X^s = \ln \tilde{X}^s + \gamma_{XS}(\ln L - \ln \tilde{L}^d)$$

and $\ln X = \ln \tilde{X}^s + \gamma_{XS}(\ln L_{\text{eff}} - \ln \tilde{L}^d)$

With some manipulation, we obtain

$$\ln L_{\text{eff}} = \ln L + \frac{1}{\gamma_{XS}} (\ln X - \ln X^s)$$

and so

$$\left(\frac{L_{\text{eff}}}{L}\right)_t = \left(\frac{X}{X^s}\right)^{1/\gamma_{XS}} = (P_{Gt})^{1/(\rho_G \cdot \gamma_{XS})}$$

Estimates of the extent of this 'excess labour' phenomenon are presented in table 3.5 (in % of the current labour force).

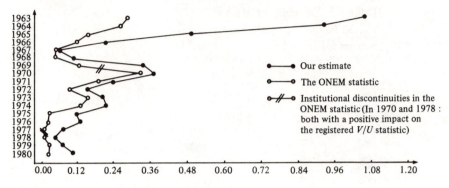

Figure 3.5. The ratio vacancies/unemployment

From these estimates, 'excess labour' appears to have been at its lowest level in the peak of 1969 (less than 1 % of the labour force) and at its highest level in 1978 (about 4.4 % of the current labour force). If there is some truth in the above results, this means that the firms (taken as an aggregate) could have produced the same output with about 36 000 workers less in 1978 and about 24 000 less in 1980.

Another statistic of interest which is often advocated as the most appropriate measure of the tension on the labour market (more appropriate at least than the conventional unemployment rate indicator) is the ratio V/U, i.e. the ratio of the number of unfilled vacancies on the number of unemployed. This statistic has been successfully introduced in the specification of a number of empirical models (see a.o. the wage equations of the French model METRIC [1977]). An estimate of this ratio is easily computed within our framework as

$$\left(\frac{V}{U}\right)_t = \frac{L_t^d - L_t}{L_t^s - L_t} = \left[\left(\frac{L^d}{L}\right)_t - 1\right] \bigg/ \left[\left(\frac{L^s}{L}\right)_t - 1\right]$$

$$= \frac{[(1 - P_{Lt})^{-1/\rho_{Lt}} - 1]}{[(P_{Lt})^{-1/\rho_{Lt}} - 1]}$$

Figure 3.5 reports our empirical estimates together with the (V/U) ratio computed on the basis of the ONEM statistics (NB the latter statistic covers the whole economy and not just the manufacturing sector).

For a number of reasons already mentioned (systematic bias, discontinuities,...), the V statistic compiled by ONEM is highly questionable,[40] so that our (V/U) estimate is in our opinion likely to be closer to the truth than its ONEM counterpart.

Conclusion

This work is intended as a step toward the development of theoretically founded and operational short-run macroeconomic models.

The theoretical framework is that of 'disequilibrium' (or 'quantity rationing') models whose basic assumption is that of prices and wages adjusting too sluggishly to achieve permanent balance of supply and demand in each market[1]. The 'first generation' empirical macro models developed along those lines, although providing some very interesting results, were however too sketchy (since they conveyed the view of the economy as jumping discontinuously between a few regimes) to be really appropriate for the effective study of short-term business developments and for economic policy analysis. Indeed, due to heterogeneity of both goods and labour markets, the real world exhibits much more continuity than is suggested by those models. A 'theory of aggregation (was) therefore a prerequisite for good econometric applications' as stated (among others) by Malinvaud [1982]. The main object of the research presented here was precisely to initiate such a theory: judging from the results reported in the preceding pages, this approach appears to be both fully workable and highly rewarding.

One of its merits lies in its *potential for appropriate policy analysis*: the sensitivity of the effect of any economic policy to prevailing economic conditions and in particular to the stage of the business cycle at which it is implemented is a very well documented fact; this phenomenon is however conventionally captured in empirical models (mostly of Keynesian inspiration) by the somewhat 'ad hoc' adjunction of 'tension indicator' terms in various equations while it arises as an inherent – and endowed with sound theoretical foundations – property of the models generated by the 'aggregation' approach.

Another main feature of this type of model is its natural *ability to exploit statistical information traditionally neglected by macroeconometric model builders*, namely business survey results. Besides their informational contribution valuable for empirical estimation, those business survey statistics have been shown above to provide, conditionally on some structural parameter estimates, direct estimators of a number of imbalances on aggregate markets but also, and more importantly for policy makers, of the multiplier effect of alternative policy measures.

Since this statistical information is the object of frequent surveys and is made available without delay (contrary to most other statistics like national accounts), its systematic use along the lines suggested in the text would enable policy makers to assess at each moment – and closely monitor – the effects of alternative policies and thus would help them determine the optimal 'policy-mix' given prevailing economic conditions. The full implementation of such an instrument for policy analysis is an ambitious project which has only been initiated here and which requires no doubt much further development (see some suggestions below) but the results already obtained seem promising in this respect.

Another interesting feature of this type of model is its *ability to take into account – and possibly endogenize – a type of structural change* which is necessarily ignored in conventional aggregate models, namely the changes in the heterogeneity of both goods and labour markets. It has been illustrated in this work with the increasing dispersion of micro demand vs. micro supply ratios on the labour market.

Beyond improvements of the above estimated empirical model (for example, refining possibly the dynamics of some spillover effects which are totally static in the present version), a number of *directions* offer themselves *for future research.*

Endogenizing the short-run adjustment process of prices and wages (which were assumed exogenous in the present 'fix-price' model) should be given in our opinion high priority, in order to analyze more appropriately the effect of some 'supply-shocks'. The type of model presented in this work is particularly well suited for such analyses, due to their giving – contrary to the traditional Keynesian-type models – equal importance to supply determinants as to demand determinants. However, when the 'supply-shocks' to analyze take the form of strong cost increases (as was the case in the seventies with the two 'oil-shocks' of 1973–74 and 1979–80), the rhythm of the transmission process of costs into prices and hence into wages matters quite a lot for supply considerations. In particular, the adjustment process of wages, with the 'real wage vs. nominal wage stickiness' issue, which has been given much attention in recent years (see a.o. Branson and Rotemberg [1980] or Bruno and Sachs [1982]), is crucial for the supply story.

Prices however are not only sensitive to costs but also to excess demand, and in this respect an aggregation procedure like that performed on quantities can also be envisaged.

Another direction for future research would point towards *exploiting other information from the business surveys*. For example, the French survey also provides direct information on the percentage of firms which are financially constrained (more precisely, which are experiencing liquidity problems)[2]. Exploiting possibly such a statistic (let us denote it P_F) along lines similar to what was done above for the P_G and P_L statistics, could be fruitful for the linkages of the 'real sphere' to the 'monetary sphere' which is up to now absent from those models. For example, since both financial constraints and insufficient demand constraints are known to play a role in the investment decision of firms, one may guess that both P_G and P_F will show up in the investment equation but the appropriate specification will have to be determined by further research[3].

Still another point on the agenda is the specification of the *formation of expectations*, which has been given only a rudimentary treatment (static expectations) in this work.

As a conclusion, an extensive research programme has still to be completed in order to develop empirical macro models which are both theoretically sound and fully operational for policy analysis; to this end, the 'aggregation approach' adopted here appears as a promising avenue, judging from the results obtained in this first attempt.

Appendixes

A Derivation of the aggregate transaction curve and the proportions of micro markets in excess demand

With the micro level demands and supplies assumed to be lognormally distributed (see the main text for a justification of this assumption), the working of any micro market j may be described as

$$\ln l_j^d = \lambda^d + \varepsilon_{dj}$$

$$\ln l_j^s = \lambda^s + \varepsilon_{sj}$$

$$\ln l_j = \min (\ln l_j^d, \ln l_j^s)$$

with

$$\begin{pmatrix} \varepsilon_d \\ \varepsilon_s \end{pmatrix} \sim N \left[\begin{pmatrix} 0 \\ 0 \end{pmatrix}, \begin{pmatrix} \sigma_{\varepsilon d}^2 & \rho \sigma_{\varepsilon d} \sigma_{\varepsilon s} \\ \rho \sigma_{\varepsilon d} \sigma_{\varepsilon s} & \sigma_{\varepsilon s}^2 \end{pmatrix} \right]$$

The 'average' demand and supply being

$$\bar{l}^d = \exp (\lambda^d + \tfrac{1}{2}\sigma_{\varepsilon d}^2)$$

$$\bar{l}^s = \exp (\lambda^s + \tfrac{1}{2}\sigma_{\varepsilon s}^2)$$

We notice that no restriction is placed on the variance–covariance matrix of the bivariate 'size distribution' $(\varepsilon_d, \varepsilon_s)$: those general assumptions may be allowed interesting interpretations (see further). Let us only say for the moment that it seems intuitively reasonable that a larger than average supply corresponds to a larger than average demand, calling for $\rho > 0$.

In order to work with aggregate instead of 'average' quantities, we change variables by multiplying through by the number of micro markets N (see the main text).

Our model becomes

$$\begin{cases} \ln D = \ln l^d + \ln N = (\lambda^d + \ln N) + \varepsilon_d = \Lambda^d + \varepsilon_d \\ \ln S = \ln l^s + \ln N = (\lambda^s + \ln N) + \varepsilon_s = \Lambda^s + \varepsilon_s \end{cases}$$

with unchanged $(\varepsilon_d, \varepsilon_s)$.

Aggregate demand and supply are

$$E(D) = \exp(\Lambda^d + \tfrac{1}{2}\sigma_{\varepsilon d}^2) = \bar{l}^d \cdot N = L^d$$

$$E(S) = \exp(\Lambda^s + \tfrac{1}{2}\sigma_{\varepsilon s}^2) = \bar{l}^s \cdot N = L^s$$

while aggregate transactions are

$$L = E[\min(D, S)]$$

This expression corresponds to equation (1.1) so that we have

$$L = \int_{-\infty}^{\infty} \int_{(\Lambda^s - \Lambda^d) + \varepsilon_s}^{\infty} \exp(\Lambda^s + \varepsilon_s) \cdot f(\varepsilon_d, \varepsilon_s) \, d\varepsilon_d \, d\varepsilon_s$$

$$+ \int_{-\infty}^{\infty} \int_{(\Lambda^d - \Lambda^s) + \varepsilon_d}^{\infty} \exp(\Lambda^d + \varepsilon_d) \cdot f(\varepsilon_d, \varepsilon_s) \, d\varepsilon_s \, d\varepsilon_d$$

$$= L_1 + L_2$$

Let us develop the integral L_1.

$$L_1 = \exp(\Lambda^s) \int_{-\infty}^{\infty} \int_{(\Lambda^s - \Lambda^d) + \varepsilon_s}^{\infty} \exp(\varepsilon_s) \cdot f(\varepsilon_d, \varepsilon_s) \, d\varepsilon_d \, d\varepsilon_s$$

since $f(\varepsilon_d, \varepsilon_s)$ is a normal density function, the product $\exp(\varepsilon_s) \cdot f(\varepsilon_d, \varepsilon_s)$ is an exponential expression which is proportional to

$$\exp -\tfrac{1}{2}(\varepsilon'\Sigma^{-1}\varepsilon - 2\varepsilon_s)$$

$$= \exp -\tfrac{1}{2}[(\varepsilon - \bar{\varepsilon})'\Sigma^{-1}(\varepsilon - \bar{\varepsilon}) - \sigma_{\varepsilon s}^2]$$

with

$$\bar{\varepsilon} = \Sigma \begin{pmatrix} 0 \\ 1 \end{pmatrix} = \begin{pmatrix} \rho\sigma_{\varepsilon d}\sigma_{\varepsilon s} \\ \sigma_{\varepsilon s}^2 \end{pmatrix}$$

L_1 may be rewritten

$$L_1 = \exp(\Lambda^s + \tfrac{1}{2}\sigma_{\varepsilon s}^2) \int_{-\infty}^{\infty} \int_{(\Lambda^s - \Lambda^d) + \varepsilon_s}^{\infty} f_N(\varepsilon | \bar{\varepsilon}, \Sigma) \, d\varepsilon_d \, d\varepsilon_s$$

with $f_N(\varepsilon | \bar{\varepsilon}, \Sigma)$ being the bivariate normal density with mean $\bar{\varepsilon}$ and variance–covariance matrix Σ.

Let us change variables from ε to η with $\eta = \varepsilon - \bar{\varepsilon}$. We have

$$\eta \sim N(0, \Sigma)$$

Then

$$L_1 = \exp\left(\Lambda^s + \tfrac{1}{2}\sigma_{es}^2\right) \int_{-\infty}^{\infty} \int_{(\Lambda^s - \Lambda^d) + \sigma_{es}^2 - \rho\sigma_{es}\sigma_{ed} + \eta_s}^{\infty} f_N(\eta \mid 0, \Sigma) \, d\eta_d \, d\eta_s$$

$$L_1 = L^s \cdot \mathrm{Pr.}\left[\eta_d > (\Lambda^s - \Lambda^d) + \sigma_{es}^2 - \rho\sigma_{es}\sigma_{ed} + \eta_s\right]$$

$$L_1 = L^s \cdot \mathrm{Pr.}\left[\eta_s - \eta_d < (\Lambda^d - \Lambda^s) + \rho\sigma_{es}\sigma_{ed} - \sigma_{es}^2\right]$$

with Pr. $(x < y)$ denoting the probability that $x < y$. Since

$$(\eta_s - \eta_d) \sim N(0, \underbrace{\sigma_{ed}^2 + \sigma_{es}^2 - 2\rho\sigma_{ed}\sigma_{es}}_{\sigma_*^2})$$

$$\left(\frac{\eta_s - \eta_d}{\sigma_*}\right) \sim N(0, 1)$$

L_1 may then be expressed as

$$L_1 = L^s \cdot F\left(\frac{\Lambda^d - \Lambda^s + \rho\sigma_{es}\sigma_{ed} - \sigma_{es}^2}{\sigma_*}\right)$$

where $F(.)$ denotes the cumulative standard normal distribution function. Defining

$$x = \frac{(\Lambda^d + \tfrac{1}{2}\sigma_{ed}^2) - (\Lambda^s + \tfrac{1}{2}\sigma_{es}^2)}{\sigma_*} = \frac{1}{\sigma_*} \ln\left(\frac{L^d}{L^s}\right)$$

we have

$$L_1 = L^s \cdot F(x - \tfrac{1}{2}\sigma_*)$$

Similarly we may compute

$$L_2 = L^d \cdot F(-x - \tfrac{1}{2}\sigma_*)$$

We get finally the expression for the aggregate transaction curve (corresponding to equation (1.1) in the main text) as

$$L = L_1 + L_2 = L^s \cdot F(x - \tfrac{1}{2}\sigma_*) + L^d \cdot F(-x - \tfrac{1}{2}\sigma_*) \tag{A.1}$$

(See Appendix B of Kooiman and Kloek [1979] for the derivation of an identical expression.)

The 'weighted proportion' of micro markets in excess demand $P_w(l^d \geqslant l^s)$ has been shown in the main text (see equation (1.3)) to be equal to

$$P_w(l^d \geqslant l^s) = \frac{1}{L} \cdot L_1 = \frac{L_1}{L_1 + L_2} = \frac{1}{1 + \dfrac{L_2}{L_1}}$$

$$P_w(l^d \geqslant l^s) = \frac{1}{1 + \dfrac{L^d}{L^s} \cdot \dfrac{F(-x - \frac{1}{2}\sigma_*)}{F(x - \frac{1}{2}\sigma_*)}} \tag{A.2}$$

It is interesting to note at this stage that we end up with equations of the form

$$\begin{cases} L = L(L^d, L^s, \sigma_*) \\ P_w(l^d \geqslant l^s) = P_w(L^d, L^s, \sigma_*) \end{cases}$$

so that, besides the aggregates L^d and L^s, the only identified parameter is σ_*, the dispersion parameter of the micro distribution of excess logdemands. The parameters $\sigma_{\varepsilon d}$, $\sigma_{\varepsilon s}$ and ρ are not separately identified so that any combination of values for those parameters that results in the same value for σ_* is equally acceptable in view of the information contained in the aggregate data L and P_w. That aggregate data will only convey information on the 'degree of mismatch' of demands vs. supplies on the micro markets.

Before proceeding to the derivation of appropriate approximations for the expressions of L and P_w, a property of this model quite analogous to a property Malinvaud derives for his model (Malinvaud [1980]) may be shown to hold and will be used later in this appendix.

Let us recall briefly the property set forth by Malinvaud: his model, slightly amended to allow easier comparison with ours, basically stands like this:

$$\begin{cases} D = L^d + \varepsilon_d \\ S = L^s + \varepsilon_s \end{cases} \qquad f(\varepsilon_d, \varepsilon_s) \text{ most general}$$

$$L = E[\min(D, S)]$$

where L, L^d, L^s designate the aggregate transactions, demand and supply respectively. The stochastic terms ε_d and ε_s, representing the distribution of micro demands and supplies, are postulated to be *additive*.

Malinvaud then shows that

$$\frac{\partial L}{\partial L^d} = P(D \leqslant S)$$

where $P(D \leqslant S)$ is the *unweighted* proportion of micro markets experiencing excess supply.

Of course we have similarly

$$\frac{\partial L}{\partial L^s} = P(S \leqslant D) = 1 - \frac{\partial L}{\partial L^d}$$

We will now derive an analogous, but more attractive, property for models with *multiplicative* instead of additive stochastic terms ε_d, ε_s.

Let the model be

$$\begin{cases} \ln D = \Lambda^d + \varepsilon_d \\ \ln S = \Lambda^s + \varepsilon_s \end{cases} \quad f(\varepsilon_d, \varepsilon_s) \text{ most general}$$

$$L = E[\min (D, S)]$$

We notice that the bivariate density function $f(\varepsilon_d, \varepsilon_s)$ need not be normal; if normality is assumed, however, we have the aggregate demand and supply

$$E(D) = L^d = \exp (\Lambda^d + \tfrac{1}{2}\sigma_{\varepsilon d}^2)$$

$$E(S) = L^s = \exp (\Lambda^s + \tfrac{1}{2}\sigma_{\varepsilon s}^2)$$

Let us compute the quantity $\partial L/\partial \Lambda^d$.

$$L = L_1 + L_2$$

$$\frac{\partial L}{\partial \Lambda^d} = \frac{\partial L_1}{\partial \Lambda^d} + \frac{\partial L_2}{\partial \Lambda^d}$$

$$\frac{\partial L_1}{\partial \Lambda^d} = \frac{\partial}{\partial \Lambda^d} \cdot \int_{-\infty}^{\infty} \int_{(\Lambda^s - \Lambda^d) + \varepsilon_s}^{\infty} \exp (\Lambda^s + \varepsilon_s) \cdot f(\varepsilon_d, \varepsilon_s) \, d\varepsilon_d \, d\varepsilon_s$$

We make use of Leibniz's rule for differentiating integrals:

$$\frac{\partial}{\partial \theta} \int_{a(\theta)}^{b(\theta)} f(u, \theta) \, du = f[b(\theta), \theta] \cdot b'(\theta)$$

$$-f[a(\theta), \theta] \cdot a'(\theta) + \int_{a(\theta)}^{b(\theta)} \frac{\partial}{\partial \theta} f(u, \theta) \, du$$

Then,

$$\frac{\partial L_1}{\partial \Lambda^d} = \int_{-\infty}^{\infty} \exp (\Lambda^s + \varepsilon_s) \cdot \left[\frac{\partial}{\partial \Lambda^d} \int_{(\Lambda^s - \Lambda^d) + \varepsilon_s}^{\infty} f(\varepsilon_d, \varepsilon_s) \, d\varepsilon_d \right] d\varepsilon_s$$

$$\frac{\partial L_1}{\partial \Lambda^d} = \int_{-\infty}^{\infty} \exp (\Lambda^s + \varepsilon_s) \cdot f(\Lambda^s - \Lambda^d + \varepsilon_s, \varepsilon_s) \, d\varepsilon_s$$

By changing variables $\Lambda = \Lambda^s + \varepsilon_s$ this can be expressed as

$$\frac{\partial L_1}{\partial \Lambda^d} = \int_{-\infty}^{\infty} \exp (\Lambda) \cdot f(\Lambda - \Lambda^d, \Lambda - \Lambda^s) \, d\Lambda$$

Now

$$\frac{\partial L_2}{\partial \Lambda^d} = \frac{\partial}{\partial \Lambda^d} \cdot \left[\int_{-\infty}^{\infty} \exp\left(\Lambda^d + \varepsilon_d\right) \int_{(\Lambda^d - \Lambda^s) + \varepsilon_d}^{\infty} f(\varepsilon_d, \varepsilon_s) \, \mathrm{d}\varepsilon_s \, \mathrm{d}\varepsilon_d \right]$$

$$= L_2 + \int_{-\infty}^{\infty} \exp\left(\Lambda^d + \varepsilon_d\right) \cdot \frac{\partial}{\partial \Lambda^d} \cdot \left[\int_{(\Lambda^d - \Lambda^s) + \varepsilon_d}^{\infty} f(\varepsilon_d, \varepsilon_s) \, \mathrm{d}\varepsilon_s \right] \mathrm{d}\varepsilon_d$$

$$= L_2 - \int_{-\infty}^{\infty} \exp\left(\Lambda^d + \varepsilon_d\right) \cdot f(\Lambda^d - \Lambda^s + \varepsilon_d, \varepsilon_d) \, \mathrm{d}\varepsilon_d$$

By changing variables $\Lambda = \Lambda^d + \varepsilon_d$ this can also be expressed as

$$\frac{\partial L_2}{\partial \Lambda^d} = L_2 - \int_{-\infty}^{\infty} \exp\left(\Lambda\right) \cdot f(\Lambda - \Lambda^s, \Lambda - \Lambda^d) \, \mathrm{d}\Lambda$$

By adding the two terms, we obtain finally

$$\frac{\partial L}{\partial \Lambda^d} = \frac{\partial L_1}{\partial \Lambda^d} + \frac{\partial L_2}{\partial \Lambda^d} = L_2$$

and so

$$\frac{\partial \ln L}{\partial \Lambda^d} = \frac{L_2}{L} = \frac{1}{1 + \dfrac{L_1}{L_2}} = P_w(l^d < l^s) \tag{A.3}$$

and of course similarly

$$\frac{\partial \ln L}{\partial \Lambda^s} = \frac{L_1}{L} = P_w(l^d \geqslant l^s)$$

The above expression is thus seen to be the counterpart in a model with multiplicative stochastic terms of the property Malinvaud derived for models with additive stochastic terms. From an empirical point of view it seems more attractive since 'weighted' proportions as opposed to unweighted ones are most likely to be the outcome of regular surveys (see the main text for discussion of this distinction).

With the additional assumption of normality for $(\varepsilon_d, \varepsilon_s)$ [i.e. of lognormality for the micro demands and supplies distribution], we have also

$$\Lambda^d = \ln L^d - \tfrac{1}{2}\sigma_{\varepsilon d}^2$$

so that $\partial \Lambda^d = \partial \ln L^d$ if $\sigma_{\varepsilon d}$ is assumed to stay constant.
The above expression then becomes

$$\frac{\partial \ln L}{\partial \ln L^d} = P_w(l^d < l^s)$$

which is easily contrasted with Malinvaud's expression

$$\frac{\partial L}{\partial L^d} = P(l^d < l^s)$$

For more comments on these expressions, refer to the main text.

We are now able to find approximations for expressions like (A.1) and (A.2) in order to get rid of the embedded cumulative standard normal distribution function and to obtain easily manageable functional forms.

Let us examine first equation (A.2):

$$P_w(l^d \geqslant l^s) = \cfrac{1}{1 + \cfrac{L^d}{L^s} \cdot \cfrac{F(-x - \frac{1}{2}\sigma_*)}{F(x - \frac{1}{2}\sigma_*)}}$$

$$= \cfrac{1}{1 + \exp(\sigma_* \cdot x) \cfrac{F(-x - \frac{1}{2}\sigma_*)}{F(x - \frac{1}{2}\sigma_*)}} = P_w(x, \sigma_*)$$

This function of (x, σ_*) has values between 0 and 1. It can easily be verified that

$$\lim_{\sigma_* \to 0} P_w(x, \sigma_*) = \cfrac{1}{1 + \cfrac{L^d \cdot F(+\infty)}{L^s \cdot F(-\infty)}} = 0 \quad \text{when } x < 0 \quad (L^d < L^s)$$

$$= \cfrac{1}{1 + \cfrac{L^d \cdot F(-\infty)}{L^s \cdot F(+\infty)}} = 1 \quad \text{when } x > 0 \quad (L^d > L^s)$$

$$\lim_{x \to -\infty} P_w(x, \sigma_*) = \cfrac{1}{1 + e^{-\infty} \cdot \cfrac{F(+\infty)}{F(-\infty)}} = 0 \qquad (L^d \ll L^s)$$

$$\lim_{x \to +\infty} P_w(x, \sigma_*) = \cfrac{1}{1 + e^{+\infty} \cdot \cfrac{F(-\infty)}{F(+\infty)}} = 1 \qquad (L^d \gg L^s)$$

$$P_w(0, \sigma_*) = \tfrac{1}{2} \qquad (L^d = L^s)$$

Since $P_w(x, \sigma_*)$ has the form of a cumulative distribution function, let us approximate it by a logistic curve

$$h(x; \rho, \alpha) = \frac{1}{1 + \exp[-\rho(x - \alpha)]} \qquad \rho > 0[1]$$

One verifies that

$$\lim_{x \to +\infty} h(x; \rho, \alpha) = 1$$

$$\lim_{x \to -\infty} h(x; \rho, \alpha) = 0$$

To determine values for the parameters ρ and α, let us suppose

$$h(x_0; \rho, \alpha) = P_w(x_0, \sigma_*)$$

and

$$h'(x_0; \rho, \alpha) = P'_w(x_0, \sigma_*)$$

at a certain base point x_0.

(1) $$h(x_0; \rho, \alpha) = P_w(x_0, \sigma_*)$$

$$-\rho(x_0 - \alpha) = \sigma_* \cdot x_0 + \ln F(-x_0 - \tfrac{1}{2}\sigma_*) - \ln F(x_0 - \tfrac{1}{2}\sigma_*)$$

and

$$\alpha = x_0 + \frac{1}{\rho}\left[\sigma_* \cdot x_0 + \ln \frac{F(-x_0 - \tfrac{1}{2}\sigma_*)}{F(x_0 - \tfrac{1}{2}\sigma_*)}\right]$$

(2) Combined with condition (1) this means

$$-\rho \cdot \exp\left[-\rho(x_0 - \alpha)\right] = \left[\exp\left(\sigma_* \cdot x_0\right)\frac{F(-\tfrac{1}{2}\sigma_* - x_0)}{F(-\tfrac{1}{2}\sigma_* + x_0)}\right]'_{x = x_0}$$

$$-\rho \cdot \exp\left[-\rho(x_0 - \alpha)\right] = \sigma_* \cdot \exp\left(\sigma_* \cdot x_0\right) \cdot \frac{F(-\tfrac{1}{2}\sigma_* - x_0)}{F(-\tfrac{1}{2}\sigma_* + x_0)}$$

$$-\exp\left(\sigma_* \cdot x_0\right)$$

$$\cdot \left[\frac{f(-\tfrac{1}{2}\sigma_* - x_0)F(-\tfrac{1}{2}\sigma_* + x_0) + f(-\tfrac{1}{2}\sigma_* + x_0)F(-\tfrac{1}{2}\sigma_* - x_0)}{[F(-\tfrac{1}{2}\sigma_* + x_0)]^2}\right]$$

We have

$$(\rho + \sigma_*)\exp\left[-\rho(x_0 - \alpha)\right] = \exp\left[-\rho(x_0 - \alpha)\right] \cdot \frac{F(-\tfrac{1}{2}\sigma_* + x_0)}{F(-\tfrac{1}{2}\sigma_* - x_0)}$$

$$\cdot \left[\frac{f(-\tfrac{1}{2}\sigma_* - x_0)F(-\tfrac{1}{2}\sigma_* + x_0) + f(-\tfrac{1}{2}\sigma_* + x_0)F(-\tfrac{1}{2}\sigma_* - x_0)}{[F(-\tfrac{1}{2}\sigma_* + x_0)]^2}\right]$$

and so

$$\rho = -\sigma_* + \frac{f(-\tfrac{1}{2}\sigma_* - x_0)}{F(-\tfrac{1}{2}\sigma_* - x_0)} + \frac{f(-\tfrac{1}{2}\sigma_* + x_0)}{F(-\tfrac{1}{2}\sigma_* + x_0)}$$

The most natural choice for the point x_0 is of course $x_0 = 0$ (i.e. the point where $L^d = L^s$) in order to have also $h(0; \rho, \alpha) = P_w(0, \sigma_*) = \tfrac{1}{2}$ which seems a reasonable requirement.

For $x_0 = 0$, the parameters α and ρ reduce to

$$\begin{cases} \alpha = 0 \\ \rho = -\sigma_* + 2 \cdot \dfrac{f(-\tfrac{1}{2}\sigma_*)}{F(-\tfrac{1}{2}\sigma_*)} \end{cases}$$

With this approximation, we may write

$$P_w(l^d \geqslant l^s) = \frac{1}{1 + \exp\left[-\rho(x)\right]}$$

Since x was defined to be $\sigma_*^{-1} \cdot \ln(L^d/L^s)$ we get

$$P_w(l^d \geqslant l^s) = \frac{1}{1 + \left(\dfrac{L^d}{L^s}\right)^{-\rho/\sigma_*}}$$

By defining a parameter

$$\rho_* = \frac{\rho}{\sigma_*} = -1 + \frac{2}{\sigma_*} \frac{f(-\tfrac{1}{2}\sigma_*)}{F(-\tfrac{1}{2}\sigma_*)} \tag{A.4}$$

we get a very attractive functional form for the 'weighted proportion' of micro markets in excess demand, namely

$$P_w(l^d \geqslant l^s) = \frac{1}{1 + \left(\dfrac{L^d}{L^s}\right)^{-\rho_*}} \tag{A.5}$$

where L^d, L^s are the aggregate demand and supply and ρ_* is a 'dispersion parameter' inversely related to the standard deviation σ_*. We can show that since $\rho_* \to +\infty$ when $\sigma^* \to 0$, (A.5) has the property that

$$\lim_{\sigma_* \to 0} P_w(l^d \geqslant l^s) = 0 \quad \text{when } L^d < L^s$$
$$= 1 \quad \text{when } L^d > L^s$$

as was shown to be the case for the exact function P_w.

The weighted proportion of micro markets in excess supply is of course

$$P_w(l^d < l^s) = 1 - P_w(l^d \geqslant l^s) = \cdots = \frac{1}{1 + \left(\dfrac{L^d}{L^s}\right)^{\rho_*}}$$

To derive a functional form for the aggregate transaction curve, we use the property that was shown to be the counterpart of Malinvaud's for our type of model, namely that

$$P_w(l^d \geqslant l^s) = \frac{\partial \ln L}{\partial \Lambda^s} = \frac{1}{1 + \exp(-\rho x)}$$

$$= \frac{1}{1 + \exp\left[-\rho_*(\Lambda^d + \frac{1}{2}\sigma_{\varepsilon d}^2 - \Lambda^s - \frac{1}{2}\sigma_{\varepsilon s}^2)\right]}$$

and

$$P_w(l^d < l^s) = \frac{\partial \ln L}{\partial \Lambda^d} = \frac{1}{1 + \exp\left[\rho_*(\Lambda^d + \frac{1}{2}\sigma_{\varepsilon d}^2 - \Lambda^s - \frac{1}{2}\sigma_{\varepsilon s}^2)\right]}$$

By integrating, we get the following expression for L:

$$L = k\{\exp\left[-\rho_*(\Lambda^d + \frac{1}{2}\sigma_{\varepsilon d}^2)\right] + \exp\left[-\rho_*(\Lambda^s + \frac{1}{2}\sigma_{\varepsilon s}^2)\right]\}^{-1/\rho_*}$$

with k being an arbitrary constant of integration. This can be rewritten as

$$L = k[(L^d)^{-\rho_*} + (L^s)^{-\rho_*}]^{-1/\rho_*}$$

from the exact expression (A.1), we know that

$$\lim_{L^d/L^s \to \infty} L = L^s \quad \text{and} \quad \lim_{L^d/L^s \to 0} L = L^d$$

which imposes the additional constraint $k = 1$.

The aggregate transaction exhibits finally a very simple CES-type functional form:

$$L = [(L^d)^{-\rho_*} + (L^s)^{-\rho_*}]^{-1/\rho_*} \tag{A.6}$$

For more comments about this expression, refer to the main text.

Finally, an approximation may also be found for $P(l^d \geqslant l^s)$, the *unweighted* proportion of micro markets in excess demand. As mentioned already, this last statistic is less relevant than its weighted counterpart since empirical data always refers to appropriately (?) weighted individual answers.

$$P(l^d \geqslant l^s) = \int_0^\infty \int_S^\infty G(D, S) \, dD \, dS$$

$$= \int_{-\infty}^{+\infty} \int_{(\Lambda^s - \Lambda^d) + \varepsilon_s}^{\infty} f(\varepsilon_d, \varepsilon_s) \, d\varepsilon_d \, d\varepsilon_s$$

$$= \text{Pr.} \, (\varepsilon_s - \varepsilon_d < \Lambda^d - \Lambda^s)$$

$$= F\left(\frac{\Lambda^d - \Lambda^s}{\sigma_*}\right)$$

A good approximation to the standard normal cumulative distribution function $F(x)$ is known to be the 'corrected' logistic curve (see Johnson and Kotz [1972]):

$$\left[1+\exp\left(-\frac{15}{16}\cdot\frac{\pi}{\sqrt{3}}\cdot x\right)\right]^{-1}$$

Let us denote

$$\theta_*=\frac{15}{16}\cdot\frac{\pi}{\sqrt{3}}\cdot\frac{1}{\sigma_*} \tag{A.7}$$

Then

$$P(l^d \geqslant l^s)=\{1+\exp\left[-\theta_*(\Lambda^d-\Lambda^s)\right]\}^{-1}$$
$$=\{1+\exp\left[-\theta_*(\Lambda^d+\tfrac{1}{2}\sigma_{\varepsilon d}^2-\Lambda^s-\tfrac{1}{2}\sigma_{\varepsilon s}^2-\tfrac{1}{2}\sigma_{\varepsilon d}^2+\tfrac{1}{2}\sigma_{\varepsilon s}^2)\right]\}^{-1}$$

If we put

$$b_*=\exp\left[\frac{\theta_*}{2}(\sigma_{\varepsilon d}^2-\sigma_{\varepsilon s}^2)\right]$$

we have the final expression:

$$P(l^d \geqslant l^s)=\frac{1}{1+b_*\left(\dfrac{L^d}{L^s}\right)^{-\theta_*}}$$

Moreover, if we quite reasonably assume $\sigma_{\varepsilon d}\simeq\sigma_{\varepsilon s}$ (which are as shown above not separately identified in view of the information conveyed by the data on L and P_w) then we end up with an expression similar to that of the weighted proportion P_w.

$$P(l^d \geqslant l^s)=\frac{1}{1+\left(\dfrac{L^d}{L^s}\right)^{-\theta_*}} \tag{A.8}$$

For relevant ranges of σ_*, θ_* appears close to but slightly greater than ρ_*.

B Intertemporal spillovers in micro markets and the 'selectivity mechanism' of unemployment

As in the basic model, micro demands and supplies are distributed lognormally but they react to *relative* disequilibrium of the *previous* period. Agents on both sides tend to move from micro markets where they have experienced worse than average situations to other ones offering (in their opinion) better than average prospects.

λ_t^d and λ_t^s representing, as in the main text, the 'average' values of $\ln l_t^d$ and $\ln l_t^s$ the model may be formalized as follows.

$$\ln l_t^d = \lambda_t^d + \varepsilon_{dt} - \gamma\{(\ln l_{t-1}^d - \ln l_{t-1}^s) - (\lambda_{t-1}^d - \lambda_{t-1}^s)\}$$

$$\ln l_t^s = \lambda_t^s + \varepsilon_{st} + \delta\{(\ln l_{t-1}^d - \ln l_{t-1}^s) - (\lambda_{t-1}^d - \lambda_{t-1}^s)\} \qquad \text{(B.1)}$$

$$\ln l_t = \min (\ln l_t^d, \ln l_t^s)$$

γ and δ are normally expected to be positive.

On the goods market, $\gamma > 0$ means that some consumers may shift from one supplier who imposed particularly long delivery lags to another one known to deliver quickly, or that they purchase some close substitute thought to be more readily available.

Similarly $\delta > 0$ means that some producers may, when feasible, reorganize production (or invest) towards products in higher demand.

On the labour market, $\gamma > 0$ means that some employers may be tempted to recruit people with less appropriate (and less demanded) qualifications instead of engaging in long and perhaps costly research for the most qualified personnel. $\delta > 0$ represents the mobility of workers moving (geographically or by professional training schemes) to better looking micro markets.

Of course, we impose $(\gamma + \delta) < 1$ to avoid 'overshooting' reactions.

Since a larger than average micro market at time $t-1$ may reasonably be expected to remain large at time t, the cross-sectional distribution variables ε_{dt} and ε_{st} are assumed to follow an autoregressive scheme.

$$\begin{cases} \varepsilon_{dt} = \rho\varepsilon_{dt-1} + u_t \\ \varepsilon_{st} = \rho\varepsilon_{st-1} + w_t \end{cases} \quad \begin{matrix} 0 \leqslant \rho < 1 \text{ being identical for demand and} \\ \text{supply only for the sake of simplicity} \end{matrix}$$

We assume

$$\begin{pmatrix} u_t \\ w_t \end{pmatrix} \sim N\left[\begin{pmatrix} 0 \\ 0 \end{pmatrix}, \begin{pmatrix} \sigma_u^2 & \rho_{uw}\sigma_u\sigma_w \\ \rho_{uw}\sigma_u\sigma_w & \sigma_w^2 \end{pmatrix}\right]$$

with all non-contemporaneous covariances being zero.

Since ε_{dt} and ε_{st} may be rewritten

$$\varepsilon_{dt} = \sum_{i=0}^{\infty} \rho^i u_{t-i}$$

$$\varepsilon_{st} = \sum_{i=0}^{\infty} \rho^i w_{t-i}$$

one verifies that

$$\operatorname{var}(\varepsilon_{dt}-\varepsilon_{st})=\operatorname{var}\left[\sum_{i=0}^{\infty}\rho^{i}(u_{t-i}-w_{t-i})\right]=\frac{\sigma_{(u-w)}^{2}}{1-\rho^{2}}\qquad\forall t$$

Similarly one computes

$$\operatorname{cov}\left[(\varepsilon_{dt}-\varepsilon_{st})(\varepsilon_{dt-j}-\varepsilon_{st-j})\right]$$

$$=E\left[\sum_{i=0}^{\infty}\rho^{i}(u_{t-i}-w_{t-i})\right]\left[\sum_{i=0}^{\infty}\rho^{i}(u_{t-i-j}-w_{t-i-j})\right]$$

$$=\cdots=\rho^{j}\frac{\sigma_{(u-w)}^{2}}{1-\rho^{2}}$$

Let us now express the model (B.1) in terms of the 'cross-sectional' dispersion variables.

By recursive substitution, system (B.1) may be rewritten:

$$\ln l_{t}^{d}=\lambda_{t}^{d}+\varepsilon_{dt}-\gamma\cdot\sum_{i=0}^{\infty}\left[-(\gamma+\delta)\right]^{i}(\varepsilon_{dt-1-i}-\varepsilon_{st-1-i})$$

$$\ln l_{t}^{s}=\lambda_{t}^{s}+\varepsilon_{st}+\delta\cdot\sum_{i=0}^{\infty}\left[-(\gamma+\delta)\right]^{i}(\varepsilon_{dt-1-i}-\varepsilon_{st-1-i})\qquad\text{(B.1*)}$$

$$\ln l_{t}=\min(\ln l_{t}^{d},\ln l_{t}^{s})$$

or equivalently

$$\begin{cases}\ln l_{t}^{d}=\lambda_{t}^{d}+\varepsilon_{dt}^{*}\\\ln l_{t}^{s}=\lambda_{t}^{s}+\varepsilon_{st}^{*}\end{cases}$$

with

$$\begin{pmatrix}\varepsilon_{dt}^{*}\\\varepsilon_{st}^{*}\end{pmatrix}\sim N\left[\begin{pmatrix}0\\0\end{pmatrix},\begin{pmatrix}\sigma_{\varepsilon_{d}^{*}}^{2}&\rho^{**}\\\rho^{**}&\sigma_{\varepsilon_{s}^{*}}^{2}\end{pmatrix}\right]$$

The parameter of interest to us (since identified) is $\operatorname{var}(\varepsilon_{dt}^{*}-\varepsilon_{st}^{*})$. Indeed, as explained in appendix A and in the main text, this parameter conditions the position of the CES transaction curve and of the U–V trade-off. Let us compute it.

$$\operatorname{var}(\varepsilon_{dt}^{*}-\varepsilon_{st}^{*})=E\left\{\sum_{i=0}^{\infty}\left[-(\gamma+\delta)\right]^{i}(\varepsilon_{dt-i}-\varepsilon_{st-i})\right\}^{2}$$

$$=E\left\{\sum_{i=0}^{\infty}\left[-(\gamma+\delta)\right]^{2i}(\varepsilon_{dt-i}-\varepsilon_{st-i})^{2}\right.$$

$$\left.+2\sum_{i=0}^{\infty}\sum_{j=i+1}^{\infty}\left[-(\gamma+\sigma)\right]^{i+j}(\varepsilon_{dt-i}-\varepsilon_{st-i})(\varepsilon_{dt-j}-\varepsilon_{st-j})\right\}$$

By substituting the above derived expression for var and cov one gets

$$\text{var}\,(\varepsilon_{dt}^{*} - \varepsilon_{st}^{*}) = \frac{\sigma_{(u-w)}^{2}}{1-\rho^{2}} \left\{ \sum_{i=0}^{\infty} [-(\gamma+\delta)]^{2i} + 2 \sum_{i=0}^{\infty} \sum_{j=1}^{\infty} [-(\gamma+\delta)]^{2i+j} \rho^{j} \right\}$$

$$= \frac{\sigma_{(u-w)}^{2}}{1-\rho^{2}} \left[\frac{1}{1-(\gamma+\delta)^{2}} \right] \left\{ 1 + 2 \left[\frac{1}{1+(\gamma+\delta)\rho} - 1 \right] \right\}$$

$$= \frac{\sigma_{(u-w)}^{2}}{1-\rho^{2}} \left[\frac{1}{1-(\gamma+\delta)^{2}} \right] \left[\frac{1-(\gamma+\delta)\rho}{1+(\gamma+\delta)\rho} \right]$$

which is of course always positive for relevant values of ρ and $(\gamma+\delta)$.

We are mostly interested in appreciating the effect on var $(\varepsilon_{dt}^{*} - \varepsilon_{st}^{*})$ of small changes in $(\gamma+\delta)$. We may compute

$$\frac{\partial \text{ var}\,(\varepsilon_{dt}^{*} - \varepsilon_{st}^{*})}{\partial(\gamma+\delta)}$$

$$= \left[\frac{\sigma_{(u-w)}^{2}}{1-\rho^{2}} \right] \cdot 2 \cdot \left\{ \frac{(\gamma+\delta)[1-\rho^{2}(\gamma+\delta)^{2}] - \rho[1-(\gamma+\delta)^{2}]}{[1+\rho(\gamma+\delta)]^{2}[1-(\gamma+\delta)^{2}]^{2}} \right\}$$

which has the sign of $(\gamma+\delta)[1-\rho^{2}(\gamma+\delta)^{2}] - \rho[1-(\gamma+\delta)^{2}]$.

This sign evidently depends on the respective values of ρ and $(\gamma+\delta)$ but for relevant values of

$$\rho \simeq 0.8, \ldots, 0.9$$

$$(\gamma+\delta) \simeq 0.1, \ldots, 0.2 \quad \text{one has}$$

$$\frac{\partial \text{ var}\,(\varepsilon_{dt}^{*} - \varepsilon_{st}^{*})}{\partial(\gamma+\delta)} < 0$$

so that a weakening of the 'intertemporal spillover effects' would amount to a leftward shift of the CES transaction curve and hence an increase of the 'inefficiency at equilibrium'.

Let us consider the labour market as an example. In the equations of model (B.1), the spillovers show up rather mechanically with γ and δ constants. But if those specifications were to be grounded on microeconomic optimizing behaviour, it would probably appear that γ and δ have to be functions of the overall situation on the labour market. For example, rising aggregate unemployment could discourage the mobility of workers by persuading them that their chances of improving anywhere are small. Similarly on the employer's side, a high level of unemployment gives fewer incentives to content oneself with less appropriate qualifications and may even induce the opposite attitude of progressively replacing less qualified employees (or those who are too young or too old) by more qualified ones (which would previously have been 'out of reach'). This last attitude could imply a parameter γ becoming negative and would correspond to the often quoted 'selectivity mechanism of unemployment'.

If these hypotheses happened to be true the 'dispersion parameter' ρ_L^* of the labour market's transaction curve should not be taken to be constant and should be negatively related to the aggregate unemployment rate. The empirical application of chapter 3 will bring evidence of such a relationship.

C   Input–output analysis in a disequilibrium context

The traditional formula of input–output analysis starts from the equation

$$Q_i = \sum_j a_{ij}Q_j + D_i + X_i - M_i \tag{C.1}$$

with Q_i = effective production of sector i;
   D_i = deliveries of sector i to the domestic final demand (private and public consumption, fixed investment and inventory accumulation);
   X_i = exports of good i;
   M_i = imports of good i.
The system of equation (C.1) may be written in matrix form

$$\mathbf{Q} = \mathbf{A} \cdot \mathbf{Q} + (\mathbf{D} + \mathbf{X} - \mathbf{M})$$

with $\mathbf{A}$ = the matrix of technical I–O coefficients.
This system may be rewritten

$$\mathbf{Q} = [\mathbf{I} - \mathbf{A}]^{-1}(\mathbf{D} + \mathbf{X} - \mathbf{M}) \tag{C.2}$$

Conventional I–O multiplier analysis then assumes implicitly a pure Keynesian regime to prevail for all sectors, i.e. $Q_i = Q_i^d < Q_i^s \; \forall i$. This is indeed the condition to write

$$\Delta\mathbf{Q} = \Delta\mathbf{Q}^d = [\mathbf{I} - \mathbf{A}]^{-1}(\Delta\mathbf{D}^d + \Delta\mathbf{X}^d - \Delta\mathbf{M}^d)$$

where $\Delta\mathbf{D}^d$ and $\Delta\mathbf{X}^d$ are the planned (or forecasted) changes in domestic final demand or exports while the induced changes in imports $\Delta\mathbf{M}^d$ are usually computed by means of fixed import coefficients.

Let us designate $\mathbf{F} = \mathbf{D} + \mathbf{X} - \mathbf{M}$. The traditional multiplier formula then looks like

$$\Delta\mathbf{Q} = [\mathbf{I} - \mathbf{A}]^{-1}\Delta\mathbf{F}^d \tag{C.3}$$

However, as soon as one departs from the generalized pure Keynesian regime, the above formula is no longer valid. Let us first consider briefly a quantity rationing setting with the discrete *min* prevailing at the sectoral level: in that framework we have at the same time $Q_i = Q_i^d < Q_i^s$ for the sectors i in excess supply and $Q_j = Q_j^s < Q_j^d$ for the sectors j in excess demand. In that case, the multiplier effects of the vector ΔF^d will be most different than in the pure Keynesian case since not only will the ΔQ_j be equal to zero but the ΔQ_i will also be less than predicted by (C.3) due to the lack of the derived demand from the sectors j^1. Moreover, in that framework, the multiplier is likely to exhibit discontinuities at the points where a sector i switches suddenly from the excess supply to the excess demand regime.

This property makes the resulting multiplier at the same time rather unrealistic and unattractive to handle.

Those limitations are overcome in the 'aggregation by integration' approach. In that approach, each sector is considered to be made up of a large number of micro markets in various disequilibrium situations, which is surely a more appropriate description, at least for aggregate I–O analysis. Intuition suggests that in such a framework, the full multiplier effect of an increase in demand depends on the proportion of micro markets still in excess supply in the various sectors. This will be seen to be the case. We will make use of a result derived in chapter 1, namely the formula of the partial derivative of transactions with respect to demand.

For sector i, this is

$$\frac{\partial Q_i}{\partial Q_i^d} = [P_w(q_i^d < q_i^s)]^{1 + (1/\rho^i)}$$

where $P_w(q_i^d < q_i^s) \triangleq (1 - P_{Gi})$ designates the weighted proportion of micro markets of sector i in excess supply and ρ_i is a parameter which is inversely related to the dispersion of demands vs. supplies at the micro level.

If the symbol Δ is used to represent small changes we can write in matrix notation

$$\Delta Q = M \Delta Q^d$$

with M being a diagonal matrix with diagonal elements $(1 - P_{Gi})^{1 + (1/\rho^i)}$ referring to each sector.

Equation (C.1) makes clear that the demand addressed to each sector is the sum of the demand for intermediate inputs and for deliveries to the final demand, so that in matrix notation we have[2]

$$\Delta Q = M \Delta Q^d = M[A \Delta Q + \Delta F^d]$$

and hence

$$\Delta Q = \{[I - MA]^{-1} M\} \Delta F^d \tag{C.4}$$

which is the general formula for I–O multiplier analysis in a disequilibrium context.

Equation (C.3) is easily seen to be a particular case of the general model (C.4): indeed, in the pure Keynesian regime there is no micromarket in excess demand so that the diagonal matrix **M** reduces to an identity matrix and the formula (C.4) reduces to (C.3).

The disequilibrium framework with discrete *min* prevailing at the sectoral level is also a polar case of the general model (4): indeed, depending on their regime the proportions P_{Gi} are either 0 (when $Q_i = Q_i^d < Q_i^s$) or 1 (when $Q_i = Q_i^s < Q_i^d$) so that the diagonal matrix **M** only contains the elements 0 and 1.

As an illustration of the effects of supply constraints on I–O multipliers, let us consider a numerical example involving a three-sectors economy.

Let us have the technical coefficients matrix

$$\mathbf{A} = \begin{pmatrix} 0.2 & 0.2 & 0.2 \\ 0.2 & 0.2 & 0.2 \\ 0.2 & 0.2 & 0.2 \end{pmatrix}$$

Let us assume that the most recent business survey indicates

$P_{G1} = 0.2$ (which means 20% of micromarkets in sector 1 are in excess demand)

$P_{G2} = 0.5$

$P_{G3} = 0.7$

Let us also assume that previous estimation has yielded the estimates $\hat{\rho}_1 = \hat{\rho}_2 = \hat{\rho}_3 = 10$ (which is about the value of ρ we estimated for the manufacturing sector in Portes' model).

The traditional I–O multiplier matrix will be

$$[\mathbf{I} - \mathbf{A}]^{-1} = \begin{pmatrix} 1.5 & 0.5 & 0.5 \\ 0.5 & 1.5 & 0.5 \\ 0.5 & 0.5 & 1.5 \end{pmatrix}$$

while the general formula taking account of supply constraints yields

$$\{[\mathbf{I} - \mathbf{MA}]^{-1}\mathbf{M}\} = \begin{pmatrix} 0.96 & 0.11 & 0.06 \\ 0.11 & 0.53 & 0.04 \\ 0.06 & 0.04 & 0.29 \end{pmatrix}$$

The comparison of the two matrices makes clear that taking account of supply constraints in I–O analysis leads us to reduce notably the multiplier effects of an exogenous demand increase (like increased government spending). When the proportion of micro markets in excess demand increases, a higher proportion of the demand increase will result in augmented imports and/or reduced exports and/or rationing of some components of final domestic demand. The effective rationing scheme may vary from one sector to the other but in any case the general formula (C.4) remains valid so long as no sector is rationed on its intermediate inputs.

D Computation of the multiplier effect of an autonomous increase in the demand for goods in the framework of Portes' model

We want to compute the multiplier effect of an exogenous increase in the demand for goods (like the demand for exports) in the framework of Portes' model of section 2.1.1.1.

Starting from the structural form (2.2), let us first express all effective trade offers as functions only of the observed transactions and the notional trade offers:

$$\ln X^d = \ln \tilde{X}^d - \gamma_{XD} \ln \tilde{L}^s + \gamma_{XD} \ln L$$

$$\ln X^s = [1 - \gamma_{XS}\gamma_{LD}]^{-1}[\ln \tilde{X}^s - \gamma_{XS} \ln \tilde{L}^d + \gamma_{XS} \ln L - \gamma_{XS}\gamma_{LD} \ln X]$$

$$\ln L^d = [1 - \gamma_{LD}\gamma_{XS}]^{-1}[\ln \tilde{L}^d - \gamma_{LD} \ln \tilde{X}^s + \gamma_{LD} \ln X - \gamma_{LD}\gamma_{XS} \ln L]$$

$$\ln L^s = \ln \tilde{L}^s$$

The definitions of notional trade offers and their specifications in implicit form sketched in section 2.1.1 make clear that

$$\frac{\partial \ln \tilde{X}^s}{\partial \ln \tilde{X}^d} = 0$$

$$\frac{\partial \ln \tilde{L}^d}{\partial \ln \tilde{X}^d} = 0$$

$$\frac{\partial \ln \tilde{L}^s}{\partial \ln \tilde{X}^d} = 0$$

We compute

$$\frac{\partial \ln X}{\partial \ln \tilde{X}^d} = \frac{\partial \ln X}{\partial \ln X^d} \cdot \frac{\partial \ln X^d}{\partial \ln \tilde{X}^d} + \frac{\partial \ln X}{\partial \ln X^s} \cdot \frac{\partial \ln X^s}{\partial \ln \tilde{X}^d}$$

$$= (1 - P_G) \cdot \frac{\partial \ln X^d}{\partial \ln \tilde{X}^d} + P_G \cdot \frac{\partial \ln X^s}{\partial \ln \tilde{X}^d}$$

From the above expressions for the effective trade offers, we derive

$$\frac{\partial \ln X^d}{\partial \ln \tilde{X}^d} = 1 + \gamma_{XD} \frac{\partial \ln L}{\partial \ln \tilde{X}^d}$$

and

$$\frac{\partial \ln X^s}{\partial \ln \tilde{X}^d} = [1 - \gamma_{XS}\gamma_{LD}]^{-1} \left[\gamma_{XS} \frac{\partial \ln L}{\partial \ln \tilde{X}^d} - \gamma_{XS}\gamma_{LD} \frac{\partial \ln X}{\partial \ln \tilde{X}^d} \right]$$

Substituting those two expressions in the equation above we write

$$\frac{\partial \ln X}{\partial \ln \tilde{X}^d} = \left[1 + P_G \left(\frac{\gamma_{XS}\gamma_{LD}}{1 - \gamma_{XS}\gamma_{LD}} \right) \right]^{-1}$$

$$\times \left\{ (1 - P_G) + \left[\gamma_{XD}(1 - P_G) + \left(\frac{\gamma_{XS}}{1 - \gamma_{XS}\gamma_{LD}} \right) P_G \right] \left(\frac{\partial \ln L}{\partial \ln \tilde{X}^d} \right) \right\}$$

$$\text{(D.1)}$$

This expression still contains the elasticity $\partial \ln L / \partial \ln \tilde{X}^d$ which has similarly to be expressed as a function of the regime proportions and the spillover coefficients.

$$\frac{\partial \ln L}{\partial \ln \tilde{X}^d} = \frac{\partial \ln L}{\partial \ln L^d} \cdot \frac{\partial \ln L^d}{\partial \ln \tilde{X}^d} + \frac{\partial \ln L}{\partial \ln L^s} \cdot \frac{\partial \ln L^s}{\partial \ln \tilde{X}^d}$$

$$= (1 - P_L) \cdot \frac{\partial \ln L^d}{\partial \ln \tilde{X}^d} + P_L \cdot \frac{\partial \ln L^s}{\partial \ln \tilde{X}^d}$$

From the expressions of the effective trade offers, we derive

$$\frac{\partial \ln L^d}{\partial \ln \tilde{X}^d} = [1 - \gamma_{LD}\gamma_{XS}]^{-1} \left[\gamma_{LD} \frac{\partial \ln X}{\partial \ln \tilde{X}^d} - \gamma_{LD}\gamma_{XS} \frac{\partial \ln L}{\partial \ln \tilde{X}^d} \right]$$

and

$$\frac{\partial \ln L^s}{\partial \ln \tilde{X}^d} = 0$$

Substituting these two expressions in the equation just above, we write

$$\frac{\partial \ln L}{\partial \ln \tilde{X}^d} = (1 - P_L)[1 - \gamma_{LD} \cdot \gamma_{XS}]^{-1}$$

$$\times \{1 + (\gamma_{LD} \cdot \gamma_{XS})(1 - P_L)(1 - \gamma_{LD} \cdot \gamma_{XS})^{-1}\}^{-1} \cdot \gamma_{LD} \cdot \frac{\partial \ln X}{\partial \ln \tilde{X}^d}$$

which simplifies into

$$\frac{\partial \ln L}{\partial \ln \tilde{X}^d} = \left[\frac{\gamma_{LD} \cdot (1 - P_L)}{1 - \gamma_{XS} \cdot \gamma_{LD} \cdot P_L} \right] \cdot \frac{\partial \ln X}{\partial \ln \tilde{X}^d} \qquad \text{(D.2)}$$

By combining equations (D.1) and (D.2) we get

$$\frac{\partial \ln X}{\partial \ln \tilde{X}^d} = \left[1 + P_G \left(\frac{\gamma_{XS} \cdot \gamma_{LD}}{1 - \gamma_{XS} \cdot \gamma_{LD}}\right)\right]^{-1}$$

$$\times \left\{(1 - P_G) + \left[\gamma_{XD} \cdot (1 - P_G) + \left(\frac{\gamma_{XS}}{1 - \gamma_{XS} \cdot \gamma_{LD}}\right) \cdot P_G\right]\right.$$

$$\left. \times \left[\frac{\gamma_{LD}(1 - P_L)}{1 - \gamma_{XS} \cdot \gamma_{LD} \cdot P_L}\right] \cdot \frac{\partial \ln X}{\partial \ln \tilde{X}^d}\right\}$$

which may be rewritten as

$$\frac{\partial \ln X}{\partial \ln \tilde{X}^d} = (1 - P_G)\left\{1 + P_G \cdot \left(\frac{\gamma_{XS} \cdot \gamma_{LD}}{1 - \gamma_{XS} \cdot \gamma_{LD}}\right) - \frac{\gamma_{XD} \cdot \gamma_{LD} \cdot (1 - P_G) \cdot (1 - P_L)}{(1 - \gamma_{XS} \cdot \gamma_{LD} \cdot P_L)}\right.$$

$$\left. - \frac{\gamma_{XS} \cdot \gamma_{LD} \cdot P_G \cdot (1 - P_L)}{(1 - \gamma_{XS} \cdot \gamma_{LD})(1 - \gamma_{XS} \cdot \gamma_{LD} \cdot P_L)}\right\}^{-1}$$

and which reduces to the final expression

$$\frac{d \ln X}{d \ln \tilde{X}^d} = \frac{(1 - P_G)(1 - \gamma_{XS} \cdot \gamma_{LD} \cdot P_L)}{1 - (1 - P_G)\gamma_{LD}[\gamma_{XS}P_L + \gamma_{XD}(1 - P_L)]}$$

We end up with a multiplier formula quite analogous to but of course not identical to that obtained under Ito's specification of the spillover terms. However, the basic properties appear to be the same:

–   Here also stability conditions imply the following restrictions on the spillover coefficients:

$$\gamma_{XD}\gamma_{LD} < 1 \quad \text{and} \quad \gamma_{XS}\gamma_{LD} < 1$$

–   Here also the multiplier appears as a continuous function of P_G and P_L defined over the same range $[0, 1/(1 - \gamma_{XD} \cdot \gamma_{LD})]$. Like its counterpart in Ito's model, the multiplier appears to be decreasing in both P_G and P_L.

–   The 'pure' regimes of the conventional disequilibrium models are obtained for P_G and P_L converging towards the extreme values 0 and 1; it is easily verified that 'Portes' multiplier' then converges towards the same values as 'Ito's multiplier' (refer to the main text for the interpretation of those values).

The multiplier effect of an autonomous increase in demand in the framework of Portes' model appears finally as a function, of course not identical but endowed with the same basic behaviour as its counterpart in

Ito's model. Since, for reasons developed in the main text, Ito's model is given both an a-priori theoretical and ex-post empirical advantage, it seems pointless to extend further the comparative analysis of both multipliers.

E   Empirical estimates of Portes' model

Here, for the same reasons as in Ito's model, we impose the constraint $\gamma_1 = \gamma_2 = \gamma$.

The FIML estimates of the parameters (with standard errors in parentheses) are reported in table E.1 while table E.2 presents some summary statistics of the estimation.

Table E.1. *FIML estimates of the parameters of Portes' model*

Parameters	Estimates		Parameters	Estimates	
$\ln(\alpha_{DUC})$	−0.076	(0.017)	γ_{LD}	0.431	(0.073)
α_1	0.264	(0.05)	γ_{XS}	5.191	(1.230)
σ	0.518	(0.055)	c_{1XD}	0.239	(0.266)
γ	0.067	(0.007)	c_{2XD}	0.774	(0.159)
δ_0	0.247	(0.053)	c_{3XD}	2.791	(0.390)
$1/\rho_G$	0.091	(0.008)	c_{0XD}	4.329	(1.970)
σ_0	0.012	(0.003)	c_{0XS}	−0.148	(0.029)
σ_1	0.421	(0.040)	c_{0LD}	0.086	(0.028)

Table E.2. *'Goodness of fit' statistics of the FIML estimation of Portes' model*

Equation		RMSE (fit) in %	R^2	DW
(3.9.1)	(X^d)	3.34	0.981	1.99
(3.9.2)	(X^s)	1.74	0.995	1.12
(3.9.3)	(DUC)	1.46	0.940	1.23
(3.9.4)	(L^d)	1.22	0.979	1.61
(3.9.5)	(L^s)	0.95	0.931	1.39

It may be verified that the majority of the parameter estimates are very close to (and not significantly different from) their corresponding estimates in Ito's model.

Since both models differ in their specification of the spillover terms, the main differences could – *a priori* – be expected in the estimates of the spillover coefficients γ_{LD} and γ_{XS}. Since those estimates are discussed extensively in section 3.5, they will not be commented on further here.

The parameters specific to the demand for goods equation (namely c_{0XD}, c_{1XD}, c_{2XD} and c_{3XD}) exhibit estimates fairly different from their Ito's correspondents but the most striking – and at first sight surprising – difference concerns the 'dispersion' parameter $1/\rho_G$, the estimated value of which is 0.091 in Portes' version and only 0.029 in Ito's version. However, the reason for such a difference is easily understood once due account is taken of the fundamental difference in the underlying concepts of output supply X^s in the two models.

This difference was highlighted in the discussion of section 2.1; in short it could be termed like this: in Ito's model, aggregate X^s is equal to the total feasible output firms could produce with their existing equipment and their present labour force, while in Portes' model aggregate X^s is equal to the total notional output supply $\tilde{X}^s$ except for the amount of goods that cannot be produced due to prevailing constraints on labour input.

Since, over most of the observation period, labour constraints have been rather weak, X^s_{Portes} was always estimated rather close to $\tilde{X}^s$ and hence significantly above X^s_{Ito}. But, as explained in chapter 1, the 'dispersion' parameter $1/\rho_G$ precisely parameterizes the position (better, the distance) of the transaction curve X with respect to *both the supply and demand curves*: the larger value of $(1/\rho_G)_{\text{Portes}}$, reflecting the greater distance between X and X^s_{Portes}, is then quite understandable. This of course unavoidably affects the position of the X^d curve, which helps explain the differences (between Portes' and Ito's results) in the estimates of the 'demand for goods parameters'.

Since, with a prevailing (throughout the observation period) situation of weak tensions on the labour market, X^s_{Portes} stays rather close to $\tilde{X}^s$, it may be verified from the specification of L^d in both models that L^d_{Portes} and L^d_{Ito} will be fairly close together. This explains (with the definition of L^s being identical in both models) the estimates of $1/\rho_L$ (or better, of σ_0 and σ_1) being very close for both models.

F   Sensitivity analysis to alternative specifications of manufacturing labour supply

The specification adopted in the main text for manufacturing labour supply assumes that the share of manufacturing employment in total employment may constitute an appropriate measure of the 'attraction potential' of the manufacturing sector on unemployed workers.

Denoting by UN (by UNR) the number of unemployed workers (resp. the unemployment rate) and using the subscript 'tot' for aggregate by opposition to 'man' for manufacturing, this amounts to assuming

$$\frac{UN_{man}}{UN_{tot}} = \frac{L_{man}}{L_{tot}}$$

which is readily seen to imply

$$UNR_{man} = UNR_{tot}$$

This specification of sectoral labour supply implicitly assumes a fair degree of labour mobility between sectors.

If, however, for a number of reasons like specialization in professional qualifications, geographical concentration of industrial activities, etc., mobility of labour between sectors is believed to be weak, then it seems more relevant to consider as 'sectoral labour supply' the sum of actual sectoral employment plus the unemployed whose previous employment was in the considered sector[1].

Defined in that way, sectoral unemployment rates[2] may then be found to diverge significantly from the aggregate unemployment rate. For example, labour developments in recent years induce one to expect *a priori* such a divergence to occur for the manufacturing sector.

Indeed, while the share of manufacturing employment in aggregate employment remained roughly constant (at the level of about 26%–27%) during the first ten years of the observation period (from 1963 to 1974), it witnessed a continuous shrinkage in recent years (from 25% in 1975 to about 20% in 1980) as a consequence of the particularly steep decline of manufacturing employment as compared to other sectors. Hence it seems reasonable to expect that UNR_{man} as computed by ONEM will show up significantly higher than UNR_{tot} in the last period. If this conjecture happened to be true, the choice between the first specification of manufacturing labour supply (implying $UNR_{man} = UNR_{tot}$) and the second one (implying $UNR_{man} \neq UNR_{tot}$) could be of (possibly serious) consequence on the overall model performance and the parameter estimates.

The comparison between the series UNR_{tot} and UNR_{man} (as computed from the ONEM statistics) is comforting in this respect, since both series appear to be extremely close as is apparent in figure F.1.

The main explanation of this *a-priori* surprising finding resides most probably in the 'labour supply management' constituted by specific programs like early retirement schemes ('preretraite' in French) which have been systematically implemented in some manufacturing subsectors[3].

Since the series UNR_{man} appears to coincide almost exactly with the series UNR_{tot}, this implies that the use of the envisaged alternative specification of manufacturing labour supply instead of the one adopted in the main text would be of almost no consequence to empirical results.

This is verified by substituting UNR_{man}[4] (as obtained from the ONEM statistics) for UNR everywhere it appears in the equations of the model and performing estimation of the final specification retained for the model [i.e. with the constraints $\theta = 1$ (Ito's version); α (the 'association coefficient') $= 0$

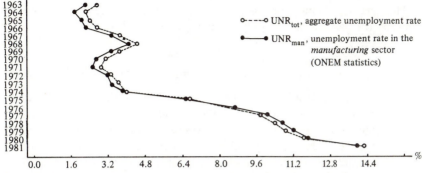

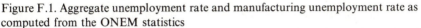

Figure F.1. Aggregate unemployment rate and manufacturing unemployment rate as computed from the ONEM statistics

Table F.1. *FIML estimates of the parameters of Ito's model with* UNR_{man} *(ONEM) as the endogenous dependent variable*

Parameters	Estimates		Parameters	Estimates	
$\ln(\alpha_{DUC})$	−0.069	(0.019)	γ_{LD}	0.485	(0.089)
α_1	0.236	(0.051)	γ_{XS}	1.482	(0.22)
σ	0.555	(0.046)	c_{1XD}	0.488	(0.187)
γ	0.069	(0.007)	c_{2XD}	0.598	(0.111)
δ_0	0.301	(0.056)	c_{3XD}	2.121	(0.278)
$1/\rho_G$	0.027	(0.006)	c_{0XD}	2.457	(1.381)
σ_0	0.015	(0.004)	c_{0XS}	−0.174	(0.03)
σ_1	0.365	(0.042)	c_{0LD}	0.124	(0.032)

and $\gamma_2 = \gamma_1$]; the resulting parameter estimates (with asymptotic standard errors in parentheses) are reported in table F.1 and are readily verified to be very close to the results of table 3.1 in section 3.6.

Although both envisaged specifications of manufacturing labour supply are found to be empirically equivalent, other specifications cannot be ruled out *a priori*.

Indeed, it could be argued that considering as sectoral potential labour only the unemployed workers previously employed in a given sector is unduly restrictive since unemployed workers may be willing to work in – and should consequently be considered available for – other sectors than just their previous one; qualifications along with previous experience should then be taken into consideration for determination of sectoral labour supply.

Confronted with the absence of a generally unquestioned definition of sectoral labour supply and having to choose one among various possible specifications, it seems interesting to examine the sensitivity of the overall empirical results to the specification chosen for L^s_{man}.

This has been done most simply by assuming the following relationship between the manufacturing and the aggregate unemployment rate:

$$UNR_{man} = (c_0 + c_1 . TREND) . UNR_{tot}$$

with the TREND variable allowed to exhibit one of two possible profiles:

– increasing steadily from the value 1 in 1960 to the value 21 in 1980.
– being set equal to zero for the period 1960 to 1973 and starting increasing only from 1974 on. This second profile of course is meant to catch the effect of the accelerated decline in manufacturing employment since 1974 which was referred to above.

Substituting the above specification for UNR_{man} in the labour supply equation, we end up with the following equation

$$\ln (P_L)_t = \rho_L \ln [1 - (c_0 + c_1 . TREND)(UNR_{tot})_t] + u_{LSt}$$

which comes instead of equation (3.8) of section 3.3 in the model proposed for estimation.

We then estimate the whole model by FIML conditionally on values imposed on the parameters c_0 and c_1, in order to assess the sensitivity of the parameter estimates to alternative specifications (i.e. combinations of values for c_0 and c_1) of the manufacturing labour supply. Various combinations of values for c_0 and c_1 were tried;[5] their results all pointed toward the same qualitative conclusions:

– The maximum likelihood value decreases somewhat for specifications implying UNR_{man} to be higher than UNR_{tot}; this may possibly contradict prior beliefs about the relative tightness of the manufacturing labour market compared to other sectoral labour markets.
– Except for the 'dispersion' parameters $1/\rho_L$ (i.e. in fact for the parameters σ_1 and/or σ_0) and to a lesser extent $1/\rho_G$, the other structural parameters appear rather insensitive to the alternative specifications of manufacturing labour supply. This is illustrated in table F.2 which reports on two experiments (namely the experiments labelled (c) and (e) in note 5) along with the results of the 'reference specification' (see section 3.6) repeated here only to ease comparison.

It is readily verified that the parameter estimates relating to the other structural equations (demand for goods; supply of goods and demand for labour) are only weakly affected by the choice of a particular specification for sectoral labour supply: this phenomenon is of course due to the fact that excess labour supply has been prevalent (to varying extents of course) through all the period of observation so that shifts of the aggregate labour supply

Table F.2. *FIML estimates of the parameters of Ito's model with alternative specifications of manufacturing labour supply*

Parameters	Reference specification		Specification (c) of note 5		Specification (e) of note 5	
max ln L	184.104		183.722		180.739	
c_0	1.0	(*)	1.5	(*)	1.0	(*)
c_1	0.0	(*)	0.0	(*)	0.1	(*)
ln (α_{DUC})	-0.075	(0.018)	-0.073	(0.018)	-0.063	(0.023)
α_1	0.235	(0.050)	0.232	(0.051)	0.258	(0.047)
σ	0.538	(0.048)	0.544	(0.048)	0.573	(0.043)
γ	0.066	(0.007)	0.067	(0.007)	0.079	(0.007)
δ_0	0.292	(0.055)	0.303	(0.056)	0.320	(0.059)
$1/\rho_G$	0.029	(0.007)	0.037	(0.007)	0.032	(0.006)
σ_0	0.0143	(0.003)	0.0217	(0.005)	0.0153	(0.008)
σ_1	0.386	(0.042)	0.593	(0.065)	0.605	(0.075)
γ_{LD}	0.480	(0.091)	0.488	(0.093)	0.463	(0.078)
γ_{XS}	1.446	(0.22)	1.250	(0.19)	1.440	(0.20)
c_{1XD}	0.484	(0.189)	0.442	(0.198)	0.459	(0.190)
c_{2XD}	0.601	(0.112)	0.631	(0.118)	0.617	(0.113)
c_{3XD}	2.180	(0.281)	2.267	(0.292)	2.055	(0.284)

schedule only have a minor impact on the other parameter estimates.

In view of those results and since our specification of sectoral labour supply has been found to coincide empirically with a most frequently adopted specification, we feel authorized to pursue the empirical analysis with this specification.

G A composite Portes–Ito model

Since no decisive theoretical argument has been provided in favour of either Portes' or Ito's model, one may be tempted to consider a composite model. The most interesting combination seems to associate Ito's effective demand for labour L_{Ito}^d with Portes' effective supply of goods X_{Portes}^s: indeed L_{Ito}^d makes more intuitive sense than L_{Portes}^d[1] while both specifications for X^s, although conveying different contents, make sense.

The suggested composite model is

$$\ln X^d = \ln \tilde{X}^d + \gamma_{XD}(\ln L - \ln \tilde{L}^s) \tag{G.1.1}$$

$$\ln X^s = \ln \tilde{X}^s + \gamma_{XS}(\ln L - \ln L^d) \quad \text{[Portes]} \tag{G.1.2}$$

$$\ln L^d = \ln \tilde{L}^d + \gamma_{LD}(\ln X - \ln \tilde{X}^s) \quad \text{[Ito]} \tag{G.1.3}$$

$$\ln L^s = \ln \tilde{L}^s \tag{G.1.4}$$

Combining those specifications with the DUC_{obs} equation, and replacing the latent variables by their expressions as functions of the observables P_G and P_L, one gets the following structural form suitable for estimation:

$$\ln X = \frac{1}{\rho_G}\ln(1-P_G) + \frac{\gamma_{XD}}{\rho_L}\ln(P_L) + \ln \tilde{X}^d \tag{G.2.1}$$

$$\ln X = \frac{1}{\rho_G}\ln(P_G) + \frac{\gamma_{XS}}{\rho_L}\ln(1-P_L) + \ln \tilde{X}^s \tag{G.2.2}$$

$$\ln \text{DUC}_{\text{obs}} = \ln \alpha_{DUC} + \frac{1}{\rho_G}\ln(P_G) + \frac{\gamma_{XS}}{\rho_L}\ln(1-P_L) \tag{G.2.3}$$

$$\ln L = \frac{\gamma_{LD}}{\rho_G}\ln(P_G) + \frac{[1+\gamma_{XS}\gamma_{LD}]}{\rho_L}\ln(1-P_L) + \ln \tilde{X}^d \tag{G.2.4}$$

$$\ln L = \frac{1}{\rho_L}\ln(P_L) + \ln \tilde{L}^s \tag{G.2.5}$$

This final structural form may be interestingly compared to its correspondents in chapter 2, namely systems of equations (2.5) (for Portes' model) and (2.7) (for Ito's model).

One verifies that the only difference with Portes' final structural form is the factor $[1+\gamma_{XS}\gamma_{LD}]$ multiplying the term '$\ln(1-P_L)$' in equation (G.2.4).

After substituting appropriate specifications (the same of course as for Portes' or Ito's model, in order to ease comparability of the results) for the notional trade offers, one may easily estimate the whole model by FIML methods. This has been done and the estimation results will be commented on below.

However, before proceeding to that point, some theoretical issues have to be discussed. It has been shown in the main text (section 2.1) that some constraints had to be imposed on the spillover coefficients in order to guarantee both *stability* and *coherency* (i.e. uniqueness of the reduced form) of the models.

For both Portes' and Ito's models, those conditions were seen to be

$$\gamma_{XD}\gamma_{LD} < 1$$

and

$$\gamma_{XS}\gamma_{LD} < 1$$

A surprising property of the *composite* Portes–Ito model will be seen to be that *its stability and coherency conditions are less severe than for both Ito's and Portes' models*.

Stability conditions may be derived, as for Portes' and Ito's model, by examining which conditions are to be required on the spillover coefficients in order to ensure that economic policy multipliers always exhibit the right sign and finite values.

Taking as an example the autonomous demand multiplier (so that comparison may be performed with Ito's multiplier of section 2.1.2 or Portes' multiplier of appendix D), we easily compute the final expression (in elasticity form):

$$\frac{d \ln X}{d \ln \tilde{X}^d} = \frac{(1 - P_G)}{\left[1 - \gamma_{XD}\gamma_{LD}(1 - P_G)(1 - P_L) + \gamma_{XS}\gamma_{LD}P_G P_L\right]}$$

The same type of comments apply here as for both Ito's and Portes' multipliers.

However, as far as stability is concerned and with $0 \leqslant P_G \leqslant 1$ and $0 \leqslant P_L \leqslant 1$, the only condition needed to ensure a positive and finite multiplier value is readily seen to be

$$\gamma_{XD}\gamma_{LD} < 1$$

while *no condition has to be imposed on the product* $\gamma_{XS}\gamma_{LD}$ (provided of course that $\gamma_{XD} \geqslant 0$; $\gamma_{XS} \geqslant 0$; $\gamma_{LD} \geqslant 0$).

This departure of the Portes–Ito model from its two 'parents' is confirmed by the analysis of the *coherency conditions*[2] in the limiting case where $\rho_G \to \infty$ and $\rho_L \to \infty$ such that the model then reduces to the aggregate switching case.

In that limiting case, the model is constituted by equations (G.1.1) to (G.1.4) plus the two *min* conditions:

$$X = \min (X^d, X^s) \quad \text{and} \quad L = \min (L^d, L^s)$$

Those equations together define a mapping from the vector of endogenous variables (X^d, X^s, L^d, L^s) to the vector $(\tilde{X}^d, \tilde{X}^s, \tilde{L}^d, \tilde{L}^s)$ consisting of (log-)linear combinations of exogenous variables and stochastic error terms.

This mapping is piecewise linear over the cones C_i, $i = K, C, R, U$ defined as

$$C_K = \{X^d \leqslant X^s, \quad L^d \leqslant L^s\}$$
$$C_C = \{X^d > X^s, \quad L^d \leqslant L^s\}$$
$$C_R = \{X^d > X^s, \quad L^d > L^s\}$$
$$C_U = \{X^d \leqslant X^s, \quad L^d > L^s\}$$

and may be expressed as

$$\begin{pmatrix} \tilde{X}^d \\ \tilde{X}^s \\ \tilde{L}^d \\ \tilde{L}^s \end{pmatrix} = f \begin{pmatrix} X^d \\ X^s \\ L^d \\ L^s \end{pmatrix}$$

with

$$f = \sum_{i=K}^{U} A_i \Pi_{ci}$$

where

$$A_K = \begin{bmatrix} 1 & 0 & -\gamma_{XD} & \gamma_{XD} \\ 0 & 1 & 0 & 0 \\ -\gamma_{LD} & \gamma_{LD} & 1 & 0 \\ 0 & 0 & 0 & 1 \end{bmatrix}$$

$$A_C = \begin{bmatrix} 1 & 0 & -\gamma_{XD} & \gamma_{XD} \\ 0 & 1 & 0 & 0 \\ 0 & 0 & 1 & 0 \\ 0 & 0 & 0 & 1 \end{bmatrix}$$

$$A_R = \begin{bmatrix} 1 & 0 & 0 & 0 \\ 0 & 1 & \gamma_{XS} & -\gamma_{XS} \\ 0 & 0 & (1+\gamma_{XS}\gamma_{LD}) & -\gamma_{XS}\gamma_{LD} \\ 0 & 0 & 0 & 1 \end{bmatrix}$$

$$A_U = \begin{bmatrix} 1 & 0 & 0 & 0 \\ 0 & 1 & \gamma_{XS} & -\gamma_{XS} \\ -\gamma_{LD} & \gamma_{LD} & (1+\gamma_{XS}\gamma_{LD}) & -\gamma_{XS}\gamma_{LD} \\ 0 & 0 & 0 & 1 \end{bmatrix}$$

and

$$\Pi_{ci} = 1 \quad \text{if } (X^d, X^s, L^d, L^s) \in C_i$$

and

$$\Pi_{ci} = 0 \quad \text{if } (X^d, X^s, L^d, L^d) \notin C_i$$

Looking for the coherency conditions amounts to finding the conditions required for the piecewise linear mapping f to be invertible. Those conditions have been derived by Gouriéroux, Laffont and Monfort (1980 b) whose theorem 1 states: if the mapping $f = \sum_i A_i \Pi_{ci}$ is continuous, a necessary and sufficient condition for f to be invertible is that all the determinants, det A_i, $i = \{K, C, R, U\}$, have the same sign.

One easily verifies that our mapping f is continuous since the mappings A_i coincide on the common boundaries of the cones C_i on which they are relevant; computing

$\det \mathbf{A}_K = 1 - \gamma_{LD}\gamma_{XD}$

$\det \mathbf{A}_C = 1$

$\det \mathbf{A}_R = 1 + \gamma_{LD}\gamma_{XS}$

$\det \mathbf{A}_U = 1$

one obtains $\gamma_{LD}\gamma_{XD} < 1$ as the only coherency condition without any other condition having to be imposed on the other product $\gamma_{LD}\gamma_{XS}$.

'Coherency analysis' of the limiting piecewise linar case thus points toward the same conclusion as the 'stability analysis', namely less severe conditions than for Ito's or Portes' model.

This might prove to be an interesting property in view of the fact that violation of such conditions by the empirical estimates was precisely the main argument for our discarding Portes' model (see section 3.5).

It will hence be of interest to look at the products of the empirical estimates $\hat{\gamma}_{LD}\hat{\gamma}_{XD}$ and $\hat{\gamma}_{LD}\hat{\gamma}_{XS}$.

However, before proceeding to the empirical estimation, two more observations involving functions of the spillover coefficients may be of interest.

(1) One knows that X^s_{Ito} and $X^s_{\text{Portes–Ito}}$ represent totally different concepts:

X^s_{Ito} represents the efficient production frontier, taking into account installed capital and the occupied labour force.

$X^s_{\text{Portes–Ito}}$ represents the notional supply of goods short of the output producers are unable to produce because of actually experienced labour constraints.

These two different concepts never coincide, except in two limiting cases where both then correspond to observable X:

(a)   either in a *pure C regime* (all firms are in the C regime).
We then easily compute:
for Ito's model: $X = X^s_{\text{Ito}} = \tilde{X}^s$
for the Portes–Ito model: $X = X^s_{\text{Portes–Ito}} = \tilde{X}^s$

(b)   or in a *pure R regime* (all firms are in the R regime).
We then easily compute:
for Ito's model: $\ln X = \ln \tilde{X}^s + \gamma_{XS}(\ln L - \ln \tilde{L}^d)$
for the Portes–Ito model: $\ln X = \ln X^s_{\text{Portes–Ito}}$

$$= \ln \tilde{X}^s + \frac{\gamma_{XS}}{1 + \gamma_{XS}\gamma_{LD}}(\ln L - \ln \tilde{L}^d)$$

Since in the pure R regime, $X = X^s$ is on the efficient production frontier, the equation above yields the specification of the efficient production frontier in the Portes–Ito model. It will hence be interesting to compare the following empirical estimates:

$$\hat{\gamma}_{XS(\text{Ito})} \quad \text{and} \quad \left(\frac{\hat{\gamma}_{XS}}{1+\hat{\gamma}_{XS}\hat{\gamma}_{LD}}\right)_{\text{Portes–Ito}}$$

(2) Knowing the specification of the efficient production frontier, one may compute (as was done in section 2.6 for Ito's model) the 'efficient' level of employment L_{eff} which would be technically needed to produce the current output X. One starts from:

$$\ln X = \ln \tilde{X}^s + \frac{\gamma_{XS}}{1+\gamma_{XS}\gamma_{LD}} (\ln L_{\text{eff}} - \ln \tilde{L}^d)$$

This may be rewritten

$$(\ln L_{\text{eff}} - \ln \tilde{L}^d) = \left(\frac{1+\gamma_{XS}\gamma_{LD}}{\gamma_{XS}}\right)[\ln X - \ln \tilde{X}^s]$$

so that

$$(\ln L_{\text{eff}} - \ln \tilde{L}^d) = -(\ln L - \ln \tilde{L}^d)$$
$$+ \left(\frac{1+\gamma_{XS}\gamma_{LD}}{\gamma_{XS}}\right)[\ln X - \ln \tilde{X}^s]$$

Substituting the terms in the right member by their expressions as functions of the observations P_G and P_L (as given by equations (G.2)), we get after some manipulation the very simple expressions

$$\frac{L_{\text{eff}}}{L} = (P_G)^{1/(\rho_G \cdot \gamma_{XS})}$$

which happens to be identical to its correspondent for Ito's model.

Here also it will be interesting to compare the empirical estimates

$$\left(\frac{1}{\hat{\rho}_G\hat{\gamma}_{XS}}\right)_{\text{Ito}} \quad \text{and} \quad \left(\frac{1}{\hat{\rho}_G\hat{\gamma}_{XS}}\right)_{\text{Portes–Ito}}$$

in order to assess the differences in the extent of the labour hoarding phenomenon as estimated under alternative specifications (models).

Imposing (as for Ito's model) the constraint $\gamma_1 = \gamma_2 = \gamma$ (Hicks neutral technical change), we estimate the entire model by FIML.

The empirical estimates (with standard errors in parentheses) are reported in table G.1, along with the estimation results of Ito's model in order to ease comparison. Table G.2 presents the RMSE statistic for each equation of both models.

Table G.1. *FIML estimates for Ito's model and for the composite Portes–Ito model*

Parameters	Ito's model		Composite Portes–Ito model	
max ln L	184.104		183.396	
ln (α_{DUC})	-0.075	(0.018)	-0.081	(0.018)
α_1	0.235	(0.050)	0.238	(0.052)
σ	0.538	(0.048)	0.525	(0.052)
γ	0.066	(0.007)	0.065	(0.007)
δ_0	0.292	(0.055)	0.273	(0.056)
$1/\rho_G$	0.029	(0.007)	0.093	(0.007)
σ_0	0.0143	(0.003)	0.0136	(0.003)
σ_1	0.386	(0.042)	0.396	(0.043)
γ_{LD}	0.480	(0.091)	0.463	(0.087)
γ_{XS}	1.446	(0.22)	4.385	(1.325)
c_{1XD}	0.484	(0.189)	0.221	(0.268)
c_{2XD}	0.601	(0.112)	0.794	(0.161)
c_{3XD}	2.180	(0.281)	2.895	(0.392)

Table G.2. *RMSE statistics as a 'goodness of fit' statistic for each equation*

Equation	Ito's model	Composite Portes–Ito model
X^d	0.0256	0.0338
X^s	0.0177	0.0178
DUC	0.0140	0.0135
L^d	0.0134	0.0132
L^s	0.0101	0.0099

First of all, one notices that the maximum likelihood value is very close to the one attained with Ito's specification, so that this criterion cannot help to discriminate between both models.

Secondly, one verifies that a majority of parameter estimates are very close to their corresponding estimates in Ito's model; significant differences arise however for the parameters $1/\rho_G$, γ_{XS} and those related to the specification of the demand for goods c_{1XD}, c_{2XD} and c_{3XD}.

Interestingly, those parameter estimates which depart significantly from their Ito's correspondents happen to be close to their Portes' correspondents (see appendix E for Portes' estimates).

One remembers that Portes' model was discarded mainly because

$$(\hat{\gamma}_{XS} \cdot \hat{\gamma}_{LD})_{\text{Portes}} > 1$$

which was unacceptable for theoretical reasons (violation of the stability and coherency conditions); one checks that here also

$$(\hat{\gamma}_{XS} \cdot \hat{\gamma}_{LD})_{\text{Portes–Ito}} > 1$$

but, as discussed above, stability and coherency do not require any conditions on this product[3].

However, it has been shown above that a sensible comparison was between the following estimates:

$$(\hat{\gamma}_{XS})_{\text{Ito}} \quad \text{and} \quad \left(\frac{\hat{\gamma}_{XS}}{1 + \hat{\gamma}_{XS}\hat{\gamma}_{LD}}\right)_{\text{Portes–Ito}}$$

which were seen to play identical roles in the specification of their respective efficient production frontier.

Both empirical estimates turn out to be extremely close:

$$(\hat{\gamma}_{XS})_{\text{Ito}} = 1.446$$

while

$$\left(\frac{\hat{\gamma}_{XS}}{1 + \hat{\gamma}_{XS}\hat{\gamma}_{LD}}\right)_{\text{Portes–Ito}} = 1.447$$

which imply identical short-run production functions in both models, despite their differences.

Another comparison which was suggested above concerns the estimated value of the product

$$\left(\frac{1}{\rho_G \cdot \gamma_{XS}}\right)$$

in both models. Although each factor exhibits very different values in each model, their combination yields

$$\left(\frac{1}{\hat{\rho}_G \cdot \hat{\gamma}_{XS}}\right)_{\text{Ito}} = 0.020$$

and

$$\left(\frac{1}{\hat{\rho}_G \cdot \hat{\gamma}_{XS}}\right)_{\text{Portes–Ito}} = 0.021$$

Hence both models yield similar estimates about the extent of the labour hoarding phenomenon.

Similarly, since we have empirically

$$\left(\frac{1}{\rho_L}\right)_{\text{Ito}} \simeq \left(\frac{1}{\rho_L}\right)_{\text{Portes–Ito}}$$

it follows that estimates of L^d and L^s according to either model will coincide.

Moreover, relying on equations (G.2.2) and (G.2.4) above and their equivalents for Ito's model (equations (2.7.2) and (2.7.4) of section 2.1), and exploiting simultaneously all the empirical equalities just discussed, namely

$$(\hat{\gamma}_{XS})_{\text{Ito}} \simeq \left(\frac{\hat{\gamma}_{XS}}{1+\hat{\gamma}_{XS}\hat{\gamma}_{LD}}\right)_{\text{Portes–Ito}}$$

$$(\hat{\rho}_G \cdot \hat{\gamma}_{XS})_{\text{Ito}} \simeq (\hat{\rho}_G \cdot \hat{\gamma}_{XS})_{\text{Portes–Ito}}$$

$$(\hat{\rho}_L)_{\text{Ito}} \simeq (\hat{\rho}_L)_{\text{Portes–Ito}}$$

$$(\hat{\gamma}_{LD})_{\text{Ito}} \simeq (\hat{\gamma}_{LD})_{\text{Portes–Ito}}$$

we obtain that

$$\hat{\tilde{X}}^s_{\text{Ito}} \simeq \hat{\tilde{X}}^s_{\text{Portes–Ito}}$$

and

$$\hat{\tilde{L}}^d_{\text{Ito}} \simeq \hat{\tilde{L}}^d_{\text{Portes–Ito}}$$

On balance, both models produce very close empirical results as far as the labour market is concerned: indeed, the estimates of L^d, L^s, L_{eff} and $\tilde{L}^d$ produced under either specification have been seen to coincide empirically.

Such an agreement is not the case for the goods market; although the estimates of the notional supply of goods $\tilde{X}^s_{\text{Ito}}$ and $\tilde{X}^s_{\text{Portes–Ito}}$ have been seen to coincide, this is not the case for the effective trade offers X^d and X^s. This difference, which is of course due to

$$\left(\frac{1}{\hat{\rho}_G}\right)_{\text{Ito}} \ll \left(\frac{1}{\hat{\rho}_G}\right)_{\text{Portes–Ito}}$$

was naturally to be expected for the effective supply of goods X^s since it embodies a different concept in each model. Hence $\hat{X}^s_{\text{Ito}} \ll \hat{X}^s_{\text{Portes–Ito}}$ only reflects the fact that they are meant to catch something different (refer to their definitions above).

The difference between $\hat{X}^d_{\text{Ito}}$ and $\hat{X}^d_{\text{Portes–Ito}}$, although fully explainable[4], is more embarrassing since both are meant to capture the same concept of effective demand for goods. $\hat{X}^d_{\text{Portes–Ito}}$ is seen to exhibit higher values and somewhat more ample fluctuations than $\hat{X}^d_{\text{Ito}}$.

Since both models were seen to be empirically equivalent on a number of issues, and in the absence of any extraneous information supporting either estimate of X^d, a discriminating criterion may lie in the 'goodness of fit' statistic reported in table G.2. While being roughly comparable for all the other equations, the RMSE statistic[5] for the 'X^d equation' turns out to be significantly higher for the Portes–Ito specification than for Ito's one, which points in favour of Ito's model.

Moreover, the Portes–Ito model fails to catch a (statistically) significant effect of the domestic demand indicator on the overall demand for domestic manufactures while such an influence is clearly captured by Ito's specification (compare in table G.1 the estimates – and their standard errors – of c_{1XD} for both models).

As a conclusion, both models yield identical results on a majority of empirical issues. They disagree as far as the effective demand for goods X^d is concerned: in this context, the available empirical results suggest Ito's specification is more appropriate.

H   Data definitions, sources and statistical series

The data used for estimation are annual data covering the period 1963–80.

Almost all the data concern a (somewhat restricted) manufacturing sector: this comprises the whole Belgian manufacturing sector as defined by the National Accounts except the subsectors

–   food processing, beverage and tobacco
–   oil refineries
–   garages
–   'other' manufacturing industries.

Most data were obtained (or computed) from more disaggregated statistical data originating from four main sources, namely:

–   the Belgian National Accounts (denoted NACC hereafter);
–   the Belgian Planning Office (denoted PB);
–   the databank of the model HERMES, a large-scale, disaggregated, multicountry model currently being constructed on behalf of the EEC (denoted HERMES);
–   the Belgian National Bank (denoted BNB).

It has already been said in the main text that the business survey data DUC, $P_G, \hat{P}_L (=P_R/P_G)$ originating from the BNB, although available on a quarterly basis, were put on a yearly basis (by computing an appropriately weighted quarterly average) for the empirical application because the other Belgian macro data are only available on an annual basis.

However, before this 'annualization' procedure, some data management had to be performed in order to get homogeneous (through time) aggregate survey results. Indeed, while the business survey on the use of capacity started for most subsectors at the end of 1962, it began somewhat later in some subsectors, namely the 'paper industry' (beginning the survey in January 1965), the 'non-ferrous metals industry' (beginning in May 1967) and the 'chemical industry' (beginning in January 1969).

To get homogeneous aggregate series starting from 1963 on, we need to compute estimates for the missing first observations of the above mentioned subsectors. This was done simply by applying a rather mechanistic procedure of the following type:

$$\hat{V}_{it} = \exp\left(\hat{c}_{i0} + \hat{c}_{i1} . \ln V_{Tt}\right) \quad t = 1, \ldots, n$$

where V = variable DUC, or P_G, or $\hat{P}_L$;

subscript i = subsectors 'paper', 'non-ferrous metals' or 'chemicals';
subscript T = aggregate manufacturing sector;
n = time index of the last missing observation;

with $\hat{c}_{i0}$ and $\hat{c}_{i1}$ being the parameter values previously obtained from estimation of the above equation on the rest of the period $t = n+1, \ldots, T$.

Comparing the final 'homogenized' aggregate variables with their original 'heterogeneous' correspondents on the subperiod $t = 1, \ldots, n$ reveal only small differences, which is most probably due to the rather modest share of the subsectors under consideration in the aggregate[1].

We now report on the data used for estimation. Definitions are given first, followed by the full display of the statistical series.

Definitions of variables referring to the manufacturing sector

X	Value-added in billions of 1975 Belgian francs (source: NACC).
L	Workers employed in thousands (source: PB).
K	Fixed capital stock in billions of 1975 Belgian francs (source: PB). This aggregate capital stock is obtained as the sum of capital stocks at the subsectoral level. Subsectoral capital stock were computed as weighted sums of past gross investments with a depreciation rate obtained from expert opinion about the average lifetime of capital in each subsector.
P	Effective production price at factor cost (source: PB).
PVA	Deflator of value-added (source: NACC).
PI	Price index of investment goods (source: NACC).
PX	Price index of manufacturing exports in Belgian francs (source: PB).
PM	Price index of manufacturing imports in Belgian francs (source: PB).
PW	Price index (converted in Belgian francs) of competitors on foreign markets (source: HERMES). This is computed as a weighted sum of our partners' import prices with weights being equal to the share of our exports to each partner in total Belgian manufacturing exports.

FORDEM   Index of 'world demand' for manufactures (source: HERMES). This is computed as the index (1975 = 1) of the weighted sum of our partners' manufacturing imports with weights being equal to the share of our exports to each partner in total Belgian manufacturing exports.

W Wage rate (cost to the employer) in thousands of Belgian francs per man/year (source: PB).

DUC   Degree of utilization of installed capacities in % as yielded by regular business surveys (source: BNB).

P_G Weighted proportion (in %) of firms in excess demand on their goods market (source: BNB).

$\hat{P}_L$ Observed 'bench-mark' value of P_L in %; computed as $\hat{P}_L = P_R / P_G$ where P_R is the weighted proportion of firms experiencing simultaneously excess demand both on their goods micro market and on their labour micro market. Refer to section 1.2 for more details (source: BNB).

Definitions of other variables

LABNAT   Aggregate employment in thousands of men (source: PB).

YDH   Disposable income of households in billions of current Belgian francs (source: *Bulletin de statistiques* – INS).

PCH   Consumer price index (source: NACC).

LI   Long-term interest rate (source: PB).

UNR   Aggregate unemployment rate as a percentage of insured labour force (source: ONEM).

Statistical series

	X	L	LABNAT	YDH	K
1963	225.583	964.600	3576.30	520.920	341.226
1964	249.902	988.600	3601.30	572.851	363.806
1965	258.712	989.300	3598.50	634.667	391.568
1966	273.440	982.500	3607.10	676.349	427.266
1967	271.987	947.700	3595.80	716.807	456.262
1968	291.439	932.300	3589.50	770.439	472.505
1969	327.700	964.400	3648.10	844.248	496.323
1970	365.915	995.400	3701.50	927.855	531.930
1971	380.002	995.800	3738.90	1018.70	563.825
1972	410.617	980.000	3736.50	1147.79	580.525
1973	459.515	993.400	3783.10	1297.08	600.182
1974	479.112	1003.80	3836.80	1517.42	636.583
1975	435.019	944.800	3783.60	1713.89	657.853
1976	478.111	903.600	3759.50	1977.73	663.660
1977	481.252	863.200	3752.70	2121.19	652.015
1978	484.119	822.500	3755.60	2267.65	636.482
1979	502.129	796.800	3801.40	2414.76	624.097
1980	492.063	781.585	3797.80	2640.94	633.137

	PVA	P	PI	PCH	PX
1963	0.651	0.531	0.546	0.528	0.608
1964	0.680	0.557	0.573	0.549	0.629
1965	0.700	0.582	0.592	0.575	0.635
1966	0.721	0.607	0.601	0.599	0.664
1967	0.739	0.617	0.615	0.613	0.665
1968	0.746	0.625	0.619	0.631	0.665
1969	0.787	0.655	0.641	0.649	0.696
1970	0.798	0.700	0.711	0.673	0.712
1971	0.792	0.733	0.746	0.708	0.709
1972	0.819	0.754	0.777	0.747	0.720
1973	0.847	0.808	0.806	0.791	0.781
1974	0.964	0.953	0.916	0.890	0.938
1975	1.000	1.000	1.000	1.000	1.000
1976	1.038	1.057	1.044	1.080	1.059
1977	1.083	1.092	1.089	1.156	1.083
1978	1.119	1.096	1.115	1.204	1.088
1979	1.121	1.128	1.148	1.245	1.150
1980	1.141	1.146	1.157	1.321	1.307

	PM	PW	W	LI	UNR	FORDEM
1963	0.649	0.653	108.769	0.0563	2.7	0.384
1964	0.660	0.664	120.345	0.0641	2.2	0.436
1965	0.665	0.687	130.814	0.0651	2.4	0.466
1966	0.689	0.698	144.397	0.0680	2.7	0.509
1967	0.685	0.685	156.473	0.0701	3.7	0.530
1968	0.683	0.674	170.013	0.0681	4.5	0.645
1969	0.709	0.711	187.109	0.0757	3.7	0.719
1970	0.753	0.742	203.902	0.0854	3.0	0.789
1971	0.761	0.750	230.890	0.0779	2.9	0.839
1972	0.756	0.729	266.898	0.0693	3.4	0.913
1973	0.800	0.781	299.616	0.0758	3.6	1.006
1974	0.957	0.965	361.064	0.0910	4.0	1.081
1975	1.000	1.000	413.060	0.0900	6.7	1.000
1976	1.063	1.026	489.437	0.0975	8.6	1.141
1977	1.071	1.036	534.622	0.0942	9.8	1.190
1978	1.092	1.027	580.555	0.0861	10.4	1.261
1979	1.183	1.106	625.648	0.0895	10.9	1.366
1980	1.313	1.213	689.917	0.1219	11.7	1.429

	DUC	P_G	P_L
1963	81.853	59.514	50.949
1964	83.925	61.562	48.567
1965	81.658	46.483	38.017
1966	81.724	41.594	25.572
1967	78.309	25.152	12.489
1968	79.606	36.193	17.844
1969	86.419	63.102	31.876
1970	86.211	58.468	33.413
1971	83.223	47.357	27.337
1972	82.555	43.688	21.688
1973	84.927	60.916	25.347
1974	82.393	52.101	26.019
1975	71.540	15.557	19.215
1976	75.355	17.980	19.674
1977	73.621	12.351	14.210
1978	73.617	11.082	9.894
1979	76.839	19.332	13.841
1980	76.286	22.047	17.932

Notes

Introduction

1 For a more thorough discussion of the issues sketched in this brief introduction, see J. P. Fitoussi [1983] for an excellent survey of current macroeconomic research trends and A. Drazen [1980] for an equally lucid survey of recent developments in macroeconomic disequilibrium theory.

2 A lot of empirical evidence is at present available on the 'sluggishness' of wages and industrial prices.

As far as the *labour market* is concerned, for those who do not regard the high recorded unemployment rates as clearly indicative of persistent disequilibrium and who still question wage rigidity, they may refer to results like those of Rosen and Quandt [1978] for example, who successfully tested the disequilibrium hypothesis for the US labour market. (See also Romer [1981] and Yatchew [1981] for clarification of some questions of Rosen's and Quandt's original work.) 'Disequilibrium' on the *market for manufactured products* is not suggested to be of the same 'lasting' nature but instead refers to the observed evidence about short-run adjustment practices on these markets: to take a recent example, the research (based on micro data) of Kawasaki, McMillan and Zimmerman [1982], [1983], on price and output decisions of firms in the German manufacturing industry highlights the fact that producers always react to changes in demand by adjusting quantities (i.e. production) but adjust prices only infrequently in response to changes in demand perceived to be of a permanent nature.

In the face of the accumulated empirical evidence, the 'fix-price' hypothesis is thus thought to be a much better approximation for short-run analysis than the opposite 'flex-price' hypothesis, where prices are postulated to adjust quickly enough to assure *permanent* equality between demands and supplies on all markets.

A number of attempts have been made to provide theoretical explanations for wage/price sluggishness. The most significant ones will be mentioned later in the text.

3 The term 'equilibrium' may have two different meanings in economics. The first refers to market equilibrium (i.e. the equality of supply and demand on markets), and was used in this sense by Marshall, Walras and most subsequent authors in the neo-classical tradition. The second meaning refers to a solution for the endogenous variables where there are no incentives to modify behaviour. Hence Sneessens [1981] distinguishes between equilibrium and disequilibrium quantity rationing models depending on the correct or possibly incorrect expectations of the agents on the prevailing regime. We will usually use the expression 'disequilibrium model' with the first meaning in mind unless otherwise stated.

4 Remember we have one such expression for each aggregate market, goods and labour.
5 More specifically, we consider simple log-linear specifications expressing the (log of the) *effective* trade offer (X^d say) as the sum of the (log of the) corresponding *notional* trade offer plus a spillover term. Portes and Ito only differ in the specification of this spillover term.

Chapter 1

1 This representation may be confusing since demands and supplies on a given market depend upon many other signals (other prices, initial endowment, perceived constraints on other markets, ...) besides the price on that market. It is used here only for graphical convenience.
2 In the sense of both sides of the aggregate market being rationed simultaneously.
3 Of course, aggregation of micro demands, supplies and transactions may only be performed on units of the same nature: hence aggregation on labour micro markets (as in the example of figure 1.2) may be performed on men (or man-hours) (possibly of different skills or qualifications); aggregation on goods micro markets is concerned with 'volumes at constant prices', i.e. physical quantities multiplied by their price of a reference year. The aggregation procedure is in this respect not different from what is conventionally assumed in empirical macro models.
4 See Hansen [1970] for an early application of this reasoning to justify the form of his smooth continuous 'employment curve'.
5 In our case, since the micro markets have been so narrowly defined, N is surely very large.
6 The factor $1/N^2$ is the Jacobian of the transformation.
7 I thank Professor J. F. Richard whose help resulted in a more straightforward derivation of the CES transaction curve than the derivation I had proposed initially.
8 See appendix B for a model involving 'intertemporal spillovers' and allowing an interpretation in terms of the 'selectivity mechanism'.
9 Although firms in modern economies typically manufacture a range of products, the assumption of the single-product firm is warranted here since (as will be seen in the following subsection) the Belgian survey asks the firms to fill one questionnaire for each product (or group of products).
10 Of course real firms also use intermediate inputs in the production process. These however will not be given explicit treatment here as the aggregate production function specified in the empirical application will be of the conventional two-factor (capital and labour) type. Indeed, from the point of view of rationing, results of the business surveys indicate that constraints (in terms of the proportion of firms declaring themselves to be constrained) on material inputs have been very weak throughout the whole observation period with the only exceptions of a few months in 1973–74 (up to 25 % constrained in January 1974) and to a lesser extent in 1969–70 (up to 14 % of firms constrained in October 1969). Still these percentages comprise a number of firms which mention shortages of material inputs simultaneously with constraints on labour and/or equipment. On the whole, constraints on material inputs appear to have been far less severe than constraints on labour and/or profitable equipment, which explains our giving the priority to the handling of the latter constraints in this first attempt to exploit such data within a 'disequilibrium' macro model.
11 The notional output supply $\tilde{X}_i^s$ and demand for labour $\tilde{L}_i^d$ are clearly *short-run* notional trade offers since they result from an optimization programme *given the firm's existing equipment*. Since we are concerned in this work with short-run modelling and do not treat investment decisions (and hence the stock of capital) as endogenous, the 'notional' trade offers throughout this text are to be understood as short-run concepts.
12 Perhaps a most appealing representation of the firm's technology is the vintage type production function whereby the firm's capital stock is viewed as heterogeneous: each vintage of capital embodies a fixed production technique with complementary factors and labour productivity is assumed to be higher the more recent the vintage. Notional output supply (resp. notional labour demand) is then easily computed as the sum of the potential output (resp. the labour requirements) of successive vintages, starting from the most recent vintage and stopping at the last vintage for which quasi-rents are positive. In such a framework, if the firm does not immediately scrap the economically obsolete equipment, its notional output

supply $\bar{X}_i^s$ may depart from (and will be lower than) maximum feasible output. Refer to chapter 3 for some empirical evidence of such a phenomenon.

13 Another, commonly mentioned, vehicle of flexibility is for industrial firms to hold inventories of finished products. However, the stabilizing role of these stocks should not be exaggerated since, as shown by Blinder [1981], the 'buffer' role of inventories is overwhelmingly played by stocks at the wholesale and retail level and manufacturers' finished goods inventories play only a minor role. Instead backlogs of unfilled orders and changes in delivery periods have been shown by V. Zarnowitz [1962] to play, by far, the major stabilizing role in the manufacturing sector. If this has to be accounted for, then X_i^d (in the model above) is to be reinterpreted as reflecting not only the instantaneous demand (incoming new orders) but also somewhat the unfilled orders in excess (or below) some optimal target level.

14 Analysis of policy multipliers will be handled in section 2.1.

15 More precisely, three times a year from 1963 to 1977 and four times a year since then.

16 Actually, for some subsectors, the survey began somewhat later. Statistical series had thus to be homogenized for the empirical application – see appendix H on data sources and management.

17 Other constraints ('availability of intermediate inputs', 'other causes') play only a minor role during the observation period (see note 10). Since they have no place in the model of the firm sketched in section 1.2.1, they are assimilated here with the 'classical' regime.

18 Remember our discussion about the four-dimensional 'size distribution' at the end of section 1.1: although the 'zero-correlation assumption' proved a convenient theoretical assumption for the derivation of an attractive structural form, it was stressed that the interpretation of the actual business survey data would have to deal with the factual possibility of non-zero correlations.

19 The precise question is: 'Do you experience difficulties at present in recruiting workers?' Unfortunately, such a question is *not* asked in the Belgian survey.

20 In view of the available evidence suggesting higher values of $\bar{\rho}^*$ during recessions (see point (i)) and since the available observations cover a period mainly characterized by depressed business conditions, the reported estimates are more likely to reflect upper bounds than average values of ρ^*.

21 This expression may be obtained as the first-order approximation (around $\psi = 1$, i.e. around $\rho^* = 0$) of the bivariate normal C-type distribution proposed by Mardia (see J. F. Richard [1980]). Interestingly, the same expression was proposed by Gumbel [1961] for the bivariate logistic distribution with $-1 \leqslant \alpha \leqslant 1$ implying $-0.3 \leqslant \rho^* \leqslant 0.3$.

22 Expressions (A.5) and (A.8) of appendix A, standing respectively for weighted and unweighted proportions, may be used to assess the numerical differences between both statistics. Substituting relevant values for the aggregate demand/supply ratios (values, say, in the range $0.85 \dots 1.15$) and the exponents ρ_* and θ_* (from the empirical estimates $\hat{\rho}$, we can infer through equation (A.4) the corresponding $\hat{\sigma}$ which allows computation via equation (A.7) of the $\hat{\theta}$ parameter), we verify that (over the relevant domain at least) numerical differences between both proportions turn out to be strikingly small, being of the order of less than 2% (for absolute differences).

23 This was done by reweighting by labour shares the $\hat{P}_L$ statistics available at the most disaggregated level (subsectoral level – 9 subsectors).

24 Although quarterly observations are available from 1978 on, the series under display have been brought (by interpolation) to a uniform periodicity of three observations per year (January, May, September) for readability of the figures. The series were put on a yearly basis for the empirical application, because other Belgian macro data are only available on an annual basis.

25 Provided the economy is not yet in the inelastic part of the supply curve (all physical capacity exhausted).

Chapter 2

1 Actually the specifications analyzed by Portes appeared in linear instead of log-linear form but this difference is inessential to the following discussion.

2 To state it more precisely, only the last two specifications may be accepted as relevant *at the aggregate level*. Of course, nothing prevents the Barro–Grossman specification from being envisaged at the micro level. Our modelling strategy has been to *specify the spillover effects directly at the aggregate level*; when combined with the hypothesis of an aggregate long-run CES production function, the resulting specifications are shown (in section 2.2) to imply a short-run aggregate production function of the VES (variable elasticity of substitution) type. This functional form is then shown to be consistent with the outcome of explicit aggregation over elementary production units in a rationing context. Another strategy, followed by P. Kooiman [1982], [1983], would be to specify first the spillover effects at the micro level and then to aggregate in order to derive the aggregate short-run production function. No simple specification seems to have resulted from this alternative approach.

3 Actually a composite Portes–Ito model may be envisaged. The extensive study of such a model, both at a theoretical and empirical level, is carried out in appendix G.

4 To the same end, Portes also advocated the adjunction of additional equations postulating some dependence of observables on excess effective demands. He referred of course in the first place to simple-minded price (or wage) equations. The role of such variables is played in our model by the (weighted) proportions P_G and P_L.

5 More precisely, as was developed in detail in subsection 1.2.3, P_L is not directly observable but stands here for its specification as a function of the observed endogenous variables P_G and $\hat{P}_L$ (or P_R). This remark is valid for the remainder of this work up to the specific handling of this point in section 3.4.

6 Both the detailed economic specification (of the notional trade offers (2.1) as well as dynamic aspects) and the estimation issues will be discussed in chapter 3.

7 Less extreme situations characterized by $P_G \neq 0$ and $P_L \neq 0$ are represented by points inside the contour $ABCD$ (like point S) as explained in the preceding paragraph.

8 The fact that X^s (in Ito's definition) may depart from observed X arises from γ_{XS} being different from $1/\gamma_{LD}$ allowing for the possibility that the firms (as a whole) be off the aggregate production frontier (see Ito [1980]) due to labour hoarding (underutilization of available labour). The general case $(0 < P_G < 1$ and $0 < P_L < 1)$ is represented by points inside the 'double wedge' AFD (see above) so that labour hoarding then appears as a permanent phenomenon whose severity however varies with prevailing and expected (but expectations are here assumed to be static ones which is not a too strong assumption for an annual model) business conditions. (Remember $X^s/X = (P_G)^{-1/\rho G}$.) This hypothesis of labour hoarding as a permanent phenomenon (at a macro level) has received ample empirical support (see Fair [1969] and Fayolle [1980] a.o.). An attempt at measurement of this phenomenon along with some more comments will be made in chapter 3.

9 From the above equation, one also gets

$$(\ln X^s_{\text{Portes}} - \ln X) = \frac{1}{1 - \gamma_{XS}\gamma_{LD}}(\ln X^s_{\text{Ito}} - \ln X)$$

which is always positive since one assumes $0 < \gamma_{XS}\gamma_{LD} < 1$. This equation makes clear that $X^s_{\text{Portes}} (\geqslant X^s_{\text{Ito}})$ converges towards X^s_{Ito} for X tending towards X^s_{Ito}, i.e. when $P_G \to 1$. Similarly it can be shown that $L^d_{\text{Portes}} (\geqslant L^d_{\text{Ito}})$ converges towards L^d_{Ito} for L tending towards L^d_{Ito}, i.e. when $P_L \to 0$.

10 Early works related to Dutch macroeconomic planning already recognized this phenomenon and tried to formalize it; see a.o. Verdoorn and Post [1964].

11 The same analysis is conducted for Portes' model in appendix D.

12 It is easily seen that

$$\frac{dX}{d\tilde{X}^d} = \frac{X}{\tilde{X}^d} \cdot \frac{d\ln X}{d\ln \tilde{X}^d} = \frac{X}{X^d} \cdot \frac{X^d}{\tilde{X}^d} \cdot \frac{d\ln X}{d\ln \tilde{X}^d} = (1 - P_G)^{1/\rho G} \cdot (P_L)^{\gamma XD/\rho L} \cdot \frac{d\ln X}{d\ln \tilde{X}^d}$$

with $\dfrac{d\ln X}{d\ln \tilde{X}^d}$ being the multiplier expression discussed above.

13 'Firm' is used here to avoid repeating 'micro production unit'. In fact, a typical firm is better viewed as the aggregation of elementary production units.

14 Besides differing in shape from the observed distributions, the theoretical distributions $\Phi(\beta)$ behind the aggregate Cobb–Douglas (see H. S. Houthakker [1955–56]) and CES function (see D. Levhari [1968]) share the unrealistic assumption that the maximum labour efficiency β_0 of expressions (2.10) and (2.11) is taken to be infinite.

Chapter 3

1 The manufacturing industry is here defined as the total manufacturing sector excluding the subsectors 'food processing, beverages and tobacco', 'oil refineries' and 'garages'. These subsectors have been excluded either because they are not covered at all by the capacity survey (tobacco, oil refineries and garages) or because their survey started only recently (in 1973 for the food and beverage subsector).

2 Except the business survey data which are quarterly observations, all the other variables are only available on an annual basis. The business surveys started in 1963 but, dropping the first observation for reasons of data reliability (the survey questions seem to have been asked slightly differently during the first year) and losing another observation because of dynamic specification results in the estimation period 1965–80.

3 For the empirical application, observed manufacturing output X will be expressed in terms of manufacturing value-added at constant prices and hence X^s and $\tilde{X}^s$, the effective and notional output supply, are also expressed in value-added terms. This is conventional practice in sectoral production studies (see a.o. Benassy, Fouquet and Malgrange [1975], Villares [1980], Kooiman and Kloek [1981]). The use of value-added instead of an index of production is usually preferable because it avoids the double counting (counting a product once as output of a firm and once more when embodied as intermediate input in another firm's output) implicit in the computation of the available indexes of production. As a consequence of this double counting, variations of the production index could follow from changes in the vertical integration within the industry even in the absence of any change in activity while the value-added statistic does not suffer from such distortions.

4 The parameter ρ showing up in the long-run production function has of course nothing to do with the 'dispersion' parameters ρ_G and ρ_L appearing in the structural form (3.1).

5 This may be shown to be the optimal long-run price policy for firms facing monopolistic competition in the case of constant returns to scale. See for example Maccini [1981] where this result is derived from a model of firm behaviour where decisions on inventories and the capital stock are explicitly integrated with price decisions.

6 Artus and Muet [1984] and Mulkay [1983] provide early attempts at estimating an investment function within a multi-regimes framework. A critical discussion of these earlier works is carried out in Lambert [1986]. Lambert and Mulkay [1987] present a first attempt to rigorously endogenize investment behaviour within a complete disequilibrium model.

7 The ECM dynamic specification which embodies the PA (partial adjustment) mechanism as a particular case has been found to be appropriate in a variety of applications. See, for example, Hendry [1980] for a recent application and for references to other works.

8 It is interesting to note that these final dynamic equations (3.6) and (3.7) could also be derived by starting from the stochastic difference equations (3.4) and (3.5) expressed in slightly different form like

$$\ln\left(\frac{\tilde{X}^s}{K}\right)_t = c_{0K}^* + (1-\sigma)\gamma_2 T + \sigma\left[\frac{\delta_{0K}+\delta_{1K}L}{1-\delta_{2K}L}\right]\ln\left(\frac{r}{p}\right)_t + \frac{u_t}{1-\delta_{2K}L}$$

with $L=$ lag operator

$$\delta_{1K} = 1 - \delta_{0K} - \delta_{2K}$$

for equation (3.4) and similarly for equation (3.5), and then substituting these stochastic specifications in equation (3.1.2) and (3.1.4) respectively. However, considering the dynamic adjustment in the framework of the ECM allows more flexibility for a differentiated treatment of short-run transitory effects and longer-run determinants as will be shown in the following.

9 See the related discussion of section 3.2.

10 PROFIT$_t$ is readily seen to be an endogenous variable since its definition involves both

endogenous variables X_t and L_t. We now have a simultaneous model of six equations (five stochastic equations + one identity) and six endogenous variables $(X_t, P_{Gt}, \text{DUC}_t, L_t, P_{Lt}, \text{PROFIT}_t)$ which will be estimated by FIML.

11 After completion of the empirical study, it was suggested to me that using the deflator of value added P_{VA} instead of the product price p in the PROFIT definition would result in a more appropriate profitability index, particularly in a period marked by serious supply shocks. However both price indexes appear to be highly correlated $[\text{corr}(p, P_{VA}) = 0.994; \text{corr}(\Delta \ln p, \Delta \ln P_{VA}) = 0.774]$ so that estimation with this alternative specification yields almost unchanged empirical results. To illustrate this, we report below the empirical estimates (obtained with the price index P_{VA}) of the main parameters of interest which are readily verified to be very close to their correspondents reported in section 3.6.

$$\max \ln L = 184.108$$

$\alpha_1 = 0.235$	$\sigma_1 = 0.385$	$\gamma_{LD} = 0.461$
(0.051)	(0.042)	(0.084)
$1/\rho_G = 0.033$	$\sigma = 0.527$	$\gamma = 0.064$
(0.007)	(0.051)	(0.007)
$\sigma_0 = 0.0143$	$\gamma_{XS} = 1.457$	
(0.003)	(0.226)	

12 Since the additional variable PROFIT only captures short-run transitory variations of the notional output supply (profitable capacity), it is not likely that, in the presence of the widely prevailing phenomenon of labour hoarding, corresponding short-run fluctuations of the notional labour demand could be perceived. Indeed the inclusion of a similar term $\beta_1 \Delta \ln \text{PROFIT}_t$ in equation (3.7) was totally inconclusive.

13 Indeed, for a majority of parameters of interest (e.g. $1/\rho_G$, σ_0, σ_1, γ_{LD}, γ_{XS}, α_1) the point estimates obtained under the various dynamic specifications are verified to cluster within an interval defined by taking *one* (asymptotic) standard error on either side of the estimate obtained under the finally selected specification. Only for two parameters (σ and γ) has the interval under consideration to be broadened by taking *two* standard errors on either side. In view of the generally small size of the asymptotic standard errors involved (verify in section 3.6 where the final empirical estimates are reported), this feature implies a significant robustness of the model with respect to the 'dynamics issue' under consideration here.

14 The maximum likelihood values attained under alternative dynamic specifications (specification (a) being adopted for the cost of use of capital) are:

ECM2 $\max \ln L = 191.7$ with $\delta_{0K}, \delta_{0L}, \delta_{2K}$ and δ_{2L} free. This is the ECM type of adjustment with possibly different adjustment speeds toward the long-run capital–output and capital–labour ratios. This dynamic scheme will be labelled ECM2.

ECM1 $\max \ln L = 188.0$ with $\delta_{0K} = \delta_{0L} = \delta_0$ and $\delta_{2K} = \delta_{2L} = \delta_2$. This is the ECM type of adjustment with the same adjustment speed assumed for both technical coefficients towards their long-run values. Let us call this scheme ECM1.

PA2 $\max \ln L = 187.7$ with $\delta_{2K} = 1 - \delta_{0K}$ and $\delta_{2L} = 1 - \delta_{0L}$. This is the PA type of adjustment with possibly different adjustment speeds for both technical coefficients. This scheme is called PA2.

PA1 $\max \ln L = 184.1$ with $\delta_{0K} = \delta_{0L} = \delta_0 = 1 - \delta_{2K} = 1 - \delta_{2L}$. This is the most restricted dynamic scheme (called PA1) since it only assumes a PA mechanism with the same adjustment speed for both technical coefficients.

15 More precisely, with definition (a) of r_t, the dynamic parameters are such that 114% of the adjustment towards the long-run capital–output ratio ($\delta_{0K} = 1.14$; $\delta_{2K} = 0.69$) and 77% of the adjustment towards the long-run capital–labour ratio ($\delta_{0L} = 0.77$; $\delta_{2L} = 0.81$) are completed *within the current period*! This is not only counterintuitive but also contradicts strongly the available evidence obtained from previous works (see in the text for some references). With definition (c) of r_t, on the other hand, things look very differently since here δ_{0K} falls below its minimum admissible value: $\delta_{0K} = -0.05$ (asymptotic standard error = 0.08). Assuming $\delta_{0K} \simeq 0$ (which is a value within its confidence interval) and combining with the estimates of

the other parameters ($\delta_{2K}=0.62$; $\delta_{0L}=0.17$; $\delta_{2L}=0.81$), the time needed for 50% of the adjustment to be completed is estimated around 2.5 years for the capital–output ratio and around 3.5 years for the capital–labour ratio. These adjustment speeds, which are lower than those reported by previous studies, are in sharp (and embarassing) contrast with the findings obtained under definition (a) of r_t.

16 By 'robustness', we mean here that the adopted dynamic scheme should at least prove acceptable for both specifications of r_t although yielding possibly far better results for one specification than for the other.

17 After completion of the whole study, we tried again to estimate the model with the PA2 dynamic scheme and definition (c) of r_t. By carefully choosing the starting values of the coefficients, we succeeded in obtaining convergence rather quickly but anyway the maximum likelihood value attained was lower (183.5) than that attained with definition (a) of r_t (187.7). However, in view of the acceptable adjustment speed implied by the obtained estimates, there is no reason any more to discard the PA2 dynamic scheme for lack of 'robustness' (in the sense of note 16). Both dynamic schemes PA2 and PA1 are thus found to yield acceptable results with an advantage to be given to PA2 due to its higher maximum likelihood value (see note 14). All things considered, the choice of the dynamic specification PA2 with definition (a) of r_t might have proven preferable to the choice effectively adopted (PA1 with definition (a) of r_t). However, this turns out to be of no serious consequence since, as already explained above (see point (iii)), the key parameter estimates are found to be fairly insensitive to the dynamic scheme adopted for the technical coefficients. This may be readily verified by comparing the empirical estimates reported here (for the dynamic scheme PA2) with those reported in section 3.6 (for the dynamic scheme PA1). The numbers in parentheses are the asymptotic standard errors.

$$\delta_{0K}=0.425 \qquad \delta_{0L}=0.238$$
$$(0.07) \qquad\qquad (0.05)$$

These estimates imply that 50% of the total adjustment is performed within 1.25 years for the capital–output ratio and within 2.55 years for the capital–labour ratio (against a common median lag of 2.01 years for the effectively adopted model).

$$\sigma=0.488 \qquad \sigma_1=0.395 \qquad c_{1XD}=0.329$$
$$(0.06) \qquad\quad (0.04) \qquad\qquad (0.18)$$

$$\gamma=0.053 \qquad \gamma_{LD}=0.556 \qquad c_{2XD}=0.671$$
$$(0.006) \qquad\quad (0.08) \qquad\qquad (0.11)$$

$$1/\rho_G=0.0239 \qquad \gamma_{XS}=1.347 \qquad c_{3XD}=1.966$$
$$(0.005) \qquad\quad (0.166) \qquad\qquad (0.26)$$

$$\sigma_0=0.0136 \qquad \alpha_1=0.242$$
$$(0.003) \qquad\quad (0.04)$$

The closeness of these estimates to those of section 3.6 entails that all our conclusions referring to economic policy issues (see section 3.6) are basically unaffected by the choice made of a particular dynamic scheme.

18 Actually, the respondents to the Belgian business survey are not given a precise definition of capacity but the formulation of various survey questions clearly refers to a concept of capacity corresponding most closely to the 'engineering' concept. For a discussion of various concepts and measures of capacity, see for example Christiano [1981]. According to that study, interviews of business survey respondents clearly indicate that most of them refer to the 'engineering' concept of capacity while answering the *DUC* question.

19 See, for example, Benassy, Fouquet and Malgrange [1975] or Vilares [1980] for a discussion of these concepts in the framework of vintage production models.

20 See a.o. Christiano [1981] and Folly and Gresh [1981].

21 Expressed in value-added terms like its supply counterpart (see note 3).

22 See note 1 for the definition of our manufacturing sector.

23 Remember that manufacturing labour only accounts for a modest part (20%–25%) of the Belgian active population. A similar simplifying assumption was also adopted by Kooiman and Kloek [1981] in their disequilibrium model for Dutch manufacturing.

24 To simplify notation – and when no confusion may arise – UNR will be written for UNR_{tot} in the remainder of this work. Since $(1 - UNR)$ is then defined as L_{tot}/L_{tot}^s, we have the following identity:

$$UNR_t = 1 - \frac{LEXO_t + L_t}{LSEXO_t}$$

where L = manufacturing labour (endogenous)
  LEXO = labour at work in the rest of the economy (exogenous)
  LSEXO = total Belgian active population (exogenous)
through which UNR is also endogenous to the model and is treated as such in the estimation.

25 Such a statistic is made available by the Belgian national employment office (ONEM).

26 Estimation is performed with the TSP package developed by B. H. Hall and R. E. Hall. Among the methods proposed for FIML estimation, the Gauss method proved to be the fastest and the most efficient one and was thus used for all subsequent estimations. Standard errors of the estimates are reported as given by the approximate inverse Hessian matrix at the optimal point.

27 The observed endogenous variables being X, L, DUC_{obs}, P_G and P_R.

28 In fact, one readily verifies that, with specification (3.9), P_L is undefined for $\alpha = 0$. The LR test was actually conducted with respect to the null hypothesis $\alpha = 0.01$.

29 Another condition for stability and existence–uniqueness results was that the product $\gamma_{XD} \cdot \gamma_{LD}$ be less than unity. It was shown in section 3.3 above that the adopted specification of X^d did not imply separate estimation of γ_{XD} but instead the direct estimation of the product $\gamma_{XD}\gamma_{LD}$ (elasticity of the demand for domestic goods with respect to production) which is represented by the parameter c_{1XD}. The condition $c_{1XD} < 1$ is empirically satisfied for both Ito's and Portes' models (see empirical results in the next section and in appendix E).

30 $\ln L_{(\theta=0;\gamma_{XS}=1.45)} = 183.109$ while $\ln L_{(\theta=0;\gamma_{XS} \text{ free})}$ was equal to 183.970 which makes clear that a LR test fails to reject the constraint $\gamma_{XS} = 1.45$.

31 The LR statistic, which in this case is asymptotically distributed as χ_1^2, is defined as:

$$LR = 2 \cdot [\ln L_{(\theta=1;\gamma_1 \text{ and } \gamma_2 \text{ free})} - \ln L_{(\theta=1;\gamma_1=\gamma_2)}]$$

Its numerical value is $LR = 2 \cdot [184.662 - 184.104] = 1.116$ which is well below the critical value of rejection for the null hypothesis.

32 In a purely Keynesian regime, γ_{LD} would be the short-run elasticity of manufacturing employment with respect to the (expected) demand for domestic manufactures.

33 See Drèze and Modigliani [1981] who report estimates from different Belgian models.

34 Indeed, among the questions of the French quarterly business survey in the manufacturing sector, three questions, which unfortunately are not asked in the corresponding Belgian survey, are of direct relevance to the issue discussed here. These questions are:

  (1) By which percentage could you increase your current production with your existing installed equipment and without hiring new labour?
  (2) Could you produce still more by hiring additional labour? If yes, by which percentage could you increase your current production with the existing installed equipment and by hiring all the additional personnel which is needed?
  (3) Which increase (in % of your current labour force) would that additional personnel represent?

The (aggregate) answers to the questions 1, 2 and 3 are denoted respectively by MSE (for the French 'marge sans embauche'), MAE ('marge avec embauche') and TES ('taux d'embauche supplémentaire'). Keeping the notation adopted in the main text we may write:

$$MAE = (\tilde{X}^s/X) - 1$$
$$MSE = (X^s/X) - 1$$
$$TES = (\tilde{L}^d/L) - 1$$

In Ito's version of our structural model, we have the relation

$$\ln X^s = \ln \tilde{X}^s + \gamma_{XS}(\ln L - \ln \tilde{L}^d)$$

and hence

$$\gamma_{XS} = \frac{(\ln X^s - \ln \tilde{X}^s)}{(\ln L - \ln \tilde{L}^d)}$$

$$\gamma_{XS} = \frac{(\ln \tilde{X}^s - \ln X) - \ln (X^s - \ln X)}{(\ln \tilde{L}^d - \ln L)}$$

$$\gamma_{XS} = \frac{\ln (1 + MAE) - \ln (1 + MSE)}{\ln (1 + TES)}$$

Estimating γ_{XS} by OLS on the French data for the period 1970–78 yields

$$\gamma_{XS} = 1.247$$
$$(0.02)$$

which, although only indicative, points strongly towards γ_{XS} significantly greater than unity. It may be noticed that a value of 1.25 falls well within the confidence region of our estimate of γ_{XS}.

35 I thank H. Sneessens for having brought to my attention the following presentation which facilitates the comparison between the conventional treatment of labour hoarding and our specification. Defining L_{eff} as the efficient level of employment corresponding to output X, we may write

$$\ln X = \ln \tilde{X}^s + \gamma_{XS}(\ln L_{eff} - \ln \tilde{L}^d)$$

which is simply the specification of the efficient production frontier (equation X^s) with X^s and L replaced by X and L_{eff} respectively.

Substituting this expression for $\ln X$ in the specification of the demand for labour L^d, and regrouping terms, we get

(a) $\qquad \ln L_t^d = \gamma_{XS}\gamma_{LD} \ln L_{eff\,t} + (1 - \gamma_{XS}\gamma_{LD}) \ln \tilde{L}_t^d$

This expression of labour demand presents an interesting similarity with the conventional PA-type specification of labour hoarding. Indeed, the PA equation in the text may be rewritten:

(b) $\qquad \ln L_t = \varphi \ln L_t^* + (1 - \varphi) \ln L_{t-1}$

Remember that no rationing is assumed in conventional models so that L_t^d may be substituted for L_t in expression (b).

Such a presentation helps to stress the similarities and differences between both treatments of labour demand (and hence of labour hoarding).

In both models, the possibility of labour hoarding is linked to numerical values of parameters: in our model (equation (a)) the product $\gamma_{XS}\gamma_{LD}$ has to be strictly less than unity for labour hoarding to be possible while in the conventional model (equation (b)), the same condition has to hold on φ. Both models differ of course in crucial respects:

- first, L_{eff} (in equation (a)) and L^* (in equation (b)) do not mean the same: L_{eff} is the efficient level of labour corresponding to the actually observed output X while L^* is a desired (or optimal) level of employment (see below);

- second, we have (in equation (a)) by definition

$$L_{eff\,t} < \tilde{L}_t^d$$

which, with $\gamma_{XS}\gamma_{LD} < 1$, entails $L_t^d > L_{eff\,t}$ and hence labour hoarding as a permanent phenomenon.

In model (b), on the contrary, L_t^* may be either larger or smaller than L_{t-1}. When $L_t^* > L_{t-1}$, adjustment costs prevent the employers to hire L_t^* immediately but anyway L_t is on the efficient production frontier and *no* labour hoarding is taking place; when $L_t^* < L_{t-1}$, L_t will be used to produce a level of output for which L_t^* would have been sufficient so that labour hoarding is *then* taking place.

36 In these expressions, ρ_{L_t} stands for its specification

$$\rho_{L_t} = \frac{1}{\sigma_0 + \sigma_1 \mathrm{UNR}_t}$$

37 Except for the difference between total installed capacity (to which the TES statistic refers) and total installed *profitable* capacity (to which our statistic $[(\tilde{L}^d/L)-1]$ refers).

38 Interpretation of the ONEM statistic calls for some caution since the series is not totally homogeneous: modifications in legislation (namely in 1970 and 1978) entail discontinuities in the registered number of unfilled vacancies.

39 This share has been computed as the share of manufacturing employment in total employment.

40 In the 'main economic indicators' publication of the OECD, the (V/U) statistic is reported for a number of countries. It is striking that, for the whole observation period, the Belgian statistics are significantly lower than their correspondents for the other countries.

Conclusion

1 Such a slow adjustment process is a fact of observation and its rationalization in terms of optimizing behaviour of agents is a main theme of the research devoted to the 'microeconomic foundations of macroeconomics'. Such a research is not the subject of this work which considers rigidity of prices and wages as a given fact.

2 This statistic has been incorporated in a somewhat 'ad hoc' way in the French model METRIC [1977] and proved significant for the explanation of short-run labour demand as well as fixed investment.

3 For recent research about the appropriate specification of investment behaviour in disequilibrium models, see a.o. Artus and Muet [1984], Lambert [1986], Lambert and Mulkay [1987] or Mulkay [1983].

Appendix A

1 This ρ parameter is not to be confused with the correlation between ε_d and ε_s, for which we used the same symbol.

Appendix C

1 It will be assumed throughout that no sector is ever rationed on its intermediate inputs. Due to the small open economy assumption, increased imports of intermediate inputs are always available to compensate when domestic suppliers are in excess demand. Without this assumption, a detailed rationing scheme for each type of intermediate input would have to be defined in order to allow for I/O analysis.

2 Here also, even if demand for *domestic* intermediate inputs may be rationed, firms are assumed to be always able to get their inputs through increased imports (see note 1).

Appendix F

1 This definition of sectoral labour supply is frequently adopted in empirical works; see a.o. Muellbauer and Winter [1980] or Pissarides [1978].

This definition, however, deliberately ignores the unemployed who just arrived on the labour market without previous professional experience and who then – by definition – do not belong to any 'sectoral labour force'. For the sake of completeness, one can thus modify the above definition by adding to the 'sectoral unemployed' a share of these 'new entrants'. Such a modified definition is behind the 'sectoral labour supply' curve L^s reported in figure 3.4 of chapter 3 (see also note 39 of chapter 3).

However, and this is the point we want to make clear, such a modification happens empirically to bring only very minor changes since the number of 'new entrants' so added is always very small compared to the number of unemployed people whose previous job was in the manufacturing sector. To give some idea of the figures involved, incorporating the 'new entrants' would result in increasing the measure of the 'manufacturing unemployment rate' by an order of *at most* 5% (i.e. bringing UNR_{man} from 10% to 10.5% for example or from 12% to 12.6%) compared to the outcome of the most commonly adopted definition.

In view of the only very modest changes brought about by this alternative definition, and since we perform further a 'sensitivity analysis' implying much more radical departures from the measured UNR_{man}, we feel authorized (since of no consequence) to adopt here the mainstream practice of empirical studies of 'sectoral labour supply' (Muellbauer and Winter, Pissarides, ...).

2 Such a statistic is made available on a rather disaggregated basis by the Belgian Employment Office (ONEM).

3 A striking example of the results of such 'labour supply management' is provided by the 'metal' sector (steel and non-ferrous metals) which is known for having reduced markedly its labour force since the first oil-shock and the unemployment rate of which nevertheless amounts to only 4% in 1981 by contrast to the 14.3% attained by the aggregate unemployment rate.

4 We now have the following identity

$$UNR_{(man)_t} = 1 - \frac{L_t}{LSMAN_t}$$

where L_t = manufacturing labour (endogenous)

$LSMAN_t$ = labour supply to the manufacturing sector (exogenous)

through which UNR_{man} is endogenous to the model and treated as such in the estimation.

5 The following combinations were tried:

(a) $(c_0 = 0.9; \quad c_1 = 0.)$
(b) $(c_0 = 1.1; \quad c_1 = 0.)$
(c) $(c_0 = 1.5; \quad c_1 = 0.)$

(d) $(c_0 = 1.0; \quad c_1 = 0.025)$ with TREND exhibiting the first profile described above implying

$$UNR_{man} = 2.7\% \text{ in } 1960 \text{ (while } UNR_{tot} = 2.7\%)$$

$$= 5.5\% \text{ in } 1974 \text{ (while } UNR_{tot} = 4.0\%)$$

$$= 17.8\% \text{ in } 1980 \text{ (while } UNR_{tot} = 11.7\%)$$

(e) $(c_0 = 1.0; \quad c_1 = 0.1)$ with TREND exhibiting the second profile described above implying

$$UNR_{man} = 2.7\% \text{ in } 1960 \text{ (while } UNR_{tot} = 2.7\%)$$

$$= 4.4\% \text{ in } 1974 \text{ (while } UNR_{tot} = 4.0\%)$$

$$= 19.9\% \text{ in } 1980 \text{ (while } UNR_{tot} = 11.7\%)$$

Appendix G

1 For example, Portes' specification assumes that in a pure repressed inflation regime, the amount of labour demanded by the producer always equals notional labour demand $\tilde{L}^d$, irrespective of the level of X (or X^d) relative to that of $\tilde{X}^s$: such behaviour seems unwarranted.

2 These are conditions for the existence and uniqueness of a fix-price equilibrium, or equivalently for the existence of a well-defined reduced form.

3 The only stability and coherency condition has been seen to be $\gamma_{XD}\gamma_{LD} < 1$; this product, which expresses the traditional 'consumption' demand response to increased output is represented here by the coefficient c_{1XD} whose estimated value is well below unity.

4 Refer to appendix E where the same phenomenon was commented upon for $\hat{X}^d_{Ito}$ vs. $\hat{X}^d_{Portes}$.

5 Since the dependent variables are expressed in logarithms, the RMSE statistic yields the 'average' error in % of the dependent variable.

Appendix H

1 In 1965, this share was of the order of 10% for the subsector 'paper' and about another 10% for the subsectors 'non-ferrous + chemicals' together.

References

Alchian, A. (1970), 'Information costs, pricing and resource unemployment'. In : *Microeconomic Foundations of Unemployment and Inflation Theory*. E. S. Phelps (ed.), Macmillan, London.

Arrow, K. J. (1959), 'Towards a theory of price adjustment'. In: *The Allocation of Economic Resources*. M. Abramowitz (ed.), Stanford University Press, Stanford, California.

Artus, P. and C. Bismut (1980), 'Substitution et coût des facteurs: un lien existe-t-il?', *Economie et Statistique* **127**, 101–14.

Artus, P., Laroque, G. and G. Michel (1984), 'Estimation of a quarterly macroeconomic model with quantity rationing', *Econometrica* **52**, 1387–414.

Artus, P. and P. A. Muet (1984), 'Investment, output and labour constraints and financial constraints: the estimation of a model with several regimes', *Recherches Economiques de Louvain*, **50**(1–2), 25–44.

Aukrust, O. (1970), 'PRIM I: a model of the price and income distribution mechanism in an open economy', *Review of Income and Wealth* **16**.

Azariadis, C. (1975), 'Implicit contracts and underemployment equilibrium', *Journal of Political Economy* **83**, 1183–202.

Baily, M. N. (1974), 'Wages and employment under uncertain demand', *Review of Economic Studies* **41**, 27–50.

Barro, R. J. and H. I. Grossman (1971), 'A general disequilibrium model of income and employment', *American Economic Review* **61**, 82–93.

Barro, R. J. and H. I. Grossman (1976), *Money, employment and inflation*, Cambridge University Press, Cambridge and New York.

Basevi, G., Blanchard, O., Buiter, W., Dornbusch, R. and R. Layard (1983), 'Macroeconomic prospects and policies for the European Community', Economic Papers no. 12, Commission of the European Community.

Benassy, J.-P. (1975), 'Neo-Keynesian disequilibrium theory in a monetary economy', *Review of Economic Studies* **42**, 503–23.

Benassy, J.-P. (1976), 'The disequilibrium approach to monopolistic price setting and general monopolistic equilibrium', *Review of Economic Studies* **43**, 69–81.

Benassy, J.-P., Fouquet, D. and P. Malgrange (1975), 'Estimation d'une fonction de production à générations de capital', *Annales de l'INSEE* **19**.

Benassy, J.-P. (1982), *The economics of market disequilibrium*, Academic Press, New York.

Bischoff, C. W. (1971), 'The effect of alternative lag distributions', in Fromm, G. (ed.), *Tax Incentives and Capital Spending*, Washington DC, The Brookings Institution.

Blinder, A. S. (1981), 'Inventories and the structure of macro models', *American Economic Association Papers and Proceedings*, 11–16.

BNB (1980), 'L'essoufflement de l'économie belge dans la décennie passée: détérioration de la balance commerciale de l'UEBL', *Bulletin de la Banque Nationale de Belgique*.

Bouissou, M. B., Laffont, J. J. and Q. H. Vuong (1984), 'Econometrie du déséquilibre sur données microéconomiques', *Annales de l'INSEE* **55–56**, 109–51.

Branson, W. H. and J. J. Rotemberg (1980), 'International adjustment with wage rigidity', *European Economic Review* **13**, 309–32.

Broeder, G. den (1983), 'A family of market transaction functions', Working paper, Netherlands Economic Institute, Erasmus University, Rotterdam.

Bruno, M. and J. Sachs (1982), 'Input price shocks and the slowdown in economic growth: the case of U.K. manufacturing', *Review of Economic Studies* **49**, 679–705.

Christiano, L. R. (1981), 'A survey of measures of capacity utilization', *IMF Staff Papers* **28**, 144–98.

Clower, R. W. (1965), 'The Keynesian counterrevolution: A theoretical appraisal'. In: *The Theory of Interest Rates*. F. H. Hahn and F. Brechling (eds.), Macmillan, London.

Cramer, J. S. (1969), *Empirical Econometrics*. North-Holland, Amsterdam.

Cuddington, J. T. (1980), 'Fiscal and exchange rate policies in a fix-price trade model with export rationing', *Journal of International Economics* **10**, 319–40.

Cuddington, J. T., Johansson, P. O. and K. G. Löfgren (1984), *Disequilibrium Macroeconomics in Open Economies*. Basil Blackwell, London.

Dixit, A. (1978), 'The balance of trade in a model of temporary equilibrium with rationing', *Review of Economic Studies* **45**, 393–404.

Dixit, A. (1980), 'The role of investment in entry-deterrence', *The Economic Journal* **90**, 95–106.

Drazen, A. (1980), 'Recent developments in macroeconomic disequilibrium theory', *Econometrica* **48**, 283–306.

Drèze, J. H. (1975), 'Existence of an equilibrium under price rigidity and quantity rationing', *International Economic Review* **16**, 301–20.

Drèze, J. H. and F. Modigliani (1981), 'The trade-off between real wages and employment in an open economy (Belgium)', *European Economic Review* **15**, 1–40.

Eaton, C. B. and R. C. Lipsey (1979), 'The theory of market preemption: The persistence of excess capacity and monopoly in growing spatial markets', *Economica* **46**, 149–58.

Fair, R. C. (1969), *The short-run demand for workers and hours*, North-Holland, Amsterdam.

Falleur, R. de (1978), 'Le travail', Rapport de la commission 2 du troisième Congrès des Economistes belges de langue française, CIFOP, Charleroi.

Fayolle, J. (1980), 'Le comportement d'investissement depuis 1974', *Economie et Statistique* **127**, 21–37.

Fitoussi, J. P. (1983), 'Modern macroeconomic theory: An overview'. In: *Modern Macroeconomic Theory*. J. P. Fitoussi (ed.), Barnes & Noble Books, Totowa, NJ, in cooperation with the European University Institute, Florence.

Folly, M. and H. Gresh (1981), 'Les marges de capacité de production industrielle inutilisées', *Economie et Statistique* **136**, 17–28.

Ginsburgh, V., Tishler, A. and I. Zang (1980), 'Alternative estimation methods for two-regime models: a mathematical programming approach', *European Economic Review* **13**, 207–28.

Gordon, R. J. (1981), 'Output fluctuations and gradual price adjustment', *Journal of Economic Literature* **19**, 493–530.

Gouriéroux, C., Laffont, J. J. and A. Monfort (1980 a), 'Disequilibrium econometrics in simultaneous equations systems', *Econometrica* **48**, 75–96.

Gouriéroux, C., Laffont, J. J. and A. Monfort (1980 b), 'Coherency conditions in simultaneous linear equation models with endogenous switching regimes', *Econometrica* **48**, 675–95.

Gouriéroux, C. and G. Laroque (1983), 'The aggregation of commodities in quantity rationing models', CEPREMAP, Discussion Paper 8305.

Grandmont, J. M. (1977), 'Temporary general equilibrium theory', *Econometrica* **45**, 535–72.

Gumbel, E. J. (1961), 'Bivariate logistic distributions', *American Statistical Association Journal*, 335–49.

Hahn, F. H. (1978), 'On non-Walrasian equilibria', *Review of Economic Studies* **45**, 1–17.

Hansen, B. (1970), 'Excess demand, unemployment, vacancies and wages', *Quarterly Journal of Economics* **84**, 1–23.

Hendry, D. F. (1980), 'Predictive failure and econometric modelling in macroeconomics: the transactions demand for money'. In: P. Ormerod (ed.), *Modelling the Economy*. Heinemann Educational Books, London.

Hildenbrand, W. (1981), 'Short-run production functions based on microdata', *Econometrica* **49**, 1095–125.

Houthakker, H. S. (1955–56), 'The Pareto distribution and the Cobb–Douglas production function in activity analysis', *Review of Economic Studies* **23**, 27–31.

Huveneers, C. (1981), 'Price formation and the scope for oligopolistic conduct in a small open economy', *Recherches Economiques de Louvain* **47**, 209–42.

Ijiri, Y. and H. A. Simon (1977), *Skew distributions and the sizes of business firms*, North-Holland, Amsterdam.

IMF (1982), 'World Economic Outlook'.

Ito, T. (1980), 'Methods of estimation for multimarket disequilibrium models', *Econometrica* **48**, 97–126.

Iwai, K. (1974), 'Towards Keynesian micro-dynamics of price, wage, sales and employment', Cowles Foundation Discussion Paper 369.

Johansen, L. (1972), *Production Functions*, North-Holland, Amsterdam–London.

Johnson, N. L. and S. Kotz (1972), *Distributions in Statistics: continuous univariate distributions*, Wiley, New York.

Kawasaki, S., McMillan, J. and K. F. Zimmermann (1982), 'Disequilibrium dynamics: an empirical study', *American Economic Review* **72**, 992–1004.

Kawasaki, S., McMillan, J. and K. F. Zimmermann (1983), 'Inventories and price inflexibility', *Econometrica* **51**, 599–610.

Kervyn, A. (1979), 'Taux de change, inflation et compétitivité externe', *Recherches Economiques de Louvain* **45**, 55–94.

Kooiman, P. and T. Kloek (1979), 'Aggregation of micro markets in disequilibrium', Working paper, Econometric Institute, Erasmus University, Rotterdam.

Kooiman, P. and T. Kloek (1980), 'An aggregate two market disequilibrium model with foreign trade', Working paper, Econometric Institute, Erasmus University, Rotterdam.

Kooiman, P. and T. Kloek (1985), 'An empirical two market disequilibrium model for Dutch manufacturing', *European Economic Review* **29**, 323–54.

Kooiman, P. (1982), 'Using business survey data in empirical disequilibrium models', Working paper, ICERD, London School of Economics.

Kooiman, P. (1983), 'The derivation of pressure of demand indicators from business survey data: a disequilibrium approach', Working paper, Econometric Institute, Erasmus University, Rotterdam.

Kooiman, P. (1984), 'Smoothing the aggregate fix-price model and the use of business survey data', *Economic Journal* **94**, 899–913.

Laffont, J. J. (1983), 'Fix-price models: A survey of recent empirical work', Cahier no. 8305, GREMAQ, Université de Toulouse.

Lambert, J. P. (1983), 'Modèles macroéconomiques de rationnement et enquêtes de conjoncture', *Recherches Economiques de Louvain* **3**, 225–45.

Lambert, J. P. (1984), *Disequilibrium macro models based on business survey data. Theory and estimation for the Belgian manufacturing sector*, Doctoral dissertation, Collection de la Faculté des Sciences Economiques, Sociales et Politiques, no. 156, Université Catholique de Louvain, Louvain-la-Neuve.

Lambert, J. P., Lubrano, M. and H. R. Sneessens (1985), 'Emploi et chômage en France de 1955 à 1982: un modèle macroéconomique annuel de rationnement', *Annales de l'INSEE* **55–56**, 39–75.

Lambert, J. P. (1986), 'Conflicting specifications for investment functions in rationing models: a reconciliation', *Recherches Economiques de Louvain* (forthcoming).

Lambert, J. P. and B. Mulkay (1987), 'Investment in a disequilibrium context, or does profitability really matter?', CORE DP 8703, Université Catholique de Louvain, Louvain-la-Neuve.

Levhari, D. (1968), 'A note on Houthakker's aggregate production function in a multifirm industry', *Econometrica* **36**, 151–4.

Lu, Y. and L. B. Fletcher (1968), 'A generalization of the CES production function', *Review of Economics and Statistics* **50**, 449–52.

Lubrano, M. and H. R. Sneessens (1982), 'A Leontieff–CES production model', CORE Discussion Paper 8219, Louvain-la-Neuve.

Maccini, L. J. (1981), 'On the theory of the firm underlying empirical models of aggregate price behaviour', *International Economic Review* **22**, 609–24.

Maddala, G. S. and F. D. Nelson (1974), 'Maximum likelihood methods for models of markets in disequilibrium', *Econometrica* **42**, 1013–30.

Malinvaud, E. (1977), *The Theory of unemployment reconsidered*, Oxford, Basil Blackwell.

Malinvaud, E. (1980), 'Macroeconomic rationing of employment'. In: E. Malinvaud and J.-P. Fitoussi (eds.), *Unemployment in Western Countries*, Macmillan.

Malinvaud, E. (1982), 'An econometric model for macro-disequilibrium analysis'. In: *Current Developments in the Interface: Economics, Econometrics, Mathematics* by Hazewinkel and Rinnooy Kan (eds.), Reidel.

Malinvaud, E. (1983), *Essais sur la Théorie du Chômage*, Calmann-Levy, Paris.

'METRIC, un modèle économétrique trimestriel de la conjoncture' (1977), *Annales de l'INSEE*, 26–7.

Muellbauer, J. (1978), 'Macrotheory vs. macroeconometrics: the treatment of disequilibrium in macro models', Birkbeck Discussion Paper 59, Birkbeck College, London.

Muellbauer, J. and R. Portes (1978), 'Macroeconomic models with quantity rationing', *The Economic Journal* **88**, 788–821.

Muellbauer, J. and D. Winter (1980), 'Unemployment, employment and exports in British manufacturing; a non-clearing markets approach', *European Economic Review* **13**, 383–409.

Mulkay, B. (1983), 'Fonctions d'investissement néoclassiques dans un modèle macroéconomique avec rationnement', *Recherches Economiques de Louvain* **49**(3), 247–76.

Neary, J. P. (1980), 'Non-traded goods and the balance of trade in a neo-Keynesian temporary equilibrium', *Quarterly Journal of Economics* **95**, 403–29.

Negishi, T. (1979), *Microeconomic Foundations of Keynesian Macroeconomics*. North-Holland, Amsterdam.

OECD (1982), *Economic Outlook*.

Okun, A. (1981), *Prices and Quantities*, Basil Blackwell, London.

Patinkin, D. (1956), *Money, Interest and Prices*, Harper and Row, New York.

Pissarides, C. A. (1978), 'The role of relative wages and excess demand in the sectoral flow of labour', *Review of Economic Studies* **45**, 453–67.

Portes, R. (1977), 'Effective demand and spillovers in empirical two-market disequilibrium models', Harvard Institute of Economic Research, Discussion Paper no. 595.

Quandt, R. E. (1982), 'Econometric disequilibrium models', *Econometric Reviews* **1**, 1–63.

Raoul, E. and J. Rouchet (1980), 'Utilisation des équipements et fléchissement de la productivité depuis 1974', *Economie et Statistique* **127**, 39–54.

Richard, J. F. (1980), 'C-type distributions and disequilibrium models', CORE, Louvain-la-Neuve, Mimeo.

Richard, J. F. (1982), 'Econometric disequilibrium models: a comment', *Econometric Reviews* **1**, 81–7.

Romer, D. (1981), 'Rosen and Quandt's disequilibrium model of the labor market: A revision', *The Review of Economics and Statistics* **63**, 145–6.

Rosen, H. S. and R. E. Quandt (1978), 'Estimation of a disequilibrium aggregate labor market', *Review of Economics and Statistics* **60**, 371–9.

Sato, K. (1975), *Production function and aggregation*, Contributions to Economic Analysis, V. 90, North-Holland, New York.

Siebrand, J. C. (1979), *Towards operational disequilibrium macroeconomics*, Martinus Nijhoff, The Hague.

Sneessens, H. R. (1981), *Theory and estimation of macroeconomic rationing models*. Springer-Verlag, Berlin.

Sneessens, H. R. (1981), *Theory and estimation of macroeconomic rationing models*, methods for quantity rationing models: A Monte Carlo comparison', *European Economic Review* **29**, 111–36.

Solow, R. M. (1980), 'On theories of unemployment', *American Economic Review* **70**, 1–11.

Spencer, P. D. (1975), 'A disequilibrium model of personal sector bank advances. 1964–1974: Some preliminary results', Working Paper, HM Treasury.

Steigum, E. (1980), 'Keynesian and classical unemployment in an open economy', *Scandinavian Journal of Economics* **82**, 147–66.

Verdoorn, P. J. and J. J. Post (1964), 'Capacity and short-term multipliers'. In: P. E. Hart *et al.* (eds.), *Econometric Analysis for National Economic Planning*, Butterworths, London.

Vilares, M. J. (1980), 'Fonctions à générations. Théorie et estimations', *Annales de l'INSEE* 38–9.

Vilares, M. J. (1981), 'Macroeconomic model with structural change and disequilibrium', Mimeo, Porto.

Yatchew, A. J. (1981), 'Further evidence on estimation of a disequilibrium aggregate labor market', *The Review of Economics and Statistics* **63**, 142–4.

Zarnowitz, V. (1962), 'Unfilled orders, price changes and business fluctuations', *Review of Economics and Statistics* **44**, 367–94.

Author index

Subject index